The Gathering of the Clan

Also by Thomas Richard Harry

The Delicate Illusion (1999)

The Gathering Of the Clan

An Independent Political Option for America

It's that simple: A philosophy of producing the greatest good for the greatest number, manifest in a policy of governing for (at least) most of the people all of the time and for all of the people most of the time.

by
Thomas Richard Harry

iUniverse, Inc.
New York Bloomington

iUniverse books may be ordered through booksellers or by contacting:

iUniverse
1663 Liberty Drive
Bloomington, IN 47403
www.iuniverse.com
1-800-Authors (1-800-288-4677)

ISBN: 978-1-4401-1750-3 (sc)
ISBN: 978-1-4401-1752-7 (dj)
ISBN: 978-1-4401-1751-0 (ebook)

Printed in the United States of America

iUniverse rev. date: 05/08/2009

To Tom, Dick, and Harry, Connie, Sue and Mary

"The struggle between Liberty and Authority is the most conspicuous feature in the portions of history with which we are earliest familiar … But in old times this contest was between subjects, or some classes of subjects, and the government. By liberty, was meant protection against the tyranny of the political rulers. The rulers were conceived … as in a necessarily antagonistic position to the people whom they ruled.

A time, however, came in the progress of human affairs, when men ceased to think it a necessity of nature that their governors should be an independent power, opposed in interest to themselves. It appeared to them much better that the various magistrates of the State should be their tenants or delegates, revocable at their pleasure. In that way alone, it seemed, could they have complete security that the powers of government would never be abused to their disadvantage. By degrees, this new demand for elective and temporary rulers became the prominent object of the exertions of the popular party, wherever any such party existed; … What was now wanted was that the rulers should be identified with the people; that their interest and will should be the interest and will of the nation. The nation did not need to be protected against its own will."

On Liberty,
John Stuart Mill

Contents

Introduction.. i

Part One

Chapter 1: Why—and Whence—Independents?....................5

Chapter 2: What It Is and What It Isn't 11

Chapter 3: The Political Status Quo.................................23

Chapter 5: Democracy and Capitalism..............................31

Chapter 6: Why Government Behaves Like It Does 37

Part Two

Chapter 7: The Rise of the Independent Voter....................69

Chapter 8: Independent Parties and Support Groups Today..............81

Chapter 9: The Independent Voter: A Profile and a Purpose 91

Chapter 10: An Independent Political Option 109

Chapter 11: The Superstructure: How It Fits Together 117

Part Three

Chapter 12: An Independent View of the Propriety
(or Impropriety) of Special-Interest Influences on Government.......141

Chapter 13: An Independent Tax Solution 157

Chapter 14: Social Security 177

Chapter 15: Working Poverty: A Minimum Wage Issue 191

Chapter 16: A Conclusion and a Message 211

Epilogue 225

Notes 227

Bibliography 237

Introduction

Political choice is the issue here. The persistent exodus of voters from the rolls of both the Republican and the Democratic parties suggests a need to consider that some change or adjustment in political choice is called for; that such consideration may be desirable, possibly even necessary, for the overall good of our country as we move ahead into the twenty-first century. The presence of such a large bloc of voters not openly affiliating with either major party begs this question regarding political choice.

In the pages that follow we endeavor to make the argument that expanded political choice is not only desirable but also necessary, for several reasons. To accomplish this, we'll see if we can't propose, not an alternative to our existing electoral or our two-party political system of the past hundred and forty-seven or so years, but an enhancement to it. Why? For a start, it's tired, it's entrenched, and it tends more and more to be focused on self-serving rather than public-serving. But that appears to be just the tip of an iceberg.

Such enhancement could take several possible forms. It could develop, at least initially, in the form of an organized, structured, and rather broad-based national interest group. It might take the form of an internal ideological/philosophical challenge to one of the two major parties. Or, as unlikely as success might seem in pursuing this route considering both historic and present circumstances, enhancement could produce an additional formal political party. The objective is to "get the attention" of both the existing political mandarins as well as that of the voting public in an effort to bring about needed (and I stress the term "needed") political change. What kind of change? Change that will once again set America heading in the right and proper direction, socially, economically, and especially politically. Such change is not only considered necessary, but as importantly in our view, it's considered possible.

I recognize that the above goal is rather abstract: "political change," "right direction." Use your imagination, your own values, and political inclinations and such abstractions can mean just about anything, which really says they mean very little. It's rhetoric, political rhetoric that is used today to suggest without really defining; to challenge without threatening; to campaign without commitment.

The purpose here is to infuse that rhetoric with political significance and meaning for those who have the ultimate responsibility for choosing our political leaders, the voter. Meaning that can be translated into action; action that can convert the abstract concepts of "change" and "direction" into an improved quality of life for most, if not all, Americans by bringing our overall society into a better, necessary, and rightful Balance. Another abstraction, admittedly, but one that will also be defined and given significance and practical application as we proceed here.

What I specifically mean by "necessary and rightful Balance" will be clarified in Chapter 9. Briefly, it represents at any one time the status quo between the three primary groups that make up our society: business, government, and the public at large.

The justification for writing about this and for making the proposals herein is a simple one: the existence of all those politically independent voters. If voters were satisfied with their existing political choice (options), or by extension satisfied with the results of government as managed by these (two) political alternatives, why would we be experiencing a steady growth of those who decide not to be, at least publically, affiliated or identified with either major party? Some suggest that today you vote the candidate, not the party, so why bother to pick a party? Possibly, but in my analysis, that's too superficial a view. Furthermore, if it's a valid explanation, then the next logical question would be, why continue to have parties? Why don't we just scrap them? Well, there are a lot of reason we don't—and shouldn't want to.

Depending upon which statistics you care to quote, the proportion of voters registering as political Independents (or who decline to state) is currently between 38 and 40 percent. That's a larger number of voters than those who declare for either of the two major parties. This is a significant fact that merits a close examination: What's occurring here? There are a number of possibilities to consider. Some counter that the number of truly independent voters is considerably smaller than this. Most, they declare, are actually "closet" Democrats or Republicans. This may well be true for many Independents, and we examine this possibility in some depth in Chapter 9. But even conceding this possibility doesn't answer the question of *why* they are registering as Independents. We will see that this rise of Independents does not seem to have moved the general voting population's political ideological profile much if at all over the past forty or so years. Therefore, if the reason for this shift isn't ideological, what is it? The supportable conclusion reached here is that it will have to do with that issue of Balance.

The generally accepted definition of political Independents is that they can't be defined, that they have no commonality, except to say that they register as unaffiliated voters. I believe this is also too superficial a view. Why? Well just consider the fact that Independents today have no place to go, politically speaking, to express what being an Independent might signify to them. Dismissing any Independent political significance or identity, aside from both parties needing to "rent them" come Election Day, is perhaps an attempt to prevent any Independent political significance or identity to solidify, to the detriment of the existing political structure. If that's the case, this is questionable wishful thinking on the part of the ideologically committed professional political punditry.

What are Independents' political options currently? (A) Vote as a conservative with the Republicans, or (B) vote as a liberal with the Democrats. That's it, for all intents and purposes. But what if neither choice, Democrat or Republican, is acceptable? Do you simply "drop out"? That would tend to say that we can't make democracy work. That outcome shouldn't be acceptable.

The thesis of this book is that if you provide the forty or so percent of registered voters another option, a practical, workable, and clearly defined option, perhaps some, perhaps many, perhaps most, if not all, would welcome it. More importantly, many might well support or even vote for it. I believe a common philosophy that Independents could coalesce around exists, if they could only recognize it; if only someone would introduce them to it.

What about today's third parties? Not probable from what we see to date. These either tend to be ideological in the extreme or suffer from being a single-issue movement. That doesn't seem like what today's Independents would be looking for. What are they looking for? I think we may have a handle on this. Quite simply, it's good, effective, representative government. I sincerely hope that's not what some call an oxymoron.

Some call this independent voting bloc (which today it really isn't) the swing vote. I believe it's America looking for that political change, looking for that "right direction." Hopefully, we can help them in their search by offering the arguments and conclusions here. It may not be the final word, but it is a start in what I believe many will agree is a valid direction.

Change is often difficult, but not necessarily bad. Often, over time and with increasing experience, understanding, technology innovation, and better information, we can see how change will improve whatever it is we are considering. But before initiating any significant change, it's wise to look beyond the moment and consider the consequences. The Introduction to Robert Ruark's 1950s novel *Something of Value*, about Africa, noted an old Basuto proverb: *"If a man does away with his traditional way of living and throws away his good customs, he had better first make certain that he has something of value to replace them."* That's good advice, especially when considering public policy matters, as I will.

A word or two concerning political philosophy: Why? Because it's necessary to lay at least a shallow foundation now that will assist in supporting an Independent political philosophy later on.

At the deep end of the philosophical pool, political philosophy is defined as the systematic elaboration of the consequences of suggested resolutions of philosophical dilemmas, or of the intractability of those dilemmas (got that?). The greatest works of political philosophy try to present those consequences in relation to fundamental cosmological, ontological, and epistemological issues. In this sense, this book is not (anywhere near) a work of political philosophy.

Near the shallower end of the pool, political philosophy tries both to make sense of what we do and to prescribe what we ought to do. In this case, this book might (possibly) be called a work of political philosophy, but it's practical as opposed to theoretical. Note in the latter definition we use the term "ought" as opposed to "should." There exists a difference in intensity, or degree, if nothing else. It is the difference between a need—ought—and a (moral) duty—should. In this sense, to the degree possible I will try and stay with "ought" in order to minimize contentious questions or issues of (moral) values. Not that values do not have a place—and a significant place—in politics; of course they do. But arguing over them here is not my primary objective.

Philosophically, the question of the proper unit to consider regarding decision making is important. Is it the individual, or is it the community of which the individual is a part? Between James M. Buchanan and Gordon Tullock's *The Calculus of Consent* and John Rawls's *Political Liberalism*, as well as Ian Shapiro's *The State of Democratic Theory*, among a number of other writers about these matters, both starting points are defended. Rawls, in his approach and arguments, is the more normative and theoretical, while Buchanan and Tullock deal more with how the system really (pragmatically) operates, in their views. This makes it a mostly positive view of the processes of decision making and governing. Their views, which are based primarily on an economic approach to decision making, are widely credible and in many instances are compatible with what we experience in the "real world."

On the other hand, in equating the needs and motivations of government, or collective decision making, with those that move and motivate capitalistic enterprise is too one-sided. An economic approach tends to equate an efficiency-oriented, single-purpose (profits) institution (capitalism) with the multiple-purpose and community-oriented institution of self-government (democracy). It makes the implicit assumption that we are all one-dimensional "Economic Man." In the real world, the (fictional) economic man in all of us is present, perhaps in many even dominant, but certainly not in everyone. The theory of utility is broader than Buchanan and Tullock's choice of the economic offshoot theory of marginal utility upon which to base decisions of a collective nature. Nonetheless, this measure of utility is broadly used in decision-making theory today, both inside government and elsewhere. Rawls, like Buchannan and Tullock, stresses the importance of self-interest, or utility, when he says, "The idea of social cooperation requires an idea of each participant's rational advantage, or good. This idea of good specifies what those who are engaged in cooperation, whether individuals, families or associations, or even the government of peoples, are trying to achieve, when the scheme is viewed from their own standpoint."

The point here is that, in one form or the other, self-interest (utility) is a principal consideration in both how we organize for collective decision making and the results this produces in the form of government and the scope of government. With this, I agree.

But whose self-interest is to be considered? Comparing individual preferences or utilities is a major difficulty for these writers—and others. Is what's good for one, just as good, better or worse for another? Buchannan and Tullock hypothesize that no external observer is presumed able to make comparisons of utility among separate individuals. However, Buchannan and Tullock do believe comparison is possible on a relative basis of "situations" and "changes in situations," in terms of their efficiency. This is the so-called Pareto rule, a "weak" ethical postulate that says the welfare of the whole group of individuals is said to be increased if (1) every individual in the group is made better off, or (2) if at least one member in the group is made better off *and* no member in the group is made worse off. This is, in reality, a very narrow concept of measuring (economic or social) utility, once you move beyond a modest number of individuals that can be unanimously polled (even considering modern-day sampling) about whether they believe themselves in fact better off. As consideration expands into very large classes, such as a national population, the assumptions required for even macro-evaluation become difficult to support. Nonetheless, government has seized upon this concept as part of its love affair of the past few decades with cost-benefit analysis.

Rawls approaches the issue of measuring individual preference, or utility, more on a basis of reciprocity. "Reasonable persons," he says "are not moved by the general good as such but desire for its own sake a social world in which they, as free and equal, can cooperate with others on terms all can accept. They insist that reciprocity should hold within that world so that each benefits along with others." I interpret this to mean that while it may not be individually measurable, reasonable people can compromise on the issue of self-interest, such that the result is (kind of) like the Pareto result: On a reciprocal basis, all should experience a result where everyone is at least no worse off than before, on a community or societal level. Obviously, that's a much wider concept than that presented in *The Calculus of Consent*. But it is also presented, Rawls concedes, as how things should work, not necessarily how they do. The question is, could they work this way? "Should" implies can; if they can't, then it is meaningless to propose it.

Rawls makes an observation that Buchannan and Tullock would, I'm sure, find difficult; but from my reading of them, not impossible to agree with: "Every interest is an interest of self (agent), but not every interest is in benefit to the self that has it. Indeed, rational agents may have all kinds of affections for persons and attachments to communities and places, including love of country and of nature; and they may select and order their ends in various ways." Furthermore, Rawls maintained, "Rational agents approach being psychopathic when their interests are solely in benefit to themselves." We remind ourselves of this in developing and presenting an Independent political philosophy.

In this author's analysis, these two views of the place of self-interest in defining the "best" method of determining how collective decision making is to be achieved are neither very different nor incompatible. They are merely put forth differently, from different points of view and scopes. This issue of self-interest, both individual and group, is significant throughout this book, especially in Chapter 6 in considering the issue of why government behaves like it does, in considering an Independent political philosophy in Chapter 9, and in Chapter 12, which considers special-interest influences on government.

A stylistic disclaimer of sorts, or at least an admonition, before proceeding further:

Those of you familiar with the novels of James Michener may find my approach here both good news and bad news. Like Michener, I believe that to fully appreciate and understand the story that will unfold, you first need to be immersed in the background and context in which it takes place. I recall to this day plowing through a hundred pages or so of setting, starting almost with Creation and the geological formation of the world, in both *Centennial* and *Chesapeake*. It was well worth it, but at the time, maintaining interest was somewhat of an effort. I trust the same is true here: it will be worth the effort. For those who simply can't tolerate such a refresher, or review, the case proper for an Independent political option will begin at Part Two. Be forewarned!

One more housekeeping item, style-wise: While the views and opinions herein are my own, or "this Independent's," unless otherwise indicated, I nonetheless prefer to use the corporate "we," or "our," when speaking with my audience rather than always referring to myself. In some instances, "we," refers to you, the reader, and me. It's idiosyncratic, no doubt, but it is a personal preference for which I ask your indulgence.

The genesis of this book dates from about 1993 or 1994, when by chance I picked up William Greider's tome, *Who Will Tell the People*. In the Introduction he stated:

> The blunt message ... is that American democracy is in much deeper trouble than most people wish to acknowledge. Behind the reassuring façade, the regular election contests and so forth, the substantive meaning of self-government has been hollowed out. What exists behind the formal shell is a systemic breakdown of the shared civic values we call democracy ... At the highest levels of government, the power to decide things has instead gravitated from the many to the few, just as ordinary citizens suspect. Instead of popular will, the government now responds more often to narrow webs of power—the interests of major economic organizations and

concentrated wealth and the influential elites surrounding them. In sum the mutual understanding between citizens and government necessary for genuine democracy is now deformed or neglected.* While democracy's decline has consequences for everyone, certain sectors of the citizenry suffer from the loss of political representation more severely and personally than everyone else. In general they are the people who already lack the advantages of higher education or social status.

Their political influence cannot depend upon private wealth since they have little or none. The atrophied political system has left them even more vulnerable to domination by others ... The democratic idea has always been most powerful in America as an unfulfilled vision of what the country might someday become—a society advancing imperfectly toward self-realization. In that sense, democracy is not so much a particular arrangement of government, but a difficult search. It is the hopeful promise the nation has made to itself.

Hyperbole, I assumed as I left his Introduction and started reading my way through the book. But it turned out it wasn't hyperbole, not if you could believe what he documented throughout the book. I was, to say the least, a bit shocked by some of the revelations he made. I was also somewhat disillusioned, disappointed, and even a bit mad at my government and those who comprised it. How dare they! As a fairly average American, now approaching senior middle-age (if I may modestly describe myself that way), who had not delved too deeply or read too widely in the political arena, I felt somewhat betrayed. I also felt a bit naïve. Had I assumed too much, trusted too easily? After all, I was raised to believe this was the most perfect of all societies and governments so far established. This was America, and I, for one, had been privileged to realize my fair share—perhaps more than my fair share—of that American Dream. America! Could what Greider described really be the case?

---

* Consider this in the context of my comment above about problems with our two-party system being just the tip of an iceberg.

Well, some thirteen or fourteen years later, after following the political arena much more closely, doing more research into this area, with one book on the subject already behind me and one unsuccessful candidacy (2000) for the U.S. Senate later, I'm sorry to say it seems plausibly to be the case. The problem is now, after this thirteen-or fourteen-year period, if democracy isn't any worse, it doesn't seem to be any better. If corrective actions (changes) as alluded to here, or by others that might also address this problem are not considered, then I would be concerned that the following observation, attributed to the journalist Robert Kaplan, could become a real possibility: *"The U.S. is evolving into a corporate oligarchy that merely wears the trappings of a democracy."* Mr. Kaplan's observation here (opinion, if you prefer) is not "the problem." It's more a projection of a possible result of the problem, absent corrective change.

My conclusion, which I reiterate throughout the following chapters, is we need a different outcome. The presence of all us Independents, not to mention the specter of Mr. Kaplan's concerns, confirms this.

So read on, read on.

T.R. Harry
June, 2008

Part One

Chapters 1 through 6 establish the justification for the argument made in this book regarding Independents, as well as the conclusions reached. In some reasonably progressive presentation, it attempts to discuss the main environment most of us live in and have to deal with, wherein the political occurs. It takes a few steps beyond simply identifying this environment and tries to say a little about why this environment is like it is: not what it should be like, but why it is like it is. This is an important distinction, because the argument herein is about correcting a status quo, about changing what is to what it needs to be, and, more importantly, can be. The argument is corrective as opposed to theoretical. Again, "should" implies "can." If something simply can't be, then the issue of should be is meaningless.

Chapter 1 gets us started thinking about the issue of Independents, especially the *why* of Independents. It highlights a certain negativism in public perceptions, as expressed in polls, about both government and politics; specifically concerning our two-party system. It asks the question, "Is there a connection between such perceptions and the growth of Independents?"

Chapter 2 begins with the analogy of family to highlight the corporate or communal nature of the problem we have: It affects us all. Why the metaphor of family? Because of its familiarity; because almost without exception, all of us care about our families. In addition, America

1

encompasses an increasing plurality of peoples and views. Hopefully, it is a reasonable plurality, to use John Rawls's term. We need some core concept around which this reasonable plurality can coalesce for basic political purposes. The idea of family expresses this. It also serves to bring out the fact that we have in politics today an infighting going on that really has very little to do with citizens (the family) in general. This is in spite of the fact that those "fighting" would have the family take sides.

Chapter 3 moves us on to the question of what we think of politics and the job our politicians are doing for us currently. The answer to these two questions appear disheartening, to say the least. It probes the issue of government itself—why we have government and the consequences of government—hopefully without turning into Civics 101. It asks questions about the role of the government as well as those governing. It sets the tenor for the next chapter, "Politically, Why We Believe What We Do."

In Chapter 4 we become a bit more theoretical. It considers the issues of values and ideologies in our views of the world and how these affect us individually and collectively. It asks the questions, "How should politics within society function," and "How does politics within society actually function?" The first is a normative issue (how should), the second a positive issue (how does). This leads us to a discussion of how society is viewed and the place of the political domain within it. This in turn takes us on a small side trip to consider the issue of democracy as an ideology (or not). Contrary to much popular belief, democracy is not necessarily democracy is not necessarily democracy. It has evolved over time in both theory and practice in different places around the world. Nonetheless, we define the basic concepts of democracy as it's generally recognized. This leads us more or less naturally into the subject of conservatism and liberalism and the question: Are these two approaches to issues themselves ideologies?

Chapter 5 explores the philosophical gorge between democracy and capitalism, two ideologies that today coexist in America and elsewhere. Both are dominant ideologies in their own fields—political and economic. One promotes equality; the other strives to achieve inequality. There is much potential conflict here, and to understand the power and influences these exert, or attempt to exert on the other, a frank and open consideration of the differences is critical to many of the conclusions reached in the latter part of this book. It *is* that big a deal. As we will show, capitalism is one of just three major players in our society and, in reality, one of only two "active" players in society. That alone makes it a big deal.

Drawing on all this and other materials, Chapter 6 attempts to explain—if just a little—why government behaves like it does. It also examines the motivations of government and how government sees its role, as determined to a large degree (as you might expect) by those holding the reins of government power. This discussion gets us into the shallow end of the pool with a bit of political theory, and we consider what some call Long Wave Theory: Cycles, or patterns, seem to appear in our society and affect the political domain, which has both influenced and been influenced by historical events and circumstances. It is a lengthy chapter, because trying to explain why government behaves like it does is complex. We begin to make recommendations for change in this chapter. These are followed up in the final part of this book as in-depth Independent political proposals.

Chapter 1

Why—and Whence—Independents?

Brook Park, Ohio, is a white, ethnic working-class suburb of Cleveland. Anthony D'Amico, president of the Brook Park Democratic Club, commented recently that Brook Park used to be 1,000 percent Democratic. Before a recent election, he looked at the registration rolls from the town's four wards, and it shocked him: Democrats, 4,448; Republicans 882; Independents, 6,508!

Loudoun County, Virginia, about a forty-minute drive west from Washington D.C., is one of the fastest growing counties in America. It has traditionally been a strong Republican bastion. Today, Loudoun County politicos say the county comprises, roughly, one-third Republicans, one-third Democrats, and one-third Independents. Voting in Loudoun County now closely mirrors that of the state at large.

In California, registration statistics for presidential primaries between 1992 and 2008 show an 83 percent increase in Independent voters, or those declining to state a party preference. Today in California, the two major parties combined share of voter preferences has declined from 87.1 percent in 1992 to 76.0 percent.

It's a documented fact: America is generating an enormous wave of apparent political discontent. An April 2008 poll found that a whopping 81 percent of Americans believe things have pretty seriously gotten off on the wrong track in the United States. This is up from 69 percent in 2007, and 35 percent in early 2002. This discontent, this building *tsunami,* is evident in the form of political dealignment, of voter abandonment of both the Democratic and Republican political parties when registering to vote. This tsunami has been building for some time now. These non-aligned voters are calling themselves "Independents." Should this wave of apparent dissatisfaction find a common shoreline, a common political landfall if you wish, watch out: The power of that wave could come crashing down, with significant implications for politics in America. Both major political parties know it. In fact, in their innermost thoughts, I believe they live in fear of it.

Not that this phenomena of Independents is entirely new. A very young John F. Kennedy, running for the House of Representatives in 1946, spoke of "the traditional parties becoming indistinguishable and ineffective amalgams of conservative and liberal elements while being challenged by the large growth of those who call themselves political independents who owe allegiance to neither party ..." During that time, his description of the parties was pretty accurate. This reflected the still-prevalent "big tent" condition of the parties.

Today, some sixty years later, the stampede of voters declaring themselves independent of party affiliation or preference (including those who decline to state) represent the largest category of registered voters in America, about 38 percent of the voting population, according to the American National Election Studies (ANES) program. In the 2004 national elections, Independents represented 33 percent of all voters going to the polls. Nonetheless, a majority of these Independents continue to vote for one or the other of the two parties. Why, if they have decided they don't want to be identified with either party? Does that make good sense?

The number of political Independents has grown, pretty consistently, from about 20 percent of voters some sixty years ago to almost double that number today. Today they represent the largest single bloc of voters in America. Just why this is seems a reasonable reason to pursue this issue of Independents and their significance or lack thereof.

One thing seems compelling: It's unlikely that this is happening for no reason at all. But is it significant? If both major parties are concerned about it, as I state above, you have think so.

It's surely no revelation that public opinion is fickle. It is also partisan. But when a preponderance of people share similar outlooks over an extended period of time, it seems to me someone should be paying attention. The old adage that where there's smoke, there is usually fire holds true. And the time to most easily handle a fire is before it gets out of control.

Regarding our political system, consider the following "smoke" from an NBC News/*Wall Street Journal* poll over the period from 1995 to 2007; an ASC News poll over the same period, and a 2006 *USA Today*/Gallup nationwide poll. The questions asked and responses were as follows:

"Which of the following statements is closest to your own view of the two-party system today, in terms of how well it defines issues and provides choices for voters …"

	Works fairly well	Has real problems	Is seriously broken	Unsure
2007	20%	47%	29%	4%
1997	15%	55%	27%	3%
1995	15%	54%	28%	3%

"Would you rate the level of ethics and honesty of members of Congress as excellent, good, not so good, or poor?"

	Excellent	Good	Not so good	Poor	Unsure
2006	1%	26%	36%	30%	7%
1995	2%	22%	42%	30%	4%

"How much confidence do you have in Congress to pass meaningful legislation to deal with the issue of corruption in Congress?"

	Great deal	Fair amount	Not much	None at all
2006	4%	28%	44%	24%

These polls cover both of our political parties in the White House over a twelve-year period as well as control of Congress split between the two. This would lead some to conclude that, there are at least widely perceived problems, if not real problems, with our generally accepted (and judicially protected) two-party system and its FPTP (First Past the Post) system of electing representatives to run government on our behalf. It also brings into question the opinion of voters concerning the general moral level of candidates the system seems to produce. Chapter 6 will delve further into this last point.

Almost by default, these inquiries and their answers beg the question, is there a cause-and-effect connection between voter perceptions and the swelling ranks of Independents? Is one driving the other? We'll see if we can't answer these questions. If asked, I would have to say it appears that what we are experiencing politically is a crisis of confidence—more specifically, a crisis of confidence and trust.

While the general level of public opinion regarding trust and confidence usually ebbs and flows during political terms, the trend here seems consistent, and it is not encouraging. Can we speculate as to why trust and confidence are shrinking? Well, consider this simple exercise in reasoning:

- Government is the result of political competition for power–
- Politics and political competition in America are ideological–
- Ideology, in practice, tends to be religious in nature–
- Religion is faith-based belief; it tends to support its own dogma and reject that of others–

- Belief based upon faith implies reliance primarily on trust and confidence—

- People vote for political parties (or their candidates) they trust and have confidence in to provide good government—

- When political parties (or their candidates) fall short of providing the kind of government most citizens want or expect, over time, trust and confidence suffer—

- Without basic confidence and trust in what you believe in, it's difficult to give your support, try as you might—

- Despite your ideology, with such experience you cease to be a supporter of that which purports to represent it—

The result of this conscious or unconscious thought process is that, as a result of distrust based upon experience, you distance yourself from that which has disappointed you; that which has asked for your trust and confidence but has failed to repay you with loyalty. The result, in this case, is a deep skepticism—distrust of politicians and of the governments they direct, irrespective of partisanship, because all appear to have disappointed. But that leads to a dilemma: Regardless of negative feelings about politics and politicians, we haven't yet figured out a (democratic) way to govern except through our present political system. So, in order to maintain government, voters continue to support a system many have come to believe, or at least suspect, does not represent them properly or adequately. Does that make a lot of good sense, at least long-term? Questionably, but what if you have no option?

What can we do about this? How can we restore trust, confidence, and loyalty among the people involved? That's going to be a large part of the subject under discussion here. Certainly the issue of good government, as well as confidence and trust in our political system responsible for delivering good government, is worthwhile spending some time considering. Over the next fifteen chapters, we will do just that. If you have any doubts about its importance, Chapter 4 will make it pretty clear. An "option" is the power or right to choose. Politically today, most of us have—or believe we have—only two options: a conservative choice, as supported by the Republican Party, or a liberal one, as proposed by the Democratic Party. Why are there only two choices, when all these Independents represent voters who, for whatever reason or reasons, appear to be rejecting both parties as their political option; their electoral party of choice?

A good part of the reason—and we will look into this in Chapter 7—is historical. America has had a two-party system based upon single-representative political districts and elections based upon FPTP voting since about 1824. The names of the parties have changed over time, but the number really hasn't. There are demonstrable benefits and advantages to such a system. Our legal system, up to and including the Supreme Court, has ruled over the years in favor of this system much more often than against it. The net result today is an accumulation of case law, as well as a formula the Court uses to weigh arguments, that may not provide exclusivity to our two political parties, but admittedly favors them and the present system.

It is against this historical background and within this legal landscape that we will consider the need for or desirability of an Independent political option. And if, after all is said and done, we decide in favor of such an option, it must also exist within the constraints of this present political/jurisprudential landscape. That is, after all, the real world, and these are real world issues.

With the belief that understanding issues brings clarity, we need to consider some background and related societal, civic, and economic issues before we can make the determination whether an Independent political option is either necessary or desirable. With this in mind, let's turn to these issues now.

Chapter 2

What It Is and What It Isn't

What it is: Let's be very clear about purpose, about what this book is *really* about. It's about our America and the liberal democracy we want to believe offers us the best quality of life that this poor old world of ours has so far experienced.

It's about family, the extended American family; the family that gets along and shares the same national homestead; the family that lives together, works together, and plays together, that competes among themselves and argues with each other, together. It's about just how the family ought to behave and contribute, as well as support each other. What should the rules of the house be? Just who in our national family has the right and obligation to set those rules? When all the smoke is cleared and the rhetoric is considered, that's what it's *really* all about. About America and the implicit promise America has always offered to those in the family who would pursue it: a better tomorrow.

Many in the family demonstrate the realization of this promise. They are better off today than they were yesterday. But at the same time, more than just a few of the family have apparently come to the conclusion that this promise may no longer be available to them. They seem to be no better off today than they were yesterday and in fact are having difficulty not being worse off, according to a variety of qualitative and quantitative yardsticks. That should be a concern to all of us; but, what to do about this?

Clive Crook, writing in the April 2007 *Atlantic Monthly*, asked the question, "What war on the middle class?" In his article "The Phantom Menace," he attempted to show that the so-called American middle class (which according to his measuring rod represents some three-quarters of the population. Based on our own self-declaration based on incomes—per the Pew Research Center— however, the number is closer to 53 percent of us) is not nearly as bad off as many seem to believe. And in a broad material sense, his question about a war on the middle class is at least superficially a good one. Crook, a recent English transplant, compared the issue of class in his native England with the USA. Class, which so many of us colonists still tend to associate with British society, was, by the time he left England in 2005, no longer a very interesting (political) subject, he contends. His experience here, he says, does not support the same conclusion. In his words, "In this country, voters and politicians seem to think and talk about little else, at least when it comes to domestic affairs."

Is there a war on America's middle class? If so, just who is waging it? Who or what, as Mr. Crook puts it, is the menace? Is it the small portion of the non-middle-class whom we refer to as the rich? Or is it the other part of that non-middle-class quarter of Americans defined as the poor who are waging the supposed war? In truth, there really is no war, just as Crook concludes. What there is instead is a need for politicians to find (in their own self-interest) some cause to champion before the voters, and to convince them of the need for such a champion in their defense. Middle-class "values" have historically proved a successful (political) cause to champion.

How often do we hear campaigning politicians proclaim, I want to "fight" for your rights, "fight" for your cause, "fight" for your values, etc., etc., etc. Fight? Is there really going to be a fight? I thought we fought to achieve our basic rights a long time ago, and against a real foe, if you will excuse me, Mr. Crook. No, that's not what it is. There isn't any fight, any middle-class war. It's all political rhetoric—the make-believe knight on the political white stallion defending our "middle class values." In the main, it's hogwash and needs to be recognized as such.

Now this is not to deny that the middle class, as well as those richer and poorer, is not facing a complex set of economic and social pressures, uncertainties, and changing times that are affecting all Americans, some more than others, to be sure. These pressures, uncertainties, and changes induce concern and dissatisfaction within our society—at all levels. We look primarily to elected government and political leadership to arbitrate and/or adjudicate these situations. But today, because of hyper-partisanship separating our two political parties, a paralysis of our government apparatus and that political leadership that should be working to resolve issues for all concerned is obvious. No one group within America, outside the two political parties, is waging war on another.

Nonetheless, the various factions of society compete constantly in their own self-interests. This contributes to conflict in many instances. But we are a country governed by the rule of law and by representatives—responsible to their constituents— elected to govern on our behalf. These two safeguards, properly empowered and applied, ought to (I reiterate, ought to) be sufficient to resolve these many conflicts, or to prevent them from becoming irreconcilable ideological issues. It's not always easy, but it is possible.

If some consider there is a war going on in America, it is only between political elites in their pursuit of power, with most Americans caught in the crossfire. I was personally reminded of this during the 2000 U.S. Senate race in Missouri. The principal candidates, or their representatives, then Senator John Ashcroft, the late governor Mel Carnahan, as well as the author who was running as a third-party candidate, were getting ready to make our pitches before an audience in Kansas City. A member of the press asked the governor how it was going. His reply was an exasperated, "It's a war out there!" So again, the question before us, what to do about all this?

What are we to do about a situation where those who are empowered to select a government (us) are limited today, in a realistic if not legalistic sense, to just two strongly opposed ideological choices, and no matter which of the two is successful at the polls, it is the other's partisan agenda to see that its adversary fails? Where, because of these extreme opposite ideological principles, compromise is usually not an option. I understand competition as well as the next person and have a healthy respect for it. Not, however, to the degree that it is either corrosive or otherwise damaging. How are the American people—ultimately affected by if not intimately involved in producing the outcomes—to make government work for them? How do we get past this partisan intramural competition for power that for so long now seems to produce nothing but political, and hence governmental, stand-offs? We deserve better. *

The answer to the question, "What to do about all this," has to be political, as Chapter 4 will explain more fully. But being political makes this question is a two-sided coin. Because a political issue, it might be due to the attitude and approach of those of the family we chose to make and administer the rules of the house, our political representatives: Do they truly represent our wants, interests, and priorities? Or perhaps the family in general is mostly responsible. (We will consider these possibilities further, classifying them as the demand for versus the supply of political goods). Are we demanding too much, or too little? Voters may have become too indifferent to, complacent with and lazy with respect to our democracy and the democratic process we depend upon to choose those who will represent our interests.

There may be a third possibility as well: undue intervention in the electoral process by some of the extended family (which I refer to as special-interest meddling). Cause and effect may be working both ways here. But either way, the answer to the question is political. And the fact that we feel the need to raise the possibility of an Independent political option here supports this contention.

Independents are not in and of themselves the answer; Independents represent the reason for the need to consider change. Why? Well, if for no other reason, Independent voters now represent the largest single category of registered voters in our country. Independents represent about 38 percent of all registered voters today and in the 2004 national elections, they represented 33 percent of all voters going to the polls.

---

* For those who might question my framing of this issue of "fighting" as strictly between political elites rather than more broadly among factions of Americans generally, they might want to pick up a copy of Ronald Brownstein's new book, *The Second Civil War* (How Extreme Partisanship has Paralyzed Washington and Polarized America). The bottom of page twelve would be a good place to start.

That sure seems significant. You better believe both parties consider it significant!

Significant or not, the issue of Independents ultimately begs the question of the need for change… or not. We want to determine as best we can the underlying reason or reasons for this rise in Independents, this de facto dealignment of the American electorate. I repeat, it is improbable that it is happening for no reason. In our examination of this issue, we more clearly define just what it is that we should expect from our national government in its ongoing role as legislator and administrator of our society. In this respect, we shall also consider just where and why so many Americans believe that government now falls short in this regard. If you question whether or not a majority share these doubts, I suggest you look at recent opinion polls—and their trends—about the degree of confidence the American voter has in both the Congress and the executive branch. Is the perception that government no longer represents the larger populace either fair or valid? We shall also consider what the role of this larger populace may be in arriving at such a conclusion. After all, through its votes, it is that larger populace that is responsible for putting our political representatives in place and then holding them accountable. Are we holding up our responsibilities in this equation?

In the political arena, many talk about responsibility, but few seem really ready or willing to accept it. And in as large and diffuse an organization as the U.S. Government, the buck is too often easily passed. Even when corporate responsibility—"we failed as a congress, or "as a party," for example— may be acknowledged, individually it usually isn't. Just why such denial exists is a mystery. The total is the sum of its parts, and if the total acknowledges responsibility, why aren't the parts held equally accountable?

In its present form, our two-party political system, which we have relied on to select those of the family who make the rules and then administer them, has endured now for over 140 years. While it has always been partisan, over the years it appears to have serviced a majority of the family; e.g., if you weren't a "big tent" Republican, you were a "big tent" Democrat, with just a few on the more extreme fringes of these opposing ideologies. Today, however, more than a few apparently feel there is no place for them in these "big tent" parties and that the parties have lost touch with the populace at large—the family, if you will. Increasingly it appears the family at large is letting this be known by the way that they declare their electoral preference when registering to vote. They increasingly opt to be neither Republican nor Democrat.

Why? What is the purpose or significance of this individual rejection of the parties? It's almost as if we are too embarrassed to be publicly associated with one or the other of them. Is that a proper description of this phenomenon, this apparent directionless movement? Is it only a meaningless gesture of individualism that has produced this phenomenon? Or is the family at large trying to send a message to the present political system? That some 25 to 40 percent of registered voters (depending upon whose statistics you cite) now declare themselves independent of political affiliation is something that the system cannot, or at least should not, ignore. Why not?

That's the question the next two chapters will address.

Chapter 3

The Political Status Quo

I implied in the Introduction that our societal equilibrium, our overall national status quo, as reflected by that significant presence of Independent voters, is out of Balance. We'll define that term—Balance with a capital "B"—in detail when we consider this issue in Chapter 9. However, to reiterate, the reason for this imbalance is political, and so here we want to focus on that aspect of the bigger issue.

First, let's clarify and then examine what we mean by the "political status quo." Let's start by defining the term "political," for which my old *Random House College* dictionary provides the following: *1. Of or pertaining to, or concerned with the science or art of politics; 2. Of or pertaining to or connected with a political party; 3. Of or pertaining to the state or its government.* For our purposes here we'll go with number 3, as it is with issues concerning government we will deal.

And status quo? Let's agree to accept the single definition my dictionary provides, which is, "*The existing state or condition.*" So, for our purposes, we define the political status quo as: the existing state or condition of our government. That's pretty straightforward.

Just what is the existing political status quo, the state or condition of our (federal) government? How would most of us characterize it? I wish the answer was as clear-cut and simple as the definition. To a large degree, it depends upon one's particular view of government, what we expect from it, and what we have experienced because of it. Bottom line, in the general sense of Americans as either the beneficiaries or victims of government, status quo is our opinions: our personal attitudes or judgments about government. But the really significant characterization about the recent government record is that it appears, based on our opinions, to please or satisfy so few. This is clearly the case if you use as your yardstick the responses (opinions) given by Americans when asked about their satisfaction with either our legislative or executive branches of government and whether Americans generally believe our country is on the right track or headed in the right direction.

Interestingly, this apparent dissatisfaction with the political status quo isn't particularly partisan or ideological. A March 2007 Pew poll showed that the proportion of people who express a positive view of the Democratic Party has declined by six points since January 2001. The proportion of people who express a positive view of the Republican Party has declined by fifteen points over the same period. Currently, Congress is even more unpopular than an unpopular White House, experiencing the lowest approval rating in 35 years.

When approval rates for these leaderships are running at such low levels and trending in these negative directions, you have to assume that a preponderance of Americans—more than just Independents—believe the existing state or condition of our government, the political status quo, is not good. Under today's conditions, that seems almost a no-brainer. We are not happy with government! In fact, *The Economist* put it a bit stronger, saying that one finding that stands out in the polls is that most Americans distrust government strongly. Just why, we'll get to, but I can tell you right now, that issue of Balance is definitely significant.

We ought to expect more from government! Expectations count. It is a truism that if you don't expect much, just about anything you do receive is considered satisfactory. Experts insist that most of us average Americans neither knows what is going on in government, nor is it in our self-interest to take the time to try and find out. Apparently, the personal cost benefit of becoming an informed voter is unprofitable for us. So, why try? This is the so-called economic view of voter participation. No single vote is going to determine or change anything, so why bother? Why expect very much? Why try? I can think of at least one good reason: to keep our democracy alive and healthy and our government representative, that's why.

To be fair, there are usually two sides to an argument. We aren't going to play the blame game here, but a couple of points have to be made, for both sides, as to why the political status quo is generally considered so unacceptable. I think it has to do with those expectations. What do most of us expect from government? Apparently not very much, and what we do expect is too often negative. Example: A 2007 Democracy Corps poll found that Americans believe, by a majority of 57 percent to 29 percent, that government makes it harder for people to get ahead in life. The same poll found that 83 percent of people believe that if the government had more money, it would probably waste it. The perception many of us have is that there is very little government can do that is positive and much it can do—and often does—that is negative.

Well, if that is the case, then why have government? Well, yes, you say, but we have to have a government. Okay, why? To make and enforce laws, you say. To provide for the public safety and defense, you add. To control the economy, to provide public-goods and social services that the non-government sector can't or won't provide, some of you toss in. To issue and control the money supply and regulate interstate commerce, reminds someone. All true. To look after the welfare of those less well off; to oversee the care and treatment of indigenous Americans; to provide educational opportunities and civil liberties and to prevent excessive economic and social inequality within our populace; to protect our environment; to guarantee us all our rights. And this is all true. These are some of the fundamental services we look to government to provide.

That's quite a list of government responsibilities, or perceived responsibilities, and it's surely not exhaustive. I say "perceived" because many of us, though not all, would accept some of these as government's rightful obligations. This may help explain why not just a few of us give government failing grades in its results. We are not happy with how it appears to be directing its efforts. Why aren't "we" getting more of government's attention? Well, government has to set priorities, like all of us, no? Maybe government sees some of these as higher priorities than others. Okay, so is it a matter of the "squeaky wheel getting the grease"? Sometimes.

Recently (August 2007), we saw government priority and attention ruled by the squeaky wheel. It appeared we might see government "grease" infrastructure spending for a time, at least until public attention was focused someplace else, because of the very visible failure of a pretty big bridge up in Minnesota. Right then, the issue of America's crumbling infrastructure was (again) highlighted in the public view. It became a political issue, so it received at least public lip service from government—the attention that it should have been getting all along. But isn't this is a good example of how government shouldn't function, and why? Look at the results: People were killed in a spectacular collapse; an entire major community enduring who knows how long until normal intra-city traffic was restored. (It was a full year!) The tragedy here is that this particular bridge was rated in "serious to poor" condition during the previous consecutive seventeen years; yet little or nothing was apparently done about this. Thirteen people died, 145 were injured; the state government is paying out thirty-eight million dollars to compensate the victims for their injuries and losses. Why should we have to put up with this? And this is simply the latest example of government attention by crisis.

Here's another potential "crisis" government may face that should have been getting serious attention starting years ago: air traffic control failure(s). Think of the horrendous potential there. When? I don't know, but I've been expecting it since at least 1997, when I penned my first book and highlighted the issue. Sadly, I continue to give it a high probability. Why? Because lack of leadership and priority at the responsible level, which is the federal government, has allowed any "fix" to drag on for years. Excuses you can hear plenty of, but those don't get you any closer to a solution. The current status of this important issue is that the House passed its version of an air traffic control modernization bill in 2007, but debate recently bogged down in the Senate amid partisan wrangling. Congress is not expected to do anything to further this issue now until 2009. Priorities and consequences, my friends; priorities and consequences. And in this sense, I don't mean the priorities of the privileged few (in the politically powerful sense of that term), but priorities that affect the many (and politically weak). That's another reason to have representative government.

That's one side of the argument, a lack of leadership and priorities. The other side is perhaps that we voting (or not), tax paying (or not) citizens are simply expecting too much from government. As our country continues to grow and expand (and the world it seems shrinks) and as our society matures, we look more and more to government to keep us safe, sound, and comfortable, almost from cradle to grave. Should we look to government for all this? Possibly, although that was arguably the original reason for government; it's questionably a good reason for it today. It may just be that somewhere along the way we lost our original sense of just why we have government. If that's the case, then is it time to "get back to basics," as the saying goes? Admittedly that would be neither easy nor painless for many. Furthermore, it's probably no longer even possible in this day and age. Government is one of the three major players in our society today. Government—big government—appears here to stay. The issue then is to focus its power and maximize its utility for all of us, not just some of us. That's a point we'll come back to.

Alexis de Tocqueville, that Frenchman who flitted around America back in the 1830s, had a lot to say about our country, our government, and our democracy. It was mostly good and laudatory. But he did point out a potential weakness in our fledgling democracy: He predicted that when a majority of voting citizens realized they can vote themselves more and more free (or at least at no direct cost to themselves) benefits, our system was liable to collapse of its own weight.[*] Are we at the point of demanding that government provide us with too much in the way of benefits— social or otherwise? This is an issue, considering the political status quo. But unlike Tocqueville, I don't think it takes a majority of voters to accomplish this collapse. I think a minority of us could do the trick, and this needs to be better understood. (I refer you back to Mr. Kaplan's purported observation/opinion highlighted in the Introduction.)

---

[*]   We'll look at another of our French ami's concerns about democracy when we wrap all this up in our final chapter.

On the surface at least, it's pretty apparent that the political status quo is today considered unacceptable by the majority of Americans. Looking at how to correct it is one of our next objectives. Let's pursue this, keeping those Independent voters in mind.

Chapter 4

Politically, Why We Believe What We Do

In the development of our own personal values and attitudes, most of us are exposed to and influenced by a variety of belief systems and institutions as we grow and mature. These include religious, social, economic, and/or political views of the world that are, or are believed to be, internally consistent and consciously held by many other people. We call these belief systems ideologies. An ideology is a belief system accepted as fact or truth by those who hold to it. It provides the believer with a picture of the world both as it is and as it should be, in accordance with those beliefs. As such, ideology organizes the tremendous complexity of the world into patterned beliefs, which are fairly simple and understandable:.

There has been considerable debate and discussion concerning the service or disservice of ideologies over the years. Karl Marx (1818–1883) described as ideological any set of political *illusions* produced by the social experience of a class. For Marx, a person's membership in a particular class produces a picture of the world shaped by the experiences of that class. Karl Mannheim (1893–1947) likened ideology to the blinders on a horse: From that perspective, an ideology allows us only a limited view of the world. Mannheim proposed what he called "the particular conception of ideology." In a nutshell, this means the belief that the other person's ideas but not ours are false representations of the world, an illusion or a mask, depending on whether they are consciously recognized or not.

Sigmund Freud (1856–1939) also made a point about beliefs such as ideologies. Like Marx, Freud held that ideological belief systems are usually illusions that delude and keep us content in a difficult, if not intolerable, condition. Freud prescribed psychoanalysis if the illusion became sufficiently pathological; Marx prescribed revolution.

Some contend that ideological politics hasn't really existed in the United States, or if it did, all that ended well over fifty years ago. Others contend that ideology is alive and operating in American politics. From the current perspective, such a debate seems a bit one-sided. Even if ideological politics have never before existed in the United States, they do now and have for well over two decades, and the roots of the contemporary situation go back to precisely the time when the debate over the end of ideology was raging in the late 1950s. However, the debate itself is interesting because it reflects an attitude toward ideology that continues to the present, at least in theory if not in practice. That is that ideology, by both sides of the debate, was seen as a bad thing. Ideological politics were seen as divisive politics; politics that made compromise impossible and drove people apart. Today, many would probably continue to agree with that viewpoint. But so far, sentiment hasn't changed very much, politically speaking. And that is something Independents would focus on.

Not to push this point too hard at this moment (we will take it up again later), it should not be concluded that we all have ideologies. We all have beliefs, in the large part gained from identification with or membership in some group. However, unless the beliefs are recognized or acted upon, it is difficult to say we have an ideology. The fact that more and more American voters are opting out of the identifiable ideological positions of being called a Republican or a Democrat may reflect just how much ideology is necessary, desirable, or tolerable in our society and politics today. Or, as suggested in Chapter 1, perhaps it is not the ideology proper, but the parties' actions and behavior that account for this.

This point leads us naturally to ask two questions: (1) How should politics within society function, and (2) How does politics within society actually function? The answer to the first question provides us with a view of our value system. The answer to the second question gives us an image of the political system within society in actual operation. Any analysis of the first question involves understanding our value system(s) as a liberal democratic society. That involves some comprehension of the theoretical or philosophical foundations thereof, which involves some familiarization with *the socialization system*, probably the most important segment of society. Socialization is the process by which individuals gain the values of the society as their own.

To answer the first question—how politics should function within society—one must look at *the social stratification system*, the way in which a society ranks groups within it. Social stratification is usually summed up within a political ideology by the question of equality. In America, social stratification, or class, has always been played down, equality played up. In fact, we have no distinct social class by purely social qualification as exists, or existed, in England, for example. Nonetheless, social stratification does exist in America. It is based generally on wealth and education, with a good deal of potential social mobility—in both directions. Only if there were no economic, social, political, or other inequalities would social stratification be absent. Such a society has never been realized, not even in the glorified Greek city-states of antiquity.

In our society, economics is the (very large) tail that wags the dog, so to speak. So quite obviously, in understanding our value system, we must consider *the economic system,* which is concerned with the production, distribution, and consumption of wealth. In America, this is basically accomplished through a modified free market capitalistic system. In recent times, most value systems reject extremes of wealth and poverty, which are deemed excessive, and all have incorporated means of correcting the extreme imbalances. Today, the Western capitalistic economic system is a model much of the rest of the world attempts to emulate. It is a star feature of our society, but one with a double edge to it as we will discuss.

Finally, we need to consider the political arena in evaluating our values and ideology. *The political system* is that segment of society that draws together or integrates all the others. Within the political system, decisions are made that are binding upon the whole of society.

To some degree, a political ideology includes all of the above aspects (*socialization system, social stratification system, economic system*). Thus, the political arena holds the key to any understanding of the overall ideological and social systems.

I suggest you reread the above paragraph. It is a short but concise explanation of just why politics is so critical to our societal well-being. It represents, in a nutshell, just why more and more Americans may be becoming skeptical of traditional party politics. What transpires in the political arena is the deciding factor in the kind of society we shall live in, not only today, but for years to come. If there are features in our society we are not happy with, it is to the political system we must look to correct them. Independents are apparently "ahead of the curve" in perceiving—if only unconsciously—this important fact.

Democracy as an Ideology

Democracy is the political and social ideology prevalent in the United States and among many other countries. But, contrary to popular conception, democracy is not democracy is not democracy. It has evolved over time through modifications, both in certain theories called democratic and in the practices of a number of countries called democratic.

For some, the term "democracy" should represent only those systems where everyone has a say in producing the laws that they are to follow. This may be either direct democracy, where everyone votes for the laws, or participatory democracy, where the people themselves may put forth laws for consideration through the initiative process. What we enjoy here in America is more of a republican form of government than a truly democratic form. A republican form of government is one whereby the people at large delegate their democracy by choosing representatives to do the governing on their behalf. The key elements of democracy, or at least those elements normally considered significant in a democracy, are:

1. Citizen involvement in political decision making (directly or through representatives)

A defining characteristic of democracy, citizen involvement means either direct or indirect (through the vote) participation in government. In an effective democratic representative system, citizen involvement should help ensure that public officials remain responsible to the people.

2. Some degree of equality among citizens
    Equality as a general concept contains five separate elements: Political equality, equality before the law, equality of opportunity, economic equality, and social equality, or equality of respect.

3. Some degree of liberty or freedom granted to or retained by citizens
    Undoubtedly, the most influential approach to liberty is found in the distinction between the rights a person has, or should have, as a human being (natural rights) and the rights derived from government (civil rights). While there is no universal agreement on specific natural rights, it is generally agreed that after the formation of government, these rights must become civil rights, or rights specifically guaranteed and protected by the government, even, or particularly, against itself.

4. A system of representation
    Practically, a system of direct democracy works only within small political units. Therefore, theories developed suggesting that this problem could be overcome by one individual representing an area or a number of people. It has been widely adopted. As a result, contemporary democracy is usually referred to as "representative democracy."

5. An electoral system—majority rule
    If citizens are to retain and exercise some control over political decision making, some method must be devised so the people can either maintain or remove the representatives from office. This is achieved through periodic elections. Many argue that the electoral system is a defining characteristic of a democracy, and majority rule is

generally considered the single most important part of the electoral system. In a representative democracy, most people participate in the political system through the electoral process. The electoral system, although seemingly only a mechanism for determining the near-term composition of the government, actually provides the major and sometimes the sole means of political participation for individuals living in a large, complex modern society. The electoral system therefore takes on particular importance in democratic theory. It is the key to whether or not the system is, in fact, really as democratic as intended. (Hold this thought! We will return to it in several contexts as we consider the need for an Independent political option.)

To recapitulate, the principles of democracy all relate to each other, and all stem from one most fundamental principle: citizen involvement. Politically, equality and freedom are both characteristics of and protection for citizen involvement. Democracy demands the freedom to vote and the equality of the vote; they are protection for citizen involvement, because a free and equal electorate can insist on the maintenance of that freedom and equality.

Aside from the above framework around which a democracy is constructed, there's a secondary consideration having to do with the role of the economic system within society. This has significance because the economic system is usually the engine that provides the power, or lack of it, for the prosperity of society and its members. As mentioned, the United States supports capitalism, or the "mixed economy," as our economic system is sometimes called, over any other as the better, more just, and certainly more efficient economic system. However, not all countries look as favorably on capitalism as we do. And there is another option besides democratic capitalism: democratic socialism. Today, however, capitalism appears to have bested socialism as a preferred economic model. The basic difference between the two is the degree of private versus public holding of the primary means of production and distribution and the reliance on the marketplace to make economic investing decisions. While remnants of socialism live on in a few countries, in its current developed form, it is not a serious ideological contender today.

But having said that, it must be added that capitalism is also no longer the original free market system it was conceived to be. We have learned that totally free markets and unregulated business are not generally compatible with democracy. Capitalism, which is theoretically compatible with slavery, does not, left to its own, interface effectively with democracy, which is more egalitarian by design.

Conservatism and Liberalism

"Well sir, if you're not a Conservative, then you must be a Liberal." But is it that simple? Is there any difference, any saving grace, as it were, in being mildly influenced by one or the other of these positions as opposed to being excessively in favor of one or the other? We call one extreme reactionary (conservative) and the other extreme radical (liberal). In our culture, these extremes are most often considered pejorative terms. What's the difference between the two?

Just where do these descriptive terms fit in with our examination and development of an Independent political option? Are these two approaches to issues of the day themselves ideologies? Well, yes, they probably are. But in our context it makes more sense to consider them as sub-ideologies within the larger philosophical value system of democracy. Here is how we most often describe the differences between these poles:

Conservatism within democracy today is best described as follows:

1. Resistance to change
2. Reverence for tradition and a distrust of human reason
3. Rejection of the use of government to improve the human condition (ambivalence regarding government activities)
4. Favoring individual freedom but willing to limit freedom to maintain traditional values
5. Anti-egalitarian (distrust of human nature)

Liberalism within democracy today can be characterized as follows:

1. Having a tendency to favor change

2. Possessing faith in human reason

3. Being willing to use government to improve the human condition

4. Favoring individual freedom but uncertain about economic freedom

5. Being ambivalent regarding human nature

The differences between these poles are obvious and significant to even the casual observer. But consider also, a quick review of these positions against the above five principles of democracy show no inconsistency with this value system. If that's the case, then just why can't they work together better in the halls of government to support and further the American promise? Probably because those who hold these contrasting views of the status quo find it ideologically distasteful to accept compromise. Liberalism and conservatism are primarily attitudes toward change within the democratic tradition. Too often, attempts are made to transform them into major ideologies with rigidly defined beliefs. This is to accord them more importance, in the long run, than they actually have. Their impact is primarily in response to current problems and issues. Again, hold this point in mind. We will consider it in some detail in Part II as we develop our Independent political option.

Okay, that's our landscape, the background against which we will consider the need or desirability of developing an Independent political option. A landscape consisting of ideology (values) and an understanding of what democracy demands in order to deliver to its citizens the benefits of freedom, liberty, and the opportunity for a better tomorrow. America was meant to guarantee the first two and to offer freely—to make available, if not guarantee—the latter. All of us, in one form or another, want to continue to believe these benefits are available to us.

Let's move on now and talk just a little about the often antagonistic relationship between democracy and capitalism and the effects upon the growing Independent phenomenon.

Chapter 5

Democracy and Capitalism

For a couple of reasons as we consider the need for an Independent political option, another look at our capitalistic economic system is an essential part of the landscape. First, as mentioned, in a macro approach, the capitalistic economic sector is one of only three players in our society. The other two are government and the people, as a group. As such, capitalism's economic influence upon our society is, as most realize, huge. Therefore, such influence can be expected to exert a comparably huge influence on the mediator of our society, government. We need to examine this point in some detail when considering any possible Independent agenda.

Secondly, there are significant, even contradictory, differences between the ideologies of capitalism and those of democracy. We need to understand these as we consider the political workings of our society. However, I want to preface my remarks here by clarifying that while we need to understand the differences, the antagonisms, and the potential threats that these pose, such comments are not intended to prejudice an economic system that has at this point in history come to dominate the economic framework of most societies and that has made America both an economic world leader and provided the wealth that we as citizens have come to take for granted—at least most of us, most of the time. Nonetheless, it is a must to keep the following issues between democracy and capitalism clearly in mind as we work our way forward here.

It is essential to recognize that democracy and capitalism, which we expect to coexist in mutual support of each other, have very different theoretical beliefs about the proper distribution of power. One believes in a completely equal distribution of power (one man, one vote); the other believes in the accumulation and restriction of power to those who either have it or can acquire it by means of driving competition for power out of the picture. Survival of the fittest is not a bad description of how capitalists view their system. To state it in its starkest form, capitalism is perfectly compatible with slavery. Democracy, normatively, is not compatible with slavery.

Over time, two main factors have allowed these two power systems, based on antithetical principles about the right distribution of power, to coexist. First, it has always been possible to convert economic power into political power or, conversely, political power into economic power. Few held one without gaining the other. This represents the potential for collusion, or concentration of power among the economic and political elites. That in turn is a potential threat to the effective and proper working of a representative democracy. Second, government historically has been actively used to alter market outcomes and generate a more equal distribution of income than would have been produced in the market if it had been left alone.

Historically, since market economies haven't produced enough economic equality to be compatible with democracy, all democracies have found it necessary to interfere in the market. In our country, a wide variety of programs were designed to promote equality and/or stop inequality from rising. In the nineteenth century, compulsory publicly financed education was followed by cheap land-grant universities. The Homestead Act gave land to Americans wishing to go west rather than making them pay for it. The railroads were regulated to prevent the owners from using their monopoly power to reduce the income of the middle-class customers. Later, antitrust laws were introduced to stop other types of monopolists from exercising their full potential market power. These were survival-of-the-fittest capitalists who were deliberately hobbled by government. The twentieth century followed, with the progressive income tax, unemployment insurance, Social Security, the GI Bill, and affirmative action for minorities. In the late 1960s, Medicare and Medicaid provided national health insurance for the elderly and the poor. At the end of all of those efforts, the United States still had a very unequal distribution of income and wealth but a much more equal distribution of purchasing power than it would have had without these programs.

Using political power to restrict market power and/or reduce market inequalities is a balancing act. If too much income is taxed away from those who have earned it under the rules of capitalism and then handed out to others who are given income on some basis other than their productive effort, capitalistic incentives may cease to function. The key question is how much economic (and hence social) inequality government can prevent before the limit is reached. Political philosophy and one's vision for society are important determinants here, obviously. But the alternative to having government step into the market on the side of those who are losing out in a market economy is to drive the economically weak out of society. Where do they go? How do they live? Are these the "lumpen proletariat" that Marx described? What would be the effect on the rest of society if they do become economically banished, in effect?

Is it possible we are seeing some evidence of such a slide toward this today in the form of income inequalities? By most measures, these inequalities are increasing such that government is, or for many may become, the provider of last resort. If the capitalistic economic system can find no market mechanism to provide for their participation and hence their means of economic support and government becomes the provider of last resort, where is government going to find the means to do so? Consider if you will the Earned Income Tax Credit, a negative income tax that compensates the working poor among us today trying to live on substandard incomes. Considering the overall levels of corporate profitability, you might properly ask if this is anything but a subsidy to the business community. (Chapter 15 expands on this issue.)

While democracy considers inequality a problem, according to capitalists, it's not their problem. Capitalism can argue that the overall economic process is fair, but it has to be agnostic about the "rightness" and "fairness" of any specific outcomes. Capitalism has a hard time defending the inequalities that it generates with an opposing set of beliefs as to why inequalities are right and fair. Within its value system, capitalism accepts no responsibility for those who fail in a free market model. For capitalism, it is simply not their responsibility. Thus it acts consistently not to accept any responsibility, absent imposed government rules and regulations. And capitalism—business, as an interest-group in our society—understandably resists such government interference to the degree it possibly can.

As a result, from the perspective of capitalism, there are few positives that government can contribute to the economy and many places where it can harmfully interfere. Such a view, however, obscures capitalism from recognizing that government is something necessary for its successful functioning. Without government providing pure public goods, such as the legal system, public education, and an infrastructure of public transportation, not to mention public safety and national defense, capitalism would be forced to pay for these activities itself, if it were to function at all. In short, what is missing in capitalism's rather negative view of government is an understanding that free markets require a supportive physical, social, intellectual, educational, and organizational infrastructure. As importantly, it requires some form of social glue if individuals are not to be constantly battling each other. At the end of the day, the issue is not individual choice versus social bonds but discovering the best mix of individual and communal actions that will allow a society to persist and flourish. The whole is the sum of its parts.

While we have highlighted the conflicts between democratic and capitalistic ideologies here and why the latter appears to be—and is—antagonistic to a democratic outlook, is there nothing positive to say for it? Sure there is; quite a lot. As a business model it has been, and continues to be, very successful. It's the dominant business ideology, worldwide. It provides opportunity for a very wide range of abilities and even personal interests. It satisfies the material needs of the preponderance of society well, from the points of view of both selection and affordability. It is both a stabilizing (conservative) factor for society as well as a vehicle that, out of necessity and self-protection, will respond to challenging changes and innovations. When push comes to shove, I'm all for it!

But at the same time, capitalism chafes under the yoke of external influence, influence concerned with its sole focus on the profit motive and short-term view of the future. Today, although there are consumer watch organizations, unions, and benevolent organizations that try to monitor business's behavior, it is still primarily the provenance of government to assure that capitalism remains society's servant and not its master. In this continuing relationship, government, as the representative of the people as well as the supporter of our economy, faces the very difficult task of balancing the needs of both sides. In its efforts to minimize undue economic inequalities, government must be ever cautious of that "too much" limit, where capitalistic incentives cease to function and capitalism ceases to produce. Government must assure the people that capitalism, while basically free to pursue its own ends, serves at least the minimum economic needs of the people it employs. This means assuring that the overall rewards from capitalism are equitably enough distributed among the people. Chapter 9 will expand on this principle.

We mentioned how economic and political power seem to go together. This is, or should be, a concern to everyone in a democracy. If genuine and effective representative democracy is to prevail in America, then those features of economic and political power that might work together for their own ends to cancel out the underlying democratic advantage must be continually monitored to assure that it doesn't happen. Democracy should be permanently committed to the goal of nurturing and defending equality in political expression. This is so even if we concede that private wealth and power will always have an advantage and that individuals will thus always be unequal in their potential to exert political influence. The ideal, one might suppose, would be to create in politics what is called a level playing field. However, our existing political system is prejudiced in the opposite direction. It actually subsidizes the political expression of those who already enjoy the advantage in resources (wealth), and we will detail exactly how this occurs. We will also suggest how this might be remedied, with prejudice to no one.

A remedy to unequal political representation is an absolute necessity, because, as pointed out, the political system is that segment of society that draws together or integrates all the others (the socialization system, social stratification system, and economic system). If we can't get the political system right, we can't expect the other segments to function harmoniously in line with the reasonable expectations of our democracy. And if not, well, there goes the hope for opportunity, the American dream of a better tomorrow, for an increasing number of us.

Chapter 6

Why Government Behaves Like It Does

Fareed Zakaria in his 2003 book *The Future of Freedom* relates the following exchange: During the 1990s, an American scholar traveled to Kazakhstan on a U.S. Government-sponsored mission to help the country's new parliament draft its electoral laws. His counterpart, a senior member of the Kaszak parliament, brushed aside the many options the American expert was outlining, saying emphatically, "We want our parliament to be just like your Congress." The American was horrified, recalling, "I tried to say something other than the three words that had immediately come screaming into my mind: *"No you don't!"* Zakaria continues, "This view is not unusual. Americans in the democracy business tend to see their own system as an unwieldy contraption that no other country should put up with." This self-held impression brings to mind Sir Winston Churchill's well-known observation that democracy is the worst form of government there is, except for all other forms we have tried to date.

Why is this? Why does our government behave like it does? The explanation lies most likely in two separate but related areas: one systemic, the other political. That is, the system our founding fathers gave us and the way that system functions under today's conditions. We can explore this phenomenon by looking at government from several angles: structurally, functionally, politically, economically, ideologically, and theoretically.

Structurally

On the surface at least, government appears to be structured and behave much like any other complex organization: in a functional and hierarchical manner, with a goal, or purpose. Not to overstress an analogy, it has a common group behind it (citizens), a "charter" (the Constitution), "board of directors" (the legislature), and "an executive" in charge of running it (the executive branch), as well as a strong and independent "legal department" (the judicial branch). The analogy to most organizations breaks down here, however, in how the powers and authorities are allocated between and among this hierarchy, and in its purpose. The charter (Constitution) provides for the stockholders (citizens) to select both the legislators and the executives, and both these authorities get to pick the legal department, or at least agree upon the senior appointments. That makes our hierarchical pyramid rather flat at the top. This makes pinpointing responsibility rather more difficult, or at the very least makes policy setting difficult and buck passing easier. Further complicating this is the fact that the charter stipulates that we need to reselect part of our directors every other year, and our executive every four years. This we could describe as the "contractarian" element in government.

Now, to this structural potpourri, we add lawmaking, which is the legislative prerogative. The charter once again lays out just what kind of lawmaking responsibility pertains to which chamber of the legislature, the House or the Senate. In general, Congress's legislative authority is stipulated in Section 8 of Article I of the Constitution. Keep in mind that our founding fathers purposely set up government in this separation of powers model in an attempt, we are told, to minimize the potential for concentration of power in the hands of one or the few. Recall the time frame: late eighteenth century. Monarchy and rule by the few over the many were still common in those countries from which America sprang. Today's government leaders have to live with this situation as best they can. So, keep in mind, organizationally, this is the hand we have been dealt. But also keep in mind the fact that the philosophy behind the U.S. Constitution—fear of accumulated or concentrated power—is no less relevant today than it was in 1789.

Functionally

To this organizational Rube Goldberg structure add a mandated multiplicity of government functions and you get, by definition, complexity. To that list of governmental responsibilities we drew up in Chapter 3, which was pretty complex, add International Relations, Transportation, Energy, and a couple of others. Today's current total is fifteen functional executive (cabinet) departments, plus the vice president, who report directly to the president or the Office of the President. In addition to this, under President George W. Bush, cabinet-level rank has also been accorded to five additional posts. Organizational gurus would confirm that that represents a fair (meaning large) span of control to deal with. That's the direct chain of command. Add to this an entirely independent layer of legislative committees—both House and Senate, in most cases—dealing with these functional departments and approving their budgets, and you not only increase complexity but add pressure and influence to complexity.

Politics and Ideology

Now add to this the fact that today we have two major opposing ideological views on the hows and whys of government: liberal and conservative, or, politically, Democrat and Republican. Because of this, we often end up with an ideologically "split" legislature and/or an executive and legislative branch that are often at political (ideological) odds as they try to run the country. Looked at in this light, it's a wonder anything gets accomplished. And the evidence, at least based on opinion polls, seems to indicate a lot of Americans don't think much of substance does in fact happen.

The ideological opposition leads naturally to politics, which by one definition is the use of intrigue or strategy to obtain any position of power or control. Power or control (domination) of course is what each ideology strives for. Political parties backed by ideologies were not an original part of our founding fathers' plans, but by early in the

1800s parties began playing a part in the pursuit of power. By Andrew Jackson's time in the 1830s, party politics—usually two major parties at any time—had become the dominant mode of American political activity. And so it remains today.

Now with all this formal structure, and built-in authorities, and powers, as I opined earlier, shouldn't we expect better? Why don't we get better, more efficient, and especially more effective representative governance? Well, it wouldn't be hard to conclude that a formula that is tantamount to the following simply doesn't add up:

> Structural complexity + mandated functionality + lack of pinpointed responsibility + defused and divided authority + frequent executive personnel turnover + political pressure and influence + opposing political ideologies = good government

That simply doesn't appear to be a formula for a win-win situation, does it? So, how can we rearrange it so it is? Certainly that's what America needs.

Before we consider that, there are at least two other areas we need to peer into to discover why government behaves like it does. These are a little less transparent than what we have looked at so far, but at the same time no secret. One is the theory or philosophy of government. The other is the consequence of dwindling political party electoral influence. Before examining these, however, I want to interject a bit of the perceived view of the public's attitude toward government as reflected by our opinions of those who compose it, at least on the elected side.

Politicians

From a broader historical perspective, many contend that the notion that today's politicians are any worse than the norm is unsupported. Yes, there have been better and worse times. (Few would pine for the "good old days" of Rutherford B. Hayes or Millard Fillmore.) But through most of our history, politicians have been pretty normal—or at least consistent—trying to survive and flourish within the system. When he was president of Harvard, Derek Bok asked the longtime Speaker of the House of Representatives Thomas P. O'Neill if he thought the quality of people elected to Congress over thirty years had gotten better or worse. "Tip" thought for a minute and replied, "The quality is clearly better, much better. But the results are definitely worse." With this in mind, ponder a bit on the following, largely having to do with politicians and the public's impressions of them.

In his latest book, *Why We Hate Politics* (2007), Colin Hay suggests that if we are to understand contemporary levels of political disengagement and disaffection, we might do well to reflect upon the assumptions we project onto politicians and our reasons for doing so. He offers several core claims, including these:

- We do tend to assume the worse of political actors.

- Although this is by no means unprecedented historically, the prevalence of such assumptions does serve to characterize the period since the 1980s in the advanced liberal democracies.

- The prevalence of such assumptions is in fact an index of the hold that a particular body of theory—public choice theory—has come to exert over public policy since the 1980s.

His first two claims will ring true for many today. His finger-pointing toward public choice theory may be less familiar to most. To follow through with Hay's important issues here about the quality and the perception of the quality of our political representatives, a bit of a detour through some history and a closer look at the issue of public choice theory is necessary.

Theory

What is public choice theory? This question gets us if not directly into, at least up close and personal to the issue of theory or philosophy of government. For our part such theory is defined as a system of principles for guidance in practical affairs. In this case, it is specifically concerned with the practical affair of governing. We will explore the question of values and ethics later on, but suffice it to say that the genus Homo sapiens (you and I) have developed a need to conduct ourselves and our relationships with others in accordance with certain developed normative beliefs, values, and ethics. "Normative" means how things should be, not necessarily how they are. Recall that a philosophy, or an ideology, is an organized system of these that rationalizes our personal actions.

Likewise, in the case of a liberal democratic society, we govern ourselves based in large part on a philosophy of governing: why and how government does what it does. We broached this subject earlier when we discussed ideology, per se. It's a little broader in scope than that, because no matter which political ideology is for the moment in power in government (liberal or conservative), there are broad and underlying government actions, functions, and purposes that both ideologies accept as necessary functions of government. For example, rule in the interest of the people, or what some define as the public good: That's a philosophy. Rule by law: That's a philosophy. Government with limited rights and authorities: That's a philosophy. Adherence to the voice of the people, through their vote, come election time: That's a philosophy. Obedience to the basic rules set out by the Constitution: That's a philosophy. No matter who is in the driver's seat, some concepts are to be respected, perpetuated, and fulfilled.

That is the normative view of how things work in government: i.e., how they ought to work. In actual practice, these issues, areas, and functions are subject to interpretation and even a bit of "fudging" to correspond more closely to the ideology of the political party in power. That's the positive view, or how things really are, and not how they ought to be. And the reason for this is the contrasting view of the philosophy of governing. People disagree on just what the proper role of government is in society. People differ in their opinions on this and have since early in our country's history. For at least since the early twentieth century (probably since about the mid-1880s), when capitalism experienced such rapid growth and expansion and our country entered a "closed-frontier" status, this issue of the proper role of government versus the private market sector has been forefront in the political and economic arenas.

Government's Proper Role in Society

Two primary and opposing ideological views of government have existed for at least the past century and a quarter. Broadly speaking, we are talking about liberals (Democrats) and conservatives (Republicans). Conservatives, philosophically, oppose an increased role of government in society, especially in the economic sector; the opposing ideology, liberals (in the American sense of this term), favor an increasing role for government, especially in the economic sector. Historically, those in favor of increased government presence cited perceived capitalist "market failures" to provide properly in contributing to the public good. The opposite position is supported by a philosophy that accused government no less than the markets of failure in this connection. Just which philosophy was publicly dominant depended primarily, of course, upon which party was in office.

Long-wave theory is the proposition that history or historical events proceed in somewhat regular cycles, or waves, which if not exactly repetitive, can be useful in looking where you are headed by examining where you've been, so to speak. The point is, some history can be read this way (take the stock market, for example), and politics or political matters seem to fit this long-wave analysis generally, if not with exact predictability.

With this wave idea in mind, consider the American economic and political scene since about the early 1880s. Here's what we see:

Mid-1880s to about 1930

Following a depressive economic period at the start came a growing (booming) economic sector and the rise of "big business," with substantial and rapid wealth accumulation by some. At least a perception that government was increasingly pro-business, to the detriment of the still significant agricultural sector and the more general welfare of its citizens. A generally conservative dominated governmental period. About mid-period, circa 1895–1905, public dissatisfaction is manifest as evidenced by the Populist movement which promoted a more balanced government approach toward rural America and the "common folks" interests. 1914 sees WWI and a liberal (Democratic) government in place for 8 years. Then a conservative (Republican) administration back in power until 1932.

Politically this era was distinguished by what we might call the staking out of modern party ideologies. To a considerable degree, it resulted from the growth of big business after the Civil War. In the 1896 presidential election, waged between Republican William McKinley and Democrat William Jennings Bryan, Bryan pointed Democrats—heretofore a small-government party favoring limited federal government role in the economy—toward their modern philosophy of activist government; regulating and reining in the power and influence of business. McKinley, on the other hand, championed his Republican Party as a partner with business in its attempt to industrialize America, favoring policies and legislation to facilitate and reward business's efforts. High tariffs protected American business from foreign competition. But the cost to the general public was high prices.

This then was the divide: Can government best promote prosperity and opportunity by challenging the free market or by deferring to it? This ideological divide between the parties and their struggle for America's electoral support has been a defining issue ever since. The 1896 election drew an ideological line in the sand. For the next forty-five years, American politics was characterized by intense rivalry between remarkably unified partisan coalitions. From 1896 through FDR's reelection in 1939, one party or the other enjoyed unified control of government, both houses of Congress and the White House, for all but six years. Clearly, with such a partitioning of power the parties had little incentive for cooperation—and pursued it only sporadically, at best. Intense partisanship and government policies primarily favoring wealth accumulation describes the dominant politics of this era.

The prevailing intellectual theory behind governmental action during his era coming off the Civil War and a period of reconstruction was heavily influenced by the classical economic principles of the late eighteenth and early nineteenth centuries: a largely laissez-faire approach to business and a largely libertarian attitude toward government. This was still a period of expansion and growth and, for awhile, an open frontier. A rationale for government action could be described as supportive of national wealth maximization. But change, and the perceived need for change, started to develop around the end of the century.

A "Progressive School" of economic thought developed in the late 1800s and the first part of the 1900s that challenged the then-current classical/libertarian theoretical basis of society. This Progressive School was supported in its development by a family of theories about the nature of law developed in the early part of the first half of the twentieth century, referred to as Legal Realism. It focused on understanding the role of human-made institutions in shaping human behavior. Among the ideas that came out of this was a belief in legal instrumentalism; i.e., the view that the law should be used as a tool to achieve social purposes and to balance competing societal interests. This evolving legal theory was conducive to and theoretically supportive of the views of the Progressive School.

An early focus of Progressives was Institutional Economics, a branch of economics that challenged the (neo) classical view of the individual as the only legitimate unit of social analysis. Institutionalists criticized the neoclassical economic conception of the individual as a rational maximizer of self-interest. They suggested that social institutions—such as norms, organizations, law, religion, ideology—create important constraints on individual behavior; therefore, they held, it makes little sense to study the behavior of groups of individuals without reference to the institutional constraints within which such individuals make decisions and act.

The Progressive School focused in part on the application of marginal-utility theory and the law of diminishing returns to the issue of wealth distribution. The central insight of the School was that, because an additional dollar is likely, on the margin, to be of more utility (value) to a poor man than a rich man, total societal utility (value) should be increased if one adopts legal mechanisms that transfer wealth from the rich to the poor. Based on such insight, "material welfarists" espoused laws to do just this, such as minimum wage laws, subsidized education, and progressive income taxes. Their arguments were remarkably successful, finding their way into not only mainstream academic literature, but also into central political debates and Supreme Court decisions.

With this background in place, we move into the next historical wave: 1932 to about 1980.

1932–1980

A serious depressive global economic period at the start, followed by the equally serious Second World War. A liberal (Democratic) administration is in power for the next almost fifty years, with but two exceptions—1952–1960 and 1968–1976.

This period, especially the early years, is characterized by a growth of government intervention in the economic sector and an increased attention to policies and practices that favor improving the economic and social opportunities and welfare for a larger stratum of citizens than heretofore experienced. Progressive social matters were considered a legitimate arena for government action. The dominant political public consensus is that the markets fail to provide these needed goods through its operations. Business none the less generally experienced a period of growth and prosperity coming out of the long depression. Most citizens experienced a steadily rising standard of living and individual levels of social well-being, at least for most and at least into the early 1970's.

Individual opportunity through social or collective programs might well describe this era. Many of the Progressive School's programs and issues were undertaken, starting, according to some, as early as the late 1920s. These include the minimum wage, support of unionism, higher rates of progressive taxation, the GI Bill, and a national policy of full employment, to name a few. During much of this period, the Progressive/Institutional legal theories of the proper role of government dominate, and liberals control the helm of government.

Politically, the first twenty-five years of this second period saw the perpetuation of strong partisan dominance. For approximately seventeen of these first twenty-five years, unity of government was the rule. The difference of course was that America's voters switched their preference from the Republican Party to the Democratic Party. As a result, policies deferring to the markets were subordinated to policies challenging them. The emphasis on *wealth maximization* (by some) was replaced by *wealth distribution* (for many). The continued trend of strong partisanship and unity in governing enabled this shift, but you must also consider the dire economic climate (the Depression) with which this second era commenced.

The last twenty-eight years of this era, roughly 1952 through the 1970s, experienced a less unified political control of government. In only twelve of those twenty-eight years did one party dominate both Congress and occupy the White House. The other sixteen years saw opposing parties (ideologies) in control at each end of Pennsylvania Avenue. As a result, administrations, while still obviously partisan, were not nearly as successful at advancing their agendas without reaching out to the other party as had been the case for the previous almost fifty years. By necessity under such conditions, the other party's consideration became impossible to ignore, if legislation was to pass. Through necessity, consultation and negotiation among and between the two parties became more of a way of life in Washington, for at least a time. Politics is remembered today, rightly or wrongly, as being less acrimonious; even less partisan, during this period than either before or since. Some have nostalgically referred to it as the age of golden statesmanship and cooperation in Congress—a sharp contrast to the unrelenting partisanship evident in our own time.

Nevertheless, by about the late 1930s, even as their agenda was being realized by government administration, the Progressive School was being marginalized by arguments against their theories as deployed by an Economic Positivist school. The principal claim of the Positivists was that the interpersonal comparisons of utilities implicit in the policies espoused by Progressives were ungrounded in empirical data (experience). Even though their criticism was based on a supposed lack of empirical data (recall, at the start we are talking about the mid- to late-1930s), their arguments focused pretty much on the theoretical: Even if it is conceded that to any one individual the second dollar is worth less than the first, what guarantee can there be that a dollar is worth more to a poor man than to a rich man, they asked? More technically, they argued, even if it is conceded that the marginal utility of wealth is diminishing, how can you defend the assumption that utility curves are identical across individuals? In the view of the Positivists, economics was being misused to provide undeserved legitimacy to the dubious social goals of Progressives. Better to limit economics to realms in which empirical data is easily found; i.e., to limit economics to markets.

For a period, the Positivists retreated to areas in which "hard" market data were more readily available to work with. In the early 1960s, however, new interest in expanding economics theory to legal theory and beyond emerged, giving new impetus to Positivists. James Buchanan and Gordon Tullock applied economic assumptions to political markets (Public Choice) in much the same way as they had been applied to economic markets. Mancur Olson used economics to analyze collective action and public good problems in law and politics. In the field of microeconomic theory, Gary Becker applied economic tools in the traditionally legal domains of discrimination and the family. In the field of institutional economics, Armen Alchian and Harold Demetz examined the economics of industrial organization, and Oliver Williamson applied economic principles to develop the transaction cost theory of contract law. Economic theory and principles were becoming the tail that wagged the development of new thinking in most areas effecting government policy. *Wealth maximization* (once again) became a mainstay of Positivist law and economics, and it underlies most of mainstream law and economics today.

What was the effect of all this on our next period of interest?

The years between 1980–2008 followed a decade that saw the end of a long and unpopular foreign war, of changing paradigms in the economic arena, especially internationally, with America leaving the dollar gold standard. The rise of OPEC, an international oil cartel, brought rising inflation and slowing real growth, leading to the coining of a new term, "stagflation." These stresses combined with an apparent public feeling of excessive liberalism in both economic and social policies. This ushers in the return of a conservative (Republican) administration in 1980 that, with the exception of the 1992–2000 administration by a conservative leaning (Centrist) Democratic administration, governs through at least 2008. The last eight years of this period are described by many as a "blatant conservative attempt" to undo many of the policies and programs instituted by the previous wave's rule (most obviously by those who are not blatant conservatives).

Uneven patterns of income distribution are evident in this period, with the highest 5 percent of income earners realizing significant benefits and income growth not generally experienced by the rest of society. "Globalization" is seen to penalize many middle and lower level American workers, as well as entire communities in some cases, with wholesale job transfers overseas. An unprecedented attack on America's homeland on September 11, 2001, sets America on the defense against an unconventional and largely invisible enemy. An increasingly unpopular and widely perceived as unnecessary foreign war, justified in large part by this 9/11 event, tries both our country's resources and its patience. The mood of the country reflects such feelings by giving the conservative government a huge vote of no confidence in the 2006 off-term congressional elections, returning both houses to liberal (Democratic) control.

In the early twenty-first century, we are back to an era of strong political partisanship.

The last fifteen or more years is often described as a period of excessive or hyper-partisanship. This very description differentiates it from earlier periods. Both parties appear to be under the influence and control of the more extreme factions of their respective ideologies: the most conservative of the conservatives in the Republican Party and the most liberal of the liberals in the Democratic Party (The tendency is thus to try and play the political game down around the ten to twenty yard lines, as will be seen later in the chapter.) There appears to be little tolerance of or for the less ideological in either party.[*] It may not be

---

[*]   This alone might well explain much of the growth of Independents

too strong a statement to say that there is no such thing as a moderate politician in government today. Those holding the political reins of leadership in government do not tolerate moderation. Their motto, in both houses and in both parties, seems to be if you aren't with us, you're against us. It would appear not only that there is no common ground between the parties, there is little within them today either.

In one sense, this says the parties are strong; they can command loyalty and obedience from their elected members in promoting their agendas. But in another sense, it reflects a narrowing of the parties' focus to their most ideological bases; to constituents that parties intend not only to promote and serve in governing, but that they need to rely on in their ongoing bids to maintain electoral dominance. The Republicans have publicly acknowledged this. Both parties have attenuated to where they represent primarily the extreme ends of their respective ideologies.

Repeated findings have demonstrated that generally Americans, be they of either persuasion, are not nearly as ideologically extreme in their political views as are the two warring parties. As with earlier periods considered, the unification of government is important in political behavior here. For six of the past eight years of a Republican administration, Republicans also controlled Congress. Under largely Republican administrations during this period, the ideological emphasis is again on *wealth accumulation*. Policies that reflect sympathy with business are given priority.

While it was high tariffs in the first period, support for "free trade" policies that favor business interests rule over those of a broader public interest today.

Admittedly, these thumbnail sketches of these periods are incomplete. What is important is to detect apparent broad patterns—waves—here. Where, in all cases, the seeds for eventual change were planted (as would be expected) before the actual political changes themselves. In many cases, well before, and in all waves, a philosophical basis for the developments in law and economics in support of the next wave was being developed and promoted, from within the ivory towers of academia.[*]

---

[*]   An observation: The usual pattern in critical thinking is to begin with a thesis, compare it with its opposite, its antithesis, and from these develop a synthesis,

Consider Wave Number One, from the mid-1880s to 1932: Pretty business dominated; the market moved by laissez-faire was seen through the eyes of Classical economics as the divine leader and provider. The only problem was it increasingly would be perceived by many as providing too little to too many and too much to too few. But in the meantime, the market ruled. We are told that Moses came down off Mt. Sinai with the complete commandments (law) from God. But other than that example, most change is the accumulation and percolation of ideas over time (even Moses was up on that mountain for some forty days getting it right) that are arranged, then rearranged into a plausible excuse for a "theory" of how and why things are and how they ought to be.

One brief example of this evolving process was a book written in 1909 by the Progressive Herbert Croley, founder of the magazine *The New Republic,* entitled *The Promise of American Life.* As a sympathizer, if not an academic member of the Progressive School, he wrote of the need for a number of (specific) social programs that, in spite of Teddy Roosevelt drawing from it in his presidential run of 1912, had to wait until the next wave rolled in with the 1930s. But he and others provided a background and platform for justifying what we might call a welfare theory of governing that guided, or theoretically justified, government actions during the coming liberal period.

The underlying premise of this theory of government action was that the market failed in some instances to provide for the economic support or opportunity for many. Hence, if this failure was to be corrected, it was up to government to either (a) do it directly or (b) see to it that the market (capitalism) did it, generally via legislation and regulation. Governing by this welfare economic approach was successful in reelecting liberal governments during most of the next fifty years.

But eventually many, especially in academia, began to perceive this governing model as being as one-sided as the previous 1880s–1932 wave became; too unbalanced to continue providing the country with what

---

or new/modified thesis. What we appear to have experienced over the past century, or so, is but an on-going struggle between thesis and antithesis (existing ideologies) for domination with no new thesis apparent. Just more of the same old struggle. Does this mean there is no "third-way," as some describe it, or no synthesis possible in our political domain?

was believed necessary. As mentioned, in this theory-forming dialog, unlike Moses' instant biblical contribution to the Jews, consensus on the right (proper) things to do and why, is an ongoing process. During this period of liberal domination of government, academia both supported and challenged the current political thinking (welfare governing). Hence, starting around the 1950s, a series of academic work stressing an economic and statistical approach to government and politics started appearing that formed the basis for considering a new or modified rationale upon which to base government action. This all pretty much came together in the mid- to late-1960s in the form, for example, of public choice theory, with a renewed emphasis on the goal of wealth maximization, as opposed to the second wave's emphasis on wealth distribution.

The underlying premise of this developing theory coming out of academia and finding its way into (especially) conservative think-tanks was that, like the liberal contention of market failure that needed to be compensated for, government could fail as well; that the markets really did a better job of providing for the general welfare than government was demonstrating. Therefore, we should look to and support the "invisible hand" of markets, of private enterprise, not government, in providing for the public good.

Institutional economics (emphasizing wealth distribution issues) was the theoretical rational for liberal government action. Public choice theory (sympathetic to wealth maximization issues) would become the theoretical rational for conservative government taking government (at least partly) out of such area. So, just what exactly is public choice theory that would justify such a reversal?

Public Choice Theory

Public choice theory is directed toward the study of politics based on economic principles. It takes the same principles economists use to analyze people's actions in the marketplace and applies them to people's actions in collective decision making. The theory aims to apply economic analysis (usually decision theory and game theory) to the political decision-making process in order to reveal certain systemic trends toward inefficient government policies. It was developed in the late 1950s and found favor beginning in the late 1960s and 1970s.

The general assumption is that the dominant motive in people's actions in the marketplace, whether they are employers, employees, or consumers, is a concern for themselves—self-interest. Public choice theorists make the same assumption that self-interest, although not necessarily the exclusive motivation, is the dominant motivation for people acting in the political marketplace, be they voters, politicians, bureaucrats, or lobbyists.

One of the basic claims that result from public choice theory is that good government policies in a democracy are an underprovided public good. This is due to the rational ignorance of the voters. Each voter is faced with a tiny probability that his vote will change the results of the election, while gathering the relevant information necessary for a well-informed voting decision requires substantial time and effort. Anthony Downs, in one of the earliest public choice books, *An Economic Theory of Democracy* (1957), suggested that the voter is largely ignorant of the details of political issues and that this ignorance is rational. Even though the result of an election may be important, an individual's vote rarely decides an election. Thus, the direct impact of casting a well-informed vote is almost nil; the voter has virtually no chance to determine the outcome of the election. So spending time following the issues is not personally worthwhile.

Evidence for Downs's claim is found in the fact that public opinion polls consistently find that less than half of all voting-age Americans can name their own congressional representative. Therefore, most voters are largely ignorant about the positions of the people for whom they vote. Except for a few highly publicized issues, they do not pay a lot of attention to what legislative bodies do. Even when they do, voters have little incentive to gain the background knowledge and analytic skill needed to understand the issues.

Public choice economists also examine the actions of legislators. Although legislators are expected to pursue the public interest, they make decisions on how to use other people's resources, not their own. Politicians may intend to spend taxpayer money wisely. Efficient decisions, however, will neither save their own money nor give them any proportion of the wealth they save for citizens. According to this thinking, there is no direct reward for opposing powerful interest groups in order to confer benefits on a public that is not even aware of the benefits or of who conferred them. Thus the incentives for good management in the public interest are weak. In contrast, interest groups are organized by people with very strong gains to be made from governmental action. They provide politicians with campaign funds and campaign workers. In return, they receive at least the "ear" of the politician and often gain support for their goals.

In other words, because legislators have the power to tax and to extract resources in other coercive ways and because voters monitor their behavior poorly, legislators behave in ways that are costly to citizens. For example, many special interest and pork-barrel projects are not in the interest of the overall public. However, it makes sense for politicians to support these projects. It may benefit them psychologically, as they feel powerful and important. It can also benefit them financially, as it may open the door to future wealth as lobbyists, after they retire. The project may be of interest to the politician's local constituency, increasing district votes or campaign contributions. The politician incurs little to no cost to gain these benefits, because public federal tax dollars are spent.

In this view, special interest lobbyists also behave rationally. They can gain government favors worth millions or billions in return for relatively small investments. They face a risk of losing out to competitors if they don't seek these favors. For example, lobbying by the domestic sugar industry might result in an inefficient subsidy—one whose costs exceed its benefits—for the production of sugar, either directly or through protectionist measures. The costs of such acts are dispersed over all citizens and therefore unnoticeable to each individual. On the other hand, a small special interest group with a strong incentive to perpetuate the policy by further lobbying shares the benefits. The vast majority of voters will be unaware of the effect due to rational ignorance. Therefore, theorists expect that numerous special interests will be able to successfully lobby for various inefficient policies. In public choice theory, such scenarios of inefficient government policies are referred to as *government failures*—a term akin to *market failures* from earlier theoretical economics.

Finally, the taxpayer is also behaving rationally. The cost of defeating any one government giveaway is very high, while the benefits to the individual taxpayer are very small. Each citizen pays only a few pennies or a few dollars for any given government favor, while the costs of ending that favor would be many times higher. Everyone involved has "rational incentives," in economic terms, to do exactly what they're doing, even though the desire of the general constituency is the opposite.

Because of its skepticism about the supposedly benign nature of government, public choice is sometimes viewed as ideologically biased, representing a conservative or libertarian branch of economics, as opposed to more liberal (that is interventionist) theories, such as Keynesian economics. This is partly correct. The emergence of public choice economics reflects dissatisfaction with the implicit assumptions, held by Keynesians, among others, that government effectively corrects market failures.

James M. Buchanan, a Nobel Prize–winning economist recognized as one of the "fathers" of public choice theory, has acknowledged the above criticism. In a speech, he defended it as follows:

> "... it is necessary to appreciate the prevailing mindset of social scientists and philosophers at the midpoint of the twentieth century when public choice arose. The socialist ideology was pervasive, and was supported by the allegedly neutral research program called 'theoretical welfare economics', which concentrated on identifying the failures of observed markets to meet idealized standards. In sum, this branch of inquiry offered theories of market failure. But failure in comparison with what? The implicit presumption was always that politicized corrections for market failures would work perfectly. In other words, market failures were set against an idealized politics.
>
> Public choice then came along and provided analyses of the behavior of persons acting politically, whether voters, politicians, or bureaucrats. These analyses exposed the essentially false comparisons that were then informing

so much of both scientific and public opinion. In a very real sense, public choice became a set of theories of governmental failures, as an offset to the theories of market failures that had previously emerged from theoretical welfare economics."

It is worthwhile to note that while Mr. Buchanan provides here what most would consider a valid justification for this analytical approach to government actions, he does not explicitly deny its ideological bias, as others have described it.

Some have condemned this theory on moral grounds. This condemnation is centered on the presumed transference of the economic theory of self interest to political analysis. Critics argue that people acting politically—for example, as voters or as legislators—do not behave as they do in markets. Individuals are differently motivated when they are choosing "for the public" rather than for themselves in private choice capacities. Buchanan acknowledges that the economic model of behavior, even if restricted to market activity, should never be taken to provide the be-all and end-all of scientific explanation. Persons act from many motives, and the economic model concentrates attention on only one of the many possible forces behind actions. Buchanan also observes that while economic motives may not be exclusive, public choice theory does incorporate the presumption that persons do not readily become economic eunuchs as they shift from market to political participation!

In a nutshell, public choice adherents stress all that is wrong with politics and government: its weak points, its inefficiencies, the inability of the voters to really understand issues or monitor government, or even stay abreast of what it is doing. They stress its susceptibility to influence and use this to demonstrate why government is not to be trusted to do the right thing. Public choice assumes that those in government service, both publicly elected and bureaucratically appointed, are primarily self-serving individuals who care little, if any, about the public interest. Unfortunately, basing their conclusions on generally accepted views of self-interest in the private sector or the marketplace, adherents attribute the same motivations to people concerned with collective issues in public life.

Politicians (Continued)

Now, with all this newfound knowledge and understanding about theory, long-waves, and public choice squirreled away in our memory banks, we can confidently return to that claim of Colin Hay about politicians, (this issue gets kind of dicey) which was: "We tend to assume the worse of political actors." He points out that while we seem to always have this opinion with us, "the prevalence of such assumption does seem to serve the period since the 1980s ..." According to him, our reasons for holding such assumptions are not especially good ones. He faults the influence of public choice theory for this.

If Hay's message is that politicians' behavior is no worse now than it was twenty-five, fifty, or maybe even a hundred years ago, I could probably support that. "Tip" O'Neill's earlier observation in his conversation with Harvard's Derek Bok would appear to support that. Generally, however, I feel myself on the opposite side of the argument on this one otherwise. Public choice theory may take a position on the self-serving nature of people, voters as well as the elected, and it may lead us to expect the worse in both motives and behavior. But the demonstrable fact is that, while we don't always perceive motives, we do witness behavior, and often it is just what public choice adherents predict: self-serving, often in the extreme. Two recent examples should suffice:

California Congressman Randy "Duke" Cunningham resigned in December 2005 after admitting he took $2.4 million in bribes. Representative Virgil Goode reportedly received more than $80,000 in "campaign donations" from the employees of MZM, a defense firm that's an alleged co-conspirator in Cunningham's case—and then he was the principal sponsor of a measure helping MZM get a contract in his district. He since offered to refund the money.

Since the 1970s, more than a dozen congressmen have been convicted in criminal court. They got caught, but how many others skate on very thin ice, ethically and even legally, who don't? According to the *Christian Science Monitor*, almost every U.S. lawmaker takes big money aimed at helping private interests win favorable government action. If they stash the cash for themselves, it's illegal. If they use it to get reelected, it's generally legal. The *Monitor* describes this as "a culture of bribery in Congress." Congress is a self-policing institution in this connection. However, in March of this year, the House approved one of the most significant changes to its ethics rules in decades, creating for the first time an independent panel empowered to initiate investigations of alleged misconduct by members of that chamber.

In today's political environment that indicates, if nothing else, an attempt to placate the public's contempt for recent scandals; the Abramoff lobbying debacle is an example. Add to this the fact that, as of this writing, FBI Director Robert S. Mueller III called targeting corrupt officials (3,500 open cases against state, local, and federal government officials) the Bureau's "top criminal priority." Considering this, I don't believe we can accept Mr. Hay's argument that this perception of politicians is unjustified. They appear, most unfortunately, to have earned it. But his argument regarding cause (what we expect) and effect (what we seem to get) merits a bit more consideration.

Why do we have the people we do as our elected representatives? Why them rather than someone else? I'm sure you can tick off a list of good probable reasons others who might run don't. Here again, the range of possibilities is probably as wide and variable as individuals. Nonetheless, there may be some common reasons or causes that keep others from throwing their hats into the ring. And this may possibly be, in the end, a reflection of the perception promoted by public choice theory, as Hay suspects.

First reason of all is the possible taint of being (or trying to become) an elected politician: Per public choice, all politicians are self-servers who, by extension in the minds of many, lie, cheat, and take bribes, and who's motives are always suspect. The above characterization of the culture of Congress as one of bribery by the *Christian Science Monitor* would seem to validate that characterization. So now, all who want to join that club, please take one step forward.

Second, electoral politics costs money—lots of it. Many of us still want to believe that what we have is Lincoln's government of, by, and for the people. But most of us don't want to pay for it, at least not by contributing to the "by the people" who want to be their representatives by running for election. So, if you are an individual running for office—well-heeled or not—you have to beg for money.

Connecticut Representative Chris Murphy recently pulled the curtain back a bit to give us a peek at what this entails, in an unusually candid description: "I and my colleagues," he said, "find that more and more of our time is spent on reelections, largely raising money. On any given day, the foot traffic to and from the national Republican and Democratic campaign offices is constant, and the conditions under which we labor are pretty depressing. I sit in a room with cubicles, surrounded by legislators, feeling more like a telemarketer than a member of Congress." We euphemistically call this soliciting campaign contributions, but it's basically begging. So okay, all you who earlier took that first step forward and want to add begging to your job description that so far also includes personal taint, take another step forward!

Third on our list of why not to run for public office, we consider personal privacy. If you value privacy, politics is not the place for you. All you have, all whom you love, and all you do will be fair game for the media (not to mention your competition), and your personal assets become (to some degree) a matter of the public record. So again, those of you having so far stayed the course and also accept the fact of the loss of privacy, take another step forward.

And to cap our list of "why not to run," we throw in cynicism. Given the perceived—and experienced—actions of your peers, your fellow politicians, how are you going to handle dealing with suspected self-serving, lying, backstabbing, and responsibility denying two-faced colleagues? Those of you still standing that are willing to accept this final personal price for representing your (suspicious, ungrateful, penny-pinching) fellow Americans, take that final fourth step forward!

Let's see what our lineup of potential candidates looks like after this thinning-out process. We seem to have people with the following general qualifications willing and eager to run for public office:

1. Candidates not afraid to be personally tainted as self-servers, cheaters, liars, and bribe takers whose motives are suspect

2. Beggars—all for a good cause, of course, which is to try and get themselves elected and reelected

3. Individuals who don't mind any and all loss of personal privacy or enduring never-ending public scrutiny

4. People who do not object to dealing with and/or being associated with other people who are likewise thought to be self-servers, liars, cheats, or bribe-takers whose motives are likewise suspect and who beg

I don't honestly know if this somewhat sarcastic approach to shaking the tree to see which apples fall for elective office makes any real-world sense. I really hope not, because the potential candidates that we come up with sure look like "bad apples" to me—just what public choice theory would predict and have you believe. It wouldn't be difficult to assume the worse, motive-wise, of people like this.

Nonetheless, this exercise makes an important point: If we expect, and truly want, people serving in government with qualifications and motivations somewhat higher than the above process suggests, we need to make two changes. First, politics needs to clean up its act, such that its (dismal) reputation does not precede it. Secondly, we need to stop the practice of making our politicians beggars. Perhaps when we do, we will encourage some otherwise competent potential candidates to stay for the elections. Unfortunately, this looks like a chicken-and-egg situation: Which needs to come first?*

So it's tempting to say that public choice theory does in some—probably too many—instances adequately describe our elected public servants today. But that's simply a verification that we need the two changes indicated above to try and correct this situation. It is not necessarily an argument that supports abandoning a government presence in providing for the public good or for turning over the public welfare as a social optimum, or goal, (in the broadest sense of this term) to the market. If it is, then public choice theory says that needed improvement isn't possible. If it is, it says that democracy, as we

---

* I thought I might send a copy of this chapter to Lee Iacocca who recently put out his latest self promoting book, *Where Have all the Leaders Gone?* (2007) It's simple, straightforward and good reading. He makes a number of relevant and even hard-hitting anecdotal points concerning the lack of leadership in government. If I'm anywhere near base on my oversimplified somewhat sarcastic analysis here, the answer to his question is herein; the result of which is, according to public choice, we aren't electing leaders, or potential leaders. It's more that we're appointing foxes to guard the hen house.

practice it, can't produce good government we can trust to promote a common good (as that good may be defined).

That means the public good becomes increasingly dependent on a sector of society that, by definition and recognition, operates on the same self-serving and self-seeking basis that the theory imputes to those charged with decision making in the collective sector—extreme self-interest. Sounds to me like that's jumping from the frying pan right into the fire. We need to consider this further, and we will.

Ideologies, Parties, and Government

Chapter 4 delved briefly into ideologies—values or belief systems. Ideologies range from individually held positions describable as extremely liberal to extremely conservative, not only about political matters but also about social, economic, and religious issues as well. In most cases our belief systems hold to all these areas pretty uniformly. So if you tend to view religious or social issues from a conservative (or liberal) perspective, chances are your political views are consistent with such an ideology.

We tend then to support, or at least be sympathetic to, political parties that proclaim our "values" and would, in our opinion, conduct government along lines that protect, promote, and expand them. Historically over the past century-plus, we have had two basic choices: Join the conservative team and be a Republican, or promote a liberal viewpoint by voting for the Democrats. And in spite of the partisan ups and downs we went through above, we seem to have muddled through. Progress has been made; Americans enjoy, by most accounts, an enviable position. But there is a risk to the nature of our liberal democracy in the political game we play.

Visualize a classic bell-shaped curve. Think of this form as that spectrum of liberal-to-conservative ideologies. The shape of the curve also approximates pretty closely the normal distribution of our political beliefs: Most of us are somewhere around the middle of the curve, ideologically speaking. That is, we have ideologies, but for most of us they tend not to be extreme (Chapter 9 will show us some figures in this connection). Toward the middle of the curve, the majority of us differ mostly in form but not greatly in content. We may find little (or a lot!) to complain about with government, irrespective of which party is governing. In fact, we may vote this election for one party and next time around for the other, depending upon the issues and the candidates—and still consider ourselves fundamentally partisan. Said differently, politically (and otherwise), Americans generally tend to be both moderate and even somewhat tolerant in their outlooks. The farther you move outward from the center of the curve, the more extreme ideology becomes; moderation and tolerance are less in evidence.

It's said that the American political game is traditionally played between the forty-yard lines. Metaphorically, this means that the important sector of the voting public that the parties must convince to vote their ticket has been around the middle of the field. The parties/candidates expect the more ideologically committed to follow them, so politicians have historically concentrated on winning those of us sitting between the forty-yard lines. This meant that to succeed once in power, they also had to govern with the middle firmly in mind.

Historically, our two parties have pretty well accommodated under their wings those of us who ideologically fit between those forty-yard lines. That represents most of us. That's what we mean when we define the Democrats and Republicans as "big tent" parties. They each have traditionally been able to represent the values of a fairly wide range of "conservatives" or "liberals." It was never perfect. The parties never represented all Americans between them. But between them, most Americans appear to have felt adequately enough represented.

There have always been political alternatives for those holding values and views at the extreme ends of that ideological curve. Most play their political game down between the five- to ten-yard lines of the political field. While an uphill battle to be sure (Chapter 8 will discuss this in more detail), these marginal political players always have the opportunity to convince others (within the rule of law) of the merits of their political views, thereby increasing both their ideological acceptance and political influence.

The risk in the political game we play is this: Those at the extreme ends of the field may convince the rest of us to play their game, ideologically speaking. By our definition and their locations on the spectrum, that game is not a moderate one. It is highly ideological and hence highly partisan. By its nature, it ignores the wills and concerns of many in its pursuit of its political objectives. A second aspect of this risk is when one or the other—or both—of the main parties, in a tight match, decides to forgo the middle and take their game down to between the five- and twenty-yard lines and settle for a highly ideological "win," if they can pull it off. The hell with the rest of us.

In the first case, the party at the extreme end succeeds in shifting the ideological balance of the country in their favor. That's largely a decision the electorate makes. In the latter case, one party or the other—or both—makes the decision not to play primarily in the middle where most of us are but to conduct their game further down the spectrum of ideology: e.g., to largely ignore any but their own party faithful, their base, so to speak. They haven't shifted the ideological balance of the country; they have simply decided, politically, it is not in their best interest—which is to win—to try and sustain a "big tent" philosophy.

Either way, however, the result tends to be the same: Broad political representation diminishes. Government focuses on pleasing a minority, not the majority. We get imbalance. We also get what we have recently been experiencing: hyper-partisanship in governing. As one or the other party attempts to govern primarily for results favoring their own ideology, the other as vigorously tries to block it. The result is that little is accomplished in the halls of government.

In their efforts to confront each other, party leadership in government increasingly demands ideological purity from our elected representatives. There is less and less room or opportunity for moderates of either ideology to influence the direction of governing. The spiral feeds on itself until, as in 2006, a sufficient number of the electorate decides they have had enough and reconfigures Congress—in this case with the other party. The problem with this under current political choice is that it becomes simply a game of musical chairs. After the music stops (the election's over) and the seats are refilled, the game remains the same. We still have but two parties, each struggling against the other to maintain political power with governing for the majority of us apparently only a secondary consideration. Little in the way of political progress should be expected. Issues that have remained unresolved will most likely continue unresolved. We are adrift.

Recapitulation

This wide-ranging and sinuous voyage attempting to explain, describe, and document why government behaves like it does is, to say the least, messy. At best it will indicate the degree of complexity we deal with in this arena. At worse, it may simply add confusion to uncertainty. But to recapitulate, and reduce all the above to the basics, it behaves like it does primarily because:

1. It is structurally complex (by design, admittedly)

2. It is functionally extensive

3. Internal power and responsibility are shared (again, mostly by design)

4. Those manipulating it are usually ideologically conflicted

5. It is internally and externally subject to competing influences and pressure

6. Turnover of political personnel is typically frequent

7. The quality of people holding public office is perceived as, and often demonstrated to be, not particularly laudable

8. The extent that the parties either represent the people, or they represent themselves influences its policies

We express our satisfaction or dissatisfaction with society—its shortcomings, the direction we feel it is taking, as opposed to the direction we feel it ought to be taking—via the political system. That's the only way we can do so—peacefully—in the democratic system we have. That's how and why government is like it is. It's our mechanism to manage a pluralistic society's status quo.

Editorially speaking, there is a need for an institutional economic outlook, or what might be termed a communitarian/welfare outlook, as well as a public choice, or, more broadly, rational choice outlook motivating government. Both of these theoretical policies, from different perspectives, aim at providing for the public good. There is a need for government to function with both theories in mind. This in itself should function as a form of check and balance. But can they? If not, then, as has been pointed out, "should" becomes meaningless. If these two theories that define the proper activities of government do no more than define the different parties at their ideological extremes, we are right back to square one: Stalemate, or worse: rule by and for the minority.

Admittedly there are failures in the market, as charged, and in government, also as charged, in providing for the public good. But few would deny that there has been progress in this direction. In all instances, there are associated costs and benefits. Who pays the cost and enjoys the benefit in our society is a major issue between these two ideologies, as well as who ought to be primarily responsible for delivering the public good. It's a fair dialog, but as dialog alone, it doesn't (and won't) accomplish much.

What we need to ensure is that this dialog as to which functions properly belong where is an open one, with all who potentially benefit from the public good having an input. What we want to avoid is allowing a single faction to dominate the dialog, by reason of theory or through economic or political power (keeping Mr. Kaplan's concern raised in the Introduction in mind here). After listening to such a fair and open dialog, then it is up to us, the voters, to make the final determination as to the direction government takes via those we choose to elect to office. It's really that simple. But keep in mind, simple is not always easy.

The Public Good

Before we leave this broad and amorphous topic, let's look a bit closer at a term we have thrown around here, the *public good*. What do we mean when we say, as above, "… benefit from the public good"? What is the public good? Does the concept that democracy ought to center around a rationally definable public good—sometimes referred to as a common good, or the public interest—have any meaning in the real world?

The historical genesis of this concept is usually associated with Jean-Jacques Rousseau's theory of the *social contract*: in particular, his contention that government decision procedures should reveal a general will that embodies the "common good." Rousseau believed this common good could be mathematically (rationally) calculated, but efforts to date have, by all accounts, failed to confirm his opinion. Still the concept is widely supported. Nonetheless, when we speak of a common good, a public good or interest, it is hard to define just what this means. Why? Simply because it's a normative concept of what "should be" and because it is subjective in the larger sense, as reasonable people with differing comprehensive or political concepts of the ideal may define. Furthermore, it's possible that sometimes peoples' interests are so irreducibly at odds, it precludes the possibility of a mutually agreed good. Therefore, in a pluralistic society such as ours, today many would pronounce a common good, or a public good, indefinable. Certainly under a partisan-party political system, common agreement seems elusive.

Elusive, perhaps; but certainly not nonexistent. Recall earlier in this chapter that we spoke of certain philosophical approaches to governing that are expected to be followed irrespective of which party (ideology) might be in control. Such expectations imply a common good, or public interest. While these may be broad philosophical examples, I believe they suffice to establish the concept. While the public good may perhaps be indefinable in a narrow (partisan) sense, for the reasons mentioned, it is nonetheless a usefully descriptive term. Most people would understand its implication, recognize its intent, and, if only on a rationally intuitive basis, concur on it being proper, desirable, or good. This holds even if their understanding of it is both normative and subjective. It is a concept that, again if only intuitively, provides meaning or intent.

If we substitute a term such as "benevolence" or "well-being" or even "happiness" for the term "public good," perhaps that would be more appropriately descriptive, in a utilitarian sense, if it is held to mean the greatest good for the greatest number. While this word substitution is not an exact solution to the mathematical quantification problem that eluded Rousseau and others, it does provide a kind of quantitative quality: The greatest for the greatest. This is a theme we will pursue.

Let's move on.

Part Two

Part One generally presented a positive (what is versus what should be) overview focused on two primary issues: of government versus politics and of democracy versus capitalism. If it did its job correctly, by this point it has become obvious that change, or correction, is called for. That continues to be the premise in this next section.

In Part Two, Chapters 7 through 11, we consider political Independents in some detail and from several perspectives. We look at the phenomena of voters rejecting (at least publicly and for the record) political affiliation, ask ourselves who these people are, and try to determine the reason, or reasons for this political dealignment. Part One already suggested possible reasons for this. But is it a significant issue ... or not? If it is, how so? If it isn't, why not? We'll consider the consequences and ramifications for our historically partisan electoral politics of a majority of America's voters being politically independent. Does this largest segment of American voters represent a political bloc—real or potential—for electoral purposes, or not? If so, what does that signify for our two traditional parties? If Independents are not a voting bloc to contend with, should they be? And finally, if they should be, how might they be?

Our inquiry is not simply academic curiosity. Independents exist and have at some level for decades. But their numbers are, historically speaking, high today. They are growing as a percentage of voters when the numbers for both traditional parties are declining—especially for the more moderate partisans. Again, this begs the question "Why?" It seems highly improbable, at least as I write this, that this phenomenon of dealignment, of shying away from political party identification, is happening coincidentally, for simply no reason

So, our first line of inquiry now is to familiarize ourselves with Independents as best we can. Hopefully this will lead us to an answer to that question "Why?" We will see that this is easier said than done, because Independents are just that, independent, and represent quite a diverse universe.

If we can unravel the apparent political enigma that presently is attributed to them, then possibly we can answer the question "Why?" We will then be in a position to determine if this is a significant issue or not. And by significant we mean as it potentially affects our present political and electoral system. If it isn't, we can all go home comfortable in the knowledge that it's no big deal! If on the other hand it appears to be significant, then we are back to the question "Why?"

Once we are comfortable with our answer here, we can consider options to deal with whatever issue or issues are involved. And again, we are not just dealing with a curiosity. We defined "significant" above as dealing with our present political and electoral landscape. If it's significant, we—all of us—will be more than remiss to ignore it.

Why?

Should you have forgotten, I urge you to go back and reread that short but crucially important paragraph in Chapter 4: "… if there are features in our society we are not happy with, it is to the political system we must look to correct them …" With this critical reality in mind, we'll show you just how instrumental Independents might be in bringing about such correction.

That's why!

Chapter 7

The Rise of the Independent Voter

I'm an Independent voter. I have several friends and acquaintances who, politically speaking, are also Independents. Therefore, we can conclude that Independent voters exist. But is that the equivalent of saying there is an Independent vote?

What is the Independent vote? Does it really exist, or is it just a political fiction? Who determines the answer, and how? Does it really make any difference in our political dynamics or the "real world" most of us inhabit? Is it but another of the many handles given to what more than a few assume represents the uncommitted middle between the two poles of political ideology? Is this the "swing vote" we hear about so often? These and other questions are worth asking, examining, and trying to answer. Why? Because we seem to be experiencing a well-documented electoral dealignment in the American political arena, resulting in a significant number of Independents.

American voters are deciding they don't want to be identified with either of our current two major political parties—at least not publicly or for the record. As such, this may represent a significant new political—and even societal—paradigm ... or not! Just exactly what does it all signify? Is it symptomatic of something deeper than mere coyness concerning public political affiliation? As a start, let's consider what part the so-called Independent vote played (or didn't play) in the national elections in November 2006.

Some pundits declared that the arguably lopsided outcome of the 2006 midterm elections was to a large extent the result of the Independent vote. If this is in fact the case, Independents have demonstrated themselves to be a potent electoral force to be reckoned with. But is this actually the case? Maybe. But it's not clearly apparent from the raw numbers. For example, the popular vote for senate seats showed 32,682,619 (53 percent) voting Democratic; 25,784,256 (42 percent) voting Republican, and just 2,260,894 (5 percent) voting either Independent or for third parties. That's hardly an impressive showing for the masses not Democrat or Republican.

On the other hand, if you look a little closer, maybe there is something to this Independent vote. For example, taking the figures for the House of Representatives rather than the Senate (because the total vote count was larger) and using the American National Election Study (ANES) voter ideology profile numbers, Independents' votes could demonstrate a significant impact.

A total vote of 68,058,000 was cast for House candidates. The ANES's voter profile figures indicate Democrats represent approximately 33 percent of the voting public and Republicans about 29 percent of the voting public, with Independents represent the remaining approximately 38 percent. So, according to ANES respondent figures as of 2004, statistically as well as actually one gets the following picture of what should have and what actually did transpire in the race for the U.S. House:

Partisanship	Expected vote at ANES calculated % of voters	Actual vote total	Difference	Difference as a % total vote received
For Democrats	22,459,000	39,268,000	+16,809,000	+ 42.8%
For Republicans	19,737,000	28,465,000	+ 8,728,000	+ 30.7%
For Independents/ Others	25,862,000	325,000	- 25,537,000	- 98.7%
	68,058,000	68,058,000	0	

At first glance the conclusion is, if there is an Independent vote, it isn't going to Independent candidates. Interesting. So just what does this Independent voter classification really mean? With the apparent influence shown in the table above, it certainly merits a closer look.

In the late 1950s approximately 20 percent of registered voters classified themselves Independents as opposed to Democrats or Republicans. In the ensuing years this number has varied, but the longer-term trend has been clearly up. In 2000, partisanship reached a new low point when 40 percent of survey respondents claimed independent status. At the time of this writing (2008), plus or minus 38 percent of registered voters declare themselves either Independents or decline to state a party affiliation. The trends of weakening partisanship are well documented, but their meaning and interpretation remains widely debated. So what? Before we can address that important question, we'd best understand just where these numbers come from and what they signify.

Since the 1950s, ANES, or simply NES, at the University of Michigan's Center for Political Studies has been measuring party affiliation as part of our voting pattern. In its modern meaning, "party identification" is a product of survey research. Democrats, Republicans, and Independents are identified by asking respondents to put themselves in one of these three categories. The portentous trend from partisanship to independence reflects an increase in the proportion of respondents who tell interviewers that they consider themselves not Republicans or Democrats, but Independents. It is a self-declared political identification, or lack thereof.

So, is that it? Yes, really. The object of this ongoing study is to identify party affiliation or preference. However, this voter classification—Democrat, Republican, or Independent—reinforces the reality that politics in the United States today is a disputation between two, and in reality only two, entrenched political ideologies. This is regardless of the fact that almost 40 percent of the voting public has decided, by its own declaration or preference, not to select either alternative. But this is not quite the end of the story.

Once so identified, respondents are asked to answer follow-up questions. One of those follow-up questions that for many years those analyzing the NES data seldom paid attention to is the key to the conclusion of the book *The Myth of the Independent Voter,* published in 1992. The authors, six recognized academics, concluded in that work that the assumption that all Independents—"the second largest group in the electorate"—share some characteristics that differentiate them in important ways from Republicans and Democrats is, in fact, a *myth.* According to their conclusion, "Independents, defined inclusively, have little in common. They are more diverse than either Republicans or Democrats. Most of them are not uncommitted, and they are not a bloc. They are largely closet Democrats and Republicans."

How did they arrive at that conclusion? The ANES questions supply the answer. The initial question is:

Generally speaking, do you usually think of yourself as a Republican, a Democrat, an Independent, or what?

If the respondent replies "Democrat" or Republican," the interviewer follows up with,

Would you call yourself a strong Republican (or Democrat) or not a very strong Republican (or Democrat)?

If the respondent replies, "Independent," the interviewer follows this up with the question,

Do you think of yourself as closer to the Republican Party or to the Democratic Party?

As it turns out, nearly two-thirds of those who initially label themselves Independents consistently concede they are closer to one party or the other. These are the so-called "leaners"; partisan Independents, you might call them, or what might be labeled Independent Republicans or Independent Democrats. Over the years, the ANES has identified a range of only about 7 to 15 percent (1958 to 2004) who constitute "pure Independents," those denying any partisan inclinations when asked about closeness to a party. In 2004 this figure was 10 percent.

Taking this information from the National Elections Studies, gathered for electoral purposes, we can disaggregate the American voter into the following seven classifications (excluding third parties):

	1958	1976	1990	2000	2004
Strong Republican	11%	9%	10%	12%	16%
Weak Republican	16%	14%	15%	12%	12%
Independent Republican	5%	10%	12%	13%	12%
Pure Independent	7%	15%	10%	12%	10%
Independent Democrat	7%	12%	12%	15%	17%
Weak Democrat	22%	25%	19%	15%	16%
Strong Democrat	27%	15%	20%	19%	17%
Apolitical	4%	1%	2%	1%	0%
Survey totals	99%	101%	100%	99%	100%

Source: Party Identification 7-point scale 1952–2004, table 2A-1, ANES Guide to Public Opinion and Electoral Behavior

While this differentiation of voters has been widely known, many opt to reduce these seven categories down to just three, for a variety of purposes which we need not go into here: Republicans, Democrats, and Independents. This condensation may serve a number of purposes, but as the authors of *The Myth of the Independent Voter* pointed out, it obscures the fact that most of these so-called Independents are, or so they claim, inclined to back one party or the other: perhaps not always, but often enough so that political strategists for both parties know that, from historical evidence, they can regularly count on the loyalty of some percentage of them. The rest is what may often be referred to as the "swing vote:" voters who decide at the last minute which party they will support based primarily upon issues then current and the particular candidates.

It is a fact today that neither major party can expect to win a national election without capturing a significant percentage of the "Independent vote," no matter how you care to break it down. When commenting upon the then upcoming 2008 New Hampshire primary, Gerald F. Seib, in his 12/4/07 *Wall Street Journal* column "Capital Journal," put it this way: "Still they [Independents] will determine the shape of the game, and the trick isn't to own them, but to rent enough of them for the day ..." Platforms, propaganda, and electioneering efforts are drawn up to specifically try and do just that—attract the swing vote—without, of course, alienating their core constituents.

It should be mentioned that the ANES system of voter classification is not exclusive. The Pew Research Center, for example, has classified voters in America in relation to ideologies to include five classifications:

Conservative, Liberal, Populist, Libertarian, and Ambivalent. For consistency and comparability, and because it is the oldest study, going back over fifty years, the ANES statistics are generally considered a reliable and representative set of data to work with.

Is that it then? Are our only political choices either Democrats or Republicans? For general purposes, and using the ANES data here, yes. There are of course third parties—lots of them. But they all fall pretty much toward the extreme ends of the liberal to conservative ideological spectrum. They are, by default, either pretty liberal or pretty conservative, or else primarily represent single issue movements. As a group, third parties have not yet proven significant in American politics, with a few exceptions at certain times in our history (early 1900s, early 1990s, for example).

Back to the question above: So what? What is the political significance of Independents being the largest bloc of voters if most of them prefer one party or the other, as concluded in *The Myth of the Independent Voter*? If this is really the case, then all the hoopla about the Independent vote seems a waste of time, irrelevant. Well, maybe. But neither major political party acts as if it believes that is the case. And if you look at the above figures, you can see exactly why.

Each party's core constituency, strong Republicans and Democrats, represents just a small percent of the total voting population. Throw in their "weak" followers and their totals as a percent of those likely to vote are still a minority. If they could hold their "Independent leaners," each party would still represent less than a majority (although Democrats would have an advantage). Therefore attracting some of the other party's leaners and some of those pure Independents becomes a must, if one or the other are to prevail come election time. So, whether they know it or not, Independents constitute a significant factor in state and national elections today.

However, consider the irony here: Independents are critically important to exactly those ideological representatives that, by the very nature of their declaration of independence, they apparently want to distance themselves from! On consideration of the numbers alone, Independents at 38 percent (2008) of voters ought to be a political force to be reckoned with in their own right. With numbers like this, one ought to expect this group to wield some major political clout, but so far that is not the case. They continue to be significant only to the two major parties winning elections.

Part of the reason of course is that as pointed out, Independents in many cases tend to prefer one ideology or the other. Closet liberal or conservative partisans, some call them, and in many instances this is probably the case. They may register as Independent, for whatever reason(s), but they vote pretty consistently for one party or the other. That itself weakens any potential to rally Independents, as a group, into a homogeneous political force for electoral purposes. As a bloc, Independents don't (and can't) exist on a one-dimensional political spectrum of conservative to liberal. Pure Independents, those believed to be truly apartisan/apolitical, account for only about 10 percent of registered Independents (including those "declined to state"). They remain the smallest of Independent factions. And when you consider that in 2004, 58 percent of independents (versus about 65 percent in 2006) expressed a preference for the Democratic Party while 42 percent (versus about 34 percent in 2006) expressed a preference for the Republican Party, it is pretty clear why, so far, no one has been able to mobilize the Independent vote for Independent (non-major party) purposes; why these mainly "leaners" continue to be considered "swing voters" to be wooed by both sides of the partisan spectrum only come election times.

The too often overlooked fact of the matter is, for the most part, they simply have no other alternative option to consider or support; it's either the liberal or conservative. Today, those are their choices. Today, those are pretty much everyone's choices. Why not for third parties? A few may vote third party, but both major parties have done a good job convincing voters that a vote for a third party is a "wasted vote." Also, limiting their appeal, today's third parties tend to be partisan in the extreme (liberally or conservatively), or to champion single issues or narrowly focused agendas (prohibition, marijuana, or the environment, for example). That's not where most Independents, as we perceive them, appear to congregate.

So again, the question: Is that it? Is that all there is to being an Independent? Being coy, wanting to be "courted" as a swing voter? If so, why bother? I mean, are Independents all really just closet partisans or political prostitutes, our vote up for grabs, sold to the highest bidder come election time? I really don't think so. Why not? Because, the dealignment of our electorate has to mean something, has to represent something. I reiterate, the growth of Independent voters isn't happening for no reason. At best registering as an Independent says, I may be a political conservative, but I don't want to be clearly identified with the Republican Party, or vice-versa for a liberal and the Democratic Party. Why not? The two parties today, in the view of today's voters, must be either (1) increasingly less necessary for influencing peoples' decisions on how to vote or (2) fall short of what these voters would like to support, what they expect, politically speaking. At worst, it may indicate that once put in the position of governing, neither party is seen to govern in a conservative/liberal manner that is acceptable and expected of them by a significant and increasing part of the voting public.

There are two other possible causes contributing to this dealignment. The first is that with a generally better educated electorate and a broader range of information and information sources about the political scene readily available, the need for relying on the parties for political guidance is much less than it was just a couple of generations ago. Many people today are much more able to make up their own minds with much less input and coaching from partisan political parties. This ties in with and perhaps helps explain why parties may be less necessary to some and thus are weakening as social/civic institutions.

The other possible influence is the tendency beginning in the 1960s for candidates for major office, especially the presidency, to appear to distance themselves from their political parties. Political historian James MacGregor Burns has described this trend in his recent book *Running Alone*. Burns argues that the proliferation of presidential campaigns centered on the candidate, not on a larger party, has turned politicians into free agents more interested in their own survival on election day than they are on governing along party lines once they are in office. This results in the packaging of candidates to make them appear to be only lightly tethered to the demands of their party's base. A not illogical conclusion that might be drawn from this is the corollary that if the candidates are not running on a dedicated party platform, why should the voter indicate any particular support for any party?

Bottom line, what does being an Independent in American politics today really mean or signify? It means, apparently, I don't want to be identified with a particular political party because (1) I don't need a party to make up my political mind for me; or (2) today we don't really vote for parties, we vote the candidates who are only nominally, or weakly, partisan; or (3) that it doesn't really matter which party eventually wins: there will be little differentiation in governing between them. So I, as an Independent, will make up my mind on which party I will favor with my vote depending upon the issues of the day and or the candidate, not based primarily on the ideology or platform of either party. I do this recognizing, practically speaking, that my alternatives are presently limited to the existing one-dimensional political spectrum.

For the two parties, is this dealignment really much of a problem? History says that they are going (to have) to vote for them anyway. Well, in some ways it is. It increasingly underscores the reality that both parties represent distinct minorities of the electorate; that they draw their most loyal supporters from opposing ends of the political spectrum; e.g., that they are increasingly ideologically partisan; that today, the "big tent" party concept under which a broad range of compatible ideology—weak to strong, populist to libertarian—could be accommodated is no longer dependable.

In a larger perspective, this Independent phenomenon says that the limited supply of political goods available in the political marketplace does not well serve the demands or preferences of a huge segment of political consumers. This is not necessarily new news, but the growth of Independents indicates that ideology, as presently represented by these parties, while still present and somewhat important according to the ANES data, is less reliable in considering electoral potential. Look again at the historical percentage of Americans who claim either a strong or a weak partisanship:

	'58	'66	'76	'82	'90	'00	'04
Strong Partisan	38%	28%	24%	30%	30%	31%	33%
Weak Partisan	39%	43%	39%	38%	34%	27%	28%
Leaning Independent	12%	16%	22%	19%	24%	28%	29%
Independent or Apolitical	11%	13%	15%	13%	12%	13%	10%

Source: Table 2A-3, The ANES Guide to Public Opinion and Electoral Behavior

If we compare these numbers and trends with the previous figures on the strength of commitment to the parties, it seems clear that those tending toward independence come from primarily the weak category of both parties. That shouldn't be a major surprise. The point here is that if you are a dyed-in-the-wool ideologue, one way or the other, not much is going to make you rethink your position. However, if you are becoming somewhat doubtful, more open-minded, or perhaps becoming less inclined to blindly follow tradition, then it certainly appears that this is the category, or categories, fueling the Independent movement. Does it then follow that these are voters unhappy or uncomfortable with the two parties for whatever their individual reasons? That does not appear to be an unreasonable assumption. Still, as reasonable as it sounds, at this point it is still just an assumption. There may be other reasons to argue for this disengagement from the party.

Issues and candidates and the perceived current state of affairs (the latter always influential come election day) are more important to many Independent voters than ideology. The hard truth here is that either major party can only expect to win by, in effect, seeming to form an implied coalition with Independents. Therefore, the need to structure platforms and package candidates that will appeal to these voters while at the same time continuing to satisfy their core partisan supporters is if nothing else, complicated. But the unfortunate reality here is that candidate packaging and these compromise-appearing platforms are primarily for campaign purpose. Once candidates are in office, Independents too often find they have been, if not misled, at a minimum marginalized in how campaign promises—actual or implied—are fulfilled. But as a group, or bloc if you will, Independents have no organized representation in that implied electoral "coalition," or access to the new administration; there is little they can do about it, except feel frustration and disappointment at once again being used and electorally abused.

Increasingly you would think that Independents should be getting the message: We need you at election time, but not otherwise. And while hope may spring eternal, until these independent-minded voters have a viable alternative to consider aside from the two existing parties, realistically, what else can they do but vote the individual(s) whose campaign promises—real or contrived for this limited purpose—appear most in line with their political preferences?

This question of Independent electoral alternatives brings us to a consideration of what active Independent political activity, if any, is going on in our political arena to try and address this reality.

Chapter 8

Independent Parties and Support Groups Today

Some may be surprised to learn that today there are Independent political parties and/or Independent political activist groups in many of the states. Some claim national standing. There also seems to be no end to individual Web sites and Web blogs offering opinion, criticism, advice, and encouragement about nonmainstream political advocacy. This does not include over thirty active third parties (of which less than half actually field candidates), such as the Libertarian Party, the Green Party of the United States, the Labor Party, the Constitution Party, and the Socialist Party USA, to list just a few. While a few of these can claim a national status, many others can't.

Some consider these to be Independents, by definition, inasmuch as they are neither Democrats nor Republicans. Of those parties that identify themselves specifically as Independents, such as the Independence Party, the American Independent Party, or the Independent American Party, these are, again, "Independent" only in the sense that they are neither Democrats nor Republicans. Their political ideologies, however, tend to be strongly the same as one or the other—liberal or conservative. The ones designated Independent here are all strongly conservative ideologically, and most draw their adherents from the disaffected extreme ends of the political spectrum, if judged by their platforms. This is to say by those who do not consider the Republican Party conservative enough.

Some may also be surprised to learn that at most elections, there are a number of Independents running for state-wide and/or federal offices, a few successfully. We use the designation Independents here in the same sense of not being a Democrat or a Republican. In the November 2006 elections, there were at least thirteen major Independent candidates for state or federal offices across the country, including successful runs for the U.S. Senate by Bernie Sanders (of Vermont) and Joe Lieberman in Connecticut (technically Independents, but pragmatically liberals; e.g., caucusing with the Democrats). One U.S. president has been an Independent, in that he was not formally affiliated with any party during his two terms. However, no one since George Washington has repeated this feat. In recent history, John Anderson tried in 1980, Elisha Shapiro in 1988, Ross Perot in 1992 and 1996, and Ralph Nader in 2004. Independents or third-party candidates traditionally do poorly in U.S. elections, and these candidates were not exceptions to this rule.

A word now about Independent political activist groups: These non-party amalgams are for the most part autonomous state and local groups formed for purposes of mounting legal, legislative, and organizational challenges to the existing partisan political process. Their stated objective usually is to remove procedural and structural barriers hindering other than the two main parties from ready access to the electoral process.

A California group, Independentvoice.org, for example, declares its mission "… grows out of a twenty-five year effort to build a non-ideological political movement at the grassroots to dramatically reorganize the self-serving partisan control of government by the Democrat and Republican parties." When confronted as to just who Independent voters are in their understanding, their response is: "As individuals we hold to a broad range of ideological and political views. Together, we share an understanding that democratic reform of the political process and of government is the urgent political necessity of the day." But note, it takes great pains to profess that it is not a political party. It wants change, it wants "democratic reform," but it does not offer, as yet, an electoral alternative to the existing liberal/conservative duopoly. You might say it is trying to gather the tools necessary to build, or to tear down, something, but as yet offers no blueprint as to just what it intends as a replacement. The glue mostly holding it together appears to be dissatisfaction. Given its broad inclusion of fellowship, of membership, one has to wonder just how consensus, even broad consensus, is going to be possible. You might also legitimately ask if after twenty-five years of efforts there shouldn't be more to show in the way of progress in this connection.

You can question whether this California organization, its philosophy/mission, purpose, composition, or results, is typical of efforts being expended by various groups toward providing Independents a real political alternative. But at least the group appears to be working toward a tangible objective: structural electoral liberalization, which could (I repeat, could) favor opening the political arena beyond just two political giants, practically speaking. Many of these scattered grassroots Independent action groups are affiliated with an organization (not a party) called the Committee for a Unified Independent Party (CUIP) in New York City. CUIP describes itself as a nonprofit, non-ideological think tank for the independent political movement.

CUIP, now also operating under the umbrella Independentvoting. org, was founded in 1994 by two veteran political activists who claim to be part of a nationwide network of Independent activists. According to the CUIP publicity releases, they have engineered and helped to shape many of the central events, organizations, and campaigns of Independent political life during the last twenty-five years. CUIP's stated mission is to act as a national strategy center and organizing hub, designing and executing "cutting edge tactics" to develop America's growing Independent movement. It mounts political, legal, and legislative actions and designs direct challenges to partisan control of the political process. It claims to have pioneered methods of organizing Independents without a political party, creating Independent voter associations to project the voice of the large percentage of the electorate that considers itself independent. Like its affiliates, not surprisingly, CUIP contends that Independents defy traditional political labels; that what they share is support for the principle that radical structural reform of the electorate process and of government is the urgent political necessity of the day, whatever that may mean to them.

Another visible independent political voice is the Independent Progressive Politics Network. This Network is said to be composed of organizations and individuals committed to the achievement of a national, nonsectarian progressive political party, or an alliance of such parties, as an alternative to the corporate-controlled Democratic/ Republican system. Its activities toward furthering this goal include providing written materials, publishing a quarterly newspaper, reaching organizations and activists, maintaining a Web site and electronic discussions, organizing conferences, and engaging in activities that further these objectives.

There are others organized, however loosely or focused, to promote political issues outside of the two major parties. Their agendas may be clearly liberal, conservative, or something else, like the recently organized Integrity Party on Long Island, New York. It describes itself as a coalition, inviting Republicans, Democrats, Independents, conservatives, and Working Families Party members who have decided to put aside ideological differences on issues like abortion and gun control and come together for the working man. Its focus, to date, has been directed toward local issues and candidates. Then there is the Third Party of America. It is a virtual, Web-based party in formation and under development, "custom-built by the American People," to quote its Web site. "Join us in creating a platform truly of and by the people," it encourages. It is an invitation to rebuild politics from scratch. Their mission: To create a president, and we are all invited to join them in deciding just how this is best done.

Interestingly, another group, this one with experience in national electoral politics—names many would recognize—went public with the intention of developing a Web-based political party called UNITY08 to select and then attempt to elect, not a nonpartisan presidential candidate, but a bipartisan political ticket. As in the case of the Third Party, UNITY08 planned to operate on the Internet. According to them, that way everyone could join the party online and participate as a delegate, helping to build the party's platform collectively rather than ceding that task to interest groups, as both major parties tend to do. Ultimately, they hoped these online delegates would select a presidential and vice-presidential candidate in an online convention to be held in 2008, just after the major-party primaries determined the Republican and Democratic nominees. They anticipated that some of those ambitious candidates not chosen by the Republicans and Democrats—as well as other Independents—would seriously consider making themselves available as potential UNITY08 third-party candidates from whom the online delegates could pick a presidential candidate from one party and a vice-presidential candidate from the other party. This whole online process would be monitored and guided, or as UNITY08 put it, "refereed," by an in-house UNITY08 rules committee. It wasn't clear whether or not the online delegates got to participate in setting the rules or not. Hardly out of the starting gate, it generated considerable speculation concerning its true intention, as well as just who the moving force behind it, financially and politically, might be. UNITY08 never really caught on with its intended online audience, nor was it able to overcome some of those electoral roadblocks at state levels. Early in 2008, it conceded defeat in its efforts.

The similarity between the Third Party and UNITY08 appears obvious, and this may well be the way of the future, politically speaking. Only time will tell. UNITY08 had been under construction since about mid-2006, and it appears that considerable time, talent, and money had been poured into it. Its stated objective was to elect a president in 2008. However, it was not specifically designed for nor aimed specifically at Independent voters. What it was aimed at is the political center, whatever that means. UNITY08 said the ticket itself would be bipartisan: one Democrat and one Republican. And if Independents with bipartisan tendencies were interested, they'd be welcome too. As such, it seems a stretch to include UNITY08 as an Independently oriented action group, or party to be. Nonetheless, with its objective of electing a bipartisan political ticket, it might have attracted a lot of Independents' interest, absent other alternatives in 2008.

The above sketch of Independent political groups and activities is certainly not exhaustive. Nonetheless, on the surface it does appear to be somewhat representative of the extent of the active Independent political activity taking place across the country. No wonder neither the Democrats nor the Republicans appear to be too concerned about this movement, if that's what it can be called. While acknowledging some scattered Independent successes at primarily local levels and on local issues, and without in any way meaning to minimize the importance of working for structural liberalization of the existing duopoly system, its total effort seems akin to an under-manned and uncoordinated assault on well-defended walled cities using only bows and arrows, supported by networks of opinion and advice—cheerleading, if you will—to the few dedicated foot soldiers down in the trenches. It's not quite the blind leading the blind; it's more like the choir singing to itself, simply for the sake of hearing itself sing. But as I say, that's what appears visible to this observer. Might there by chance be anything deeper, more profound, going on here than all this surface agitation that is not evident? If there is, it is really being kept well under wraps.

It's perhaps too easy to criticize here, to fault these so-called Independent "activists," to say that actions speak louder than words; e.g., why aren't you doing more? In fact, they face what must appear to be an insurmountable task: On the surface, nothing short of upending America's entire system of electoral politics is going to accomplish their objectives. And as it is not only the existing political establishment but the American judicial system that would have to allow this, you can guess what the chances are of that happening. Let's look at a bit of reality here.

Plurality Voting, Duverger's Law, and Third Parties

As everyone notices, the United States is hugely dominated by two parties. Every presidential election after 1824 has been won by one of the (then) two major parties. This primarily holds true for the Senate as well. In the 2004 presidential election, the top two parties' candidates got 50.7 percent and 48.3 percent of the votes. No other party or candidate got more than 0.38 percent, with all the others combined getting just 1 percent.

In America, our electoral system is constructed around a single-member district plurality election concept (SMDP), using a first-past-the-post (FPTP) voting system. A two-party system often develops (as ours has) spontaneously from such an electoral system. This trend develops out of the inherent qualities of a SMDP that discourages the development of third parties while rewarding the two major parties. Examining this phenomenon, French political scientist Maurice Duverger found that an electoral system that featured both FPTP vote counting and SMDP would always tend toward producing a stable two-party system. This is the so-called Duverger's Law.

The reasons for this are both psychological and mechanical. Psychologically, voters do not like to waste their votes. They will tend to vote for the party/candidate closest to their view that has a chance to win. Mechanically, parties that win less than a majority of the votes do not win any elections. This lack of success reduces the incentives to support such a party, for most. Self-interested politicians and supporters stick with the existing major parties, which are thereby strengthened.

Independent advocacies must obviously recognize that the existence of the two-party option is not the result of the behavior of the parties; it is the result of SMDP/FPTP elections. So, they are not necessarily wrong in their efforts to try and change the system itself, though such attempts are futile, for at least two good reasons. The first is, as already explained, this system benefits a two-party political environment; as it is these two parties among themselves who make the political laws and regulations, it is fruitless to think they will voluntarily dismantle a system that is self-beneficial.

The other reason is that the First and Fourteenth Amendment rights the Supreme Court has decided to recognize in the field of election law are consistent with "natural duopoly" regulation; i.e., a strong two-party system. Though courts have used a variety of theoretical assumptions in producing election law jurisprudence, almost all of the actual holdings in primary ballot access cases follow the natural-monopoly model of regulation. Thus the Supreme Court has permitted states to favor a two-party system, its thinking (apparently) paralleling an economic philosophy that it is "inefficient" to replicate firms/parties in natural monopoly situations. This allows the two parties to compete freely, unfettered by any real threat of competition to their privileged standing.

Why would the courts take such a position? Basically—in their views—to try and ensure that the goal central to democratic politics be realized. This can be characterized as responsiveness to the interests and views of citizens, i.e., good representation. A part of how the

Court defines this is that the results of elections must produce clear and decisive winners. This results in political legitimacy and acceptance of election results. This in turn gives government the ability to make difficult choices without worrying about internal political strife: Losers of societal debates will be less likely to dispute government decisions if it is clear that these decisions represent the will of the people. In theory, this rational is difficult to dispute.

Given all this, the apparently ineffective activities of Independents in the furtherance of their cause(s) may be more understandable, even if not more excusable. It's difficult to make a lot of headway when swimming against a strong current. Sometimes working harder is not the answer; working smarter is.

In the end, these groups and associations (but not parties) will have to come out of the political shadows and advocate specifics; something more than just a generic rally for change and, perhaps, offer opinions and technical advice on how to go about challenging the system's structural barriers to wider electoral choice. As I say, these are laudable objectives. And let's assume that somehow (given all of the above) they are successful, or at least successful enough to open up our electoral politics to challenge. Who is going to do the challenging, and on what basis, ideology or platform? A rallying cry beyond dissatisfaction with the status quo is going to be called for; a movement is going to have to be formed and developed, either within the familiar liberal to conservative spectrum or on some other basis.

Until some credible potential challenge is formulated, then articulated, and promoted, these well-meaning people and their aspirations are going nowhere, and the existing duopoly is going to continue to ignore them and their calls for "change" or "reform." They are toothless. Even after such positive attempts, the attempt may still go nowhere, if the Independents they claim to champion see no real difference or advantage over what is currently available. The devil you know is often a better option than the one you don't.

Some of the leadership in these Independent movements have had experience in and/or with third parties and have apparently come to the conclusion that a third-party approach or threat is simply not viable in our present political environment. They may well be right. If so, then they need to come up with an alternative approach. Fusion?

As we will see, this is not a real option either in today's political environment or in dealing with those issues we believe Independents are independent for. Fusion still yields a lesser of two evils, choice-wise, not an Independent political option. What about an Independent, simply running independently?

An example: Michael Bloomberg, the mayor of New York City, was said to be considering entering the 2008 presidential race as an Independent. Such a move had been rumored and speculated upon since he changed his political party affiliation from Democrat to Republican and then to Independent in 2007. Bloomberg was rumored to have "tested the waters" for an Independent candidacy for over a year, possibly more, while he professed he was not—but not expressly denying that he would not be—running as an Independent presidential candidate. I don't blame him. In spite of the fact many people would probably have welcomed him as an alternative to what either major-party is liable to field as their candidate and their agenda, he had only one potential asset to support such an effort, well, possibly two: his own wealth (big asset!) and no doubt, his desire to be president. But aside from that, what did he have? No visible organization or support outside his personal entourage; no platform other than his (like the other's) offer to correct things in Washington (political rhetoric?); and no differential political philosophy or ideology to offer to voters to support such a candidacy.

How do you suppose he would have been viewed by many, if not most, of the voters? I would guess as an opportunist and little more. Now, if we had had an opportunity to hear him on the campaign trail for a reasonable period of time, these comments may have proven off-base. That would be nice, but I simply do not see this as how Independents are going to ride into Washington and make a lasting and significant difference, and making a difference is what we are talking about. Furthermore, simply holding the reins of the White House isn't going to do it either.

But I'm getting ahead of myself.

Chapter 9

The Independent Voter: A Profile and a Purpose

Now to the nub of this: As we have seen, an Independent voter is a statistical category, based upon a self-declaration of party preference, or in this case, nonparty preference. But that description doesn't tell us very much. All it says is that the person prefers not to be (openly) associated with a particular political party. It says nothing about their particular political ideology, i.e., conservative or liberal. So is that all we really know about these people? Well, no, we know a bit more. We know, as already mentioned, that, under present circumstances, a lot of these Independents have expressed a preference for one or the other major party; they, the so-called leaners have said so. That gives us some indication of ideological tendency. But what we don't know is just why these Independents have chosen this route. We don't know, or don't think we know, a lot about them.

There seems to be no end to people talking about Independents and/or organizations pushing for Independent political actions, coalitions, or such. However, in spite of all this, there seems to be a pretty complete void concerning discussion, proposals, or agreement on just what constitutes an Independent; why an Independent is an

Independent, or concerning an Independent philosophy, if there really is one.

For a start, how does one define an Independent (aside from how they register to vote)? You might ask, what is it that is defined by what it is not, but once defined, would cease to be? Answer: An Independent voter by current standards (I agree: that's not all that informative or helpful). Can we be a bit more specific? Yes, possibly, if we look closely at what we know about them and, perhaps, what we don't know about them. What is evident is hazy at best, aside from the fact that he/she declares not to support Democratic, Republican, or any other third-party platforms or ideologies—even if they do vote Democrat or Republican much of the time.

What are their demographics? Do they "fit" a specific demographic? Studies indicate many tend to be younger voters, mostly males. Do they remain Independents as they mature? Some indications are that they might, but we're not sure yet. Are they clustered in any particular sections of the country? Maybe just bit more than usual in the West and Southwest, according to some. Education? Conflicting analysis in this area, but all education levels appear to be represented. Economic status? Again, inconclusive, but some data to indicate they tend toward the middle and lower rungs of the income ladder. Not a high comfort level concerning the demographics at this point. But we seem to be improving in this area.

Many assume that because of Independent rejection of, or at best a weak attachment to, either persuasion that they must represent "the middle" of American political preference. This appears to be a very common assumption about Independents. But upon reflection, that's not necessarily a given: a middle of what? What is "a middle"? Is it moderate conservatism, or moderate liberalism? Is it apathy or simple ignorance and laziness about who stands for what? Are they simply "swing voters," political lemmings sometimes running in one direction, sometimes in the other? Where does political preference stop being conservative and become liberal? Are those the only choices, conservative or liberal? Is it issue-specific, or ideologically general? Is there a "no-man's land" between ideologies where Independents see themselves? If so, what do they see, insofar as political preference or ideology? Or do they see any? What are they looking for? If they have a preference for something other than what we label conservative or liberal, in the broadest sense, what is it?

If that zone on the political spectrum that Independents are presumed to populate is not what the middle is assumed to represent, is it some form of centrism? But again, centrism of what? Some combination of the two ideologies, say being conservative on fiscal and economic matters but more liberal on social issues? That's not an uncommon assumption. Well, if so, maybe we should call these voters "Republicrats," not Independents. That may adequately define some of them. Nonetheless, that label really doesn't satisfactorily define or further our understanding as to just why an Independent is an Independent.

The proliferation of Independent voters does not seem to have moved the general voting population's political ideology profile significantly over the past thirty-five to forty years as their numbers have increased. Periodic Harris Polls show that the percentage of respondents who list their ideology as Conservative, Moderate, or Liberal has hardly moved:

	CONSERVATIVE	MODERATE %	LIBERAL
1970s	32	40	18
1980s	36	40	18
1990s	38	41	18
2000s	35	40	18

Source: Harris Poll (January –December 2004) Table 4, "Decade Means of Political Philosophy." Author's note: A modest increase in the Conservative category noted.

Independents are in here with everyone else. The logical conclusion one draws from these figures is that Independents' increasing declaration of independence doesn't seem to be primarily ideologically motivated. Voters are not becoming significantly more conservative, moderate, or liberal in our political leanings, according to our own declarations. We need to look further at just why Independents might be Independents.

It isn't fair to call Independents fence-straddlers. However, most of the time under current conditions, that's pretty much what they are politically consigned to. Their option is probably one of least preferred, not most preferred, political choices. And as we are speaking here of a pretty constant 25 percent to 30 percent (Harris) or 38 percent (ANES) of American voters at any one time, that's strongly indicative of political alternatives that are unacceptable to a significant number of Americans. And if you further consider actual party inclination, about 34 percent for Democrats (liberals) and about 31 percent for Republicans (conservatives), per Harris again, that leads to a pretty clear conclusion: The present one-dimensional two-party system does not offer a balanced political environment under which most Americans feel comfortable, either ideologically or for some other reason or reasons. While there has been some academic research done that questions the actual impact of Independents (*The Myth of the Independent Voter*, for example), even this work acknowledges their existence and thus reinforces this issue of a balanced political environment.

An Issue of Outcome

So, considering all this, back to the question: Why is someone an Independent? Upon examination, one is drawn to the conclusion that what is rejected by Independents in the present political environment must be *outcome*. This seems compelling. We saw earlier that the increased presence of Independents has not resulted in any apparent long-term ideological shift of the American electorate to any significant degree. (A possible exception was toward conservatism in the 1980s and 1990s, apparently swinging back in the early 2000s.) So, basic ideological shift does not appear to be the answer. Therefore, the difference that most Independents are looking for, politically, has to be a desire for a *difference in outcome*.

What do I mean by outcome? It means no correction in or acceptable movement toward Balance, as I will shortly describe it. Experience has apparently demonstrated to these nonaligned and weakly aligned voters that electing either persuasion today results in government that produces no difference in outcome. They must reject either party in the two-party system as unevenly representing the interests of too few at the expense of too many. The question why (again) needs to be considered, if this is a legitimate argument by Independents: why does the two-party duopoly unevenly represent interests of too few at the expense of too many others?

One reason is probably due to the nature of American party politics: by design (or maybe by default), they are not very democratic.

American Democracy, in Practice

In practice, our democracy leans toward an elitist approach to governing. This theory argues, in effect, that classical (citizen) representative or direct (participatory) democracy does not, even cannot, work in the modern world. J. L. Walker, in his 1966 book *A Critique of the Elitist Theory of Democracy* asserts that this approach to democracy is a decision-making method that ensures efficiency in administration and policy making and yet requires some measure of responsiveness to popular opinion on the part of the ruling elites. In this view, citizen involvement serves primarily as a check on the actions of political leaders. It also, purportedly, maintains competition among rival elites. The citizen casting his or her vote is, in this view, simply a mechanism for deciding between competing elites. This description does appear to describe in large measure the working of the American political arena, at least during the twntieth and early twenty-first centuries, like it or not.

Closely related to this argument is political pluralism. In pluralism, society is seen as composed of groups of elites competing for political power. This competition, so it is contended, is the major means of protecting citizen involvement and individual rights. As long as competition exists and is reasonably fair, no single group or elite can dominate. Also, when it comes to the making of policy, diverse groups with differing interests keep any one group from getting too much power. Advocates of political pluralism contend it is a major protection for freedom.

Critics of such pluralism make two major points. First, pluralism as understood in this sense represents a cynical disregard of all values except the manipulation of power. According to anti-pluralists, the only thing of interest to the competing elites is staying in office. All democratic, all human values are secondary to this overriding goal. Thus the suggestion that pluralism protects freedom is largely false. Pluralism is a protection for freedom, or any other value, only as long as protecting such value politically benefits the competing elites.

Ponder the implications of this elitist/pluralistic theory for a moment, its pros and cons, and then argue in favor of it if you can. In theory and in today's ever more complicated and integrated society, an elitist approach to governing may be the only one with any reliable probability of success. But when its primary objective becomes one of power as opposed to good governing, governing for more than just the few, then it has probably gone to excess and needs to be reined in.

Consider: In only four of the past forty years of biannual surveys asking the question whether or not government is run for the benefit of all (1964–2004) has a majority of respondents—and pretty slim ones at that (64 percent in 1964, 53 percent in '66, 51 percent in both 1968 and 2004)—indicated belief that government was run for the benefit of all. Whether or not this perception is true, it certainly appears to be shared by the overwhelming number of people who vote. Now, consider the growth of Independents and ask yourself if there isn't a good argument for cause and effect here.

That this, an elitist system, is what we have as an option (the option) governing us today seems beyond reasonable argument. We hear more about mutually agreed gerrymandering, about those structural impediments to non-major party participation in American politics (put in place of course by the ruling elites), about the reelection rates of incumbents. We get the impression, at least some of us do, that politics, politics leading to good representation and good government is no longer an avocation or calling. Politics is a profession like any other, and as in any profession, the primary goal is to keep one's job and move up in your profession.

Do you suppose it is some combination of such feelings, such insight, even if only on the subconscious or gut levels, into just what it is that is motivating the majority of our elite political establishment that is making more and more of us decide we don't really want to be associated with it? Why we want a different outcome? Why we need an Independent political option? But would that make Independents anything other than negative in their outlooks?

Independents, and those leaning Independent, if they are honestly concerned about and oppose the self-serving ends of the dominant one-dimensional left-right political establishment, may be much more than just negative, given the opportunity. If a different outcome is in fact their objective, then we may possibly be able to project the kind of political policies they would eagerly support. That would make Independents positively as opposed to negatively definable. Hence, we need to consider ideology and then determine specific actions that these Independents might be expected to support in social, civil, economic, and political policies. Why would they support such specific actions? Because they would view them as providing what they seek: the difference in outcome we are assuming is their ultimate quest, which we have been alluding to here as an Independent agenda, leading to an Independent political option.

An Independent Political Philosophy

Does this mean that, like present political parties, Independents also have an ideology, a political philosophy around which they could coalesce (if they could recognize it)? Yes, it does. We mere mortals require some form of rationale, a philosophy and/or guiding set of ethics underpinning our lives and how we live them and how we deal with others. And inasmuch as none have yet apparently attempted to characterize such an Independent position, conceptually, I offer the following for consideration.

Politically, Independents would define the proper end of government actions much as Bentham did, wherein the objective of democracy is to produce the greatest good (happiness) for the greatest number. Independents recognize that you cannot please all of the people all of the time but would adhere to the philosophy that it is representative government's responsibility to at least try to fairly and consistently represent (at least) most of the people all of the time, and all of the people, at least most of the time. It's that simple: A philosophy of producing the greatest good for the greatest number, manifest in a policy of governing for (at least) most of the people all of the time and for all of the people most of the time.

Their philosophy is thus primarily utilitarian. It isn't the process (deliberation) leading to the act itself, nor the motivation or ideology behind the act that is determining for Independents, it's the end that the act produces that counts. It is the antithesis in this sense to the increasingly partisan direction the existing two major parties appear to be heading.

That is the "what" of the base Independent ideology. The two big-tent parties might well argue that they too adhere to such a philosophy. Perhaps. But the simple fact that they are ideologically partisan weakens such protestation. Ask yourself, how can any such political movement that at best represents and promotes the views of less than 40 percent of the populace govern for even most of the people at least some of the time? Also, going from the "what" to the "how" is where their wheels leave the steel: One party favors policies of one sort; the other party favors pretty much the opposite. Independents are not wedded to ideological extremes, not even their own (one would like to believe). What they are committed to is the above concept of governing for all most of the time and for most all of the time. And that means eschewing partisan or dogmatic approaches to solving issues that do not provide, as realistically and fairly as possible, the most benefit for the most people.

This philosophy does not (necessarily) look to an economic basis for its rationale or as a decision basis for its policies. This philosophy is not guided by a Pareto-like principle; it does not favor a Kaldor-Hicks-type exception for an end-run around policies it favors but cannot otherwise justify, according to its core criteria. It is not a welfare-oriented outlook, in the sense that Independents support an inherent entitlement to anyone or any one class of citizens over another from public funds. It is guided by a proper application (balance) of both the principle of wealth maximization and wealth distribution.

So, while Independents have a political philosophy—the "what"—of equal importance in their approach to governing would be the "how." The difference they advocate on the "how" deals with two fundamentals. The first relates to voters; the second to dealing with the issues. Both aim at making a difference in outcomes. The first, dealing with the voters, we will defer until Chapter 10, when we take up the subject of Independents' unity of purpose. Here we will consider how Independents would deal with issues in governing.

In dealing with the issues, the need to develop a core agenda, a platform of objectives they will work toward accomplishing, at least superficially they do not differ greatly from the major parties.

However, unlike those of the major parties, their approach to issues is not ideologically or "swings" driven. They are outcome driven. Their approach to issues will reflect, to the degree possible, accomplishing the objective that the results of representative democracy provide the greatest good for the greatest number. In this sense, and in most instances, an approach of "trickle down" benefits would be difficult, very difficult, to get past them.

Assuming for the moment the existence of an active Independent electoral party, for Independents you might say that purpose trumps personality. If someone wished to run for office as an Independent, he or she would have to publicly commit to promote the core agenda of Independent issues, the platform, in toto and in detail, as widely presented to the electorate, in order to receive the party's endorsement and support. This commitment to support the Independent philosophy is important for at least two reasons: First, the platform needs to be an explicit pact between the represented and the representative; it must be presented in a transparent form voters can easily grasp. This platform will represent the issues *and* the approach to resolving them, which Independents candidates offer to voters *before* going to the polls. To keep faith with them, it is important that those elected actually attempt to do what they said they would (remember "Read my lips …").

Secondly, the platform is a measure against which Independent results can and need to be judged. Finally, it clarifies—and sets in their-(the representatives') minds—just what it is they must focus on, both the "what" but as importantly, the "how." This may all be summed up as you vote the cause, or the party, not the person. In this way, you might say that Independents are reaching back to making promises and commitments as a movement, as a party if you prefer, not as individuals running for office with their fingers crossed.

This emphasis on candidates' publicly supporting the cause, the movement, or the party, whichever term you prefer, reflects the Independent's attempt to correct two shortcomings, or at least to reverse the trend of political obfuscation, apparent in today's political arena, which are eroding the public's confidence in our political system. First is the present tendency to center campaigns around individual candidates, not on the larger ideologically positioned parties. This "packaging" of candidates, as author James MacGregor Burns earlier described it, is largely to make them appear to be somewhat distanced from the stronger ideological demands of their party's base. Why? To try and win that necessary Independent vote that is *critical* to either major party winning elections. Consider the strategies employed in both primary and general elections. In the first instance, the candidates must convince the party base of their ideological conformity. In the latter, they must try and minimize it to win over Independent voters. Commitment to the platform also emphasizes the political objectives of the movement, not the political ambitions of the individual. It is also consistent with our view that politics needs to "clean up its act," as expressed in Chapter 6. This is a goal for Independents.

The second shortcoming is the now-absent concept of responsibility in the political scene. As reflected upon earlier, what good is it for individual politicians to acknowledge corporate (group) responsibility ("We failed as a Congress," or "… as a party") and then duck any individual responsibility for the failure? If those individually responsible for the corporate decisions taken, or not taken, in governing are able to opt out of individual responsibility for the outcomes (there's that term again) that they as individuals or as party candidates purported to support when running for election, then the blame is theirs individually, and they should be held accountable come the next election cycle. The only instance when this logic wouldn't hold up is when, as members of a party, those individuals did perform as they promised but, as part of a minority voice, could not achieve the goal they supported. Evidence of such support needs to be tangible and credible.

This raises the issue of a representative's proper responsibility. Is it exclusively or even primarily to those who elected him or her to office, or is there a larger responsibility to govern for the benefit of "the country" (all of the people)? Conceptually, and constitutionally, the representative is the chosen voice of those who elected him or her and should be expected to be so. But what to do in matters where local and larger issues appear to conflict? Here, people often fall back on "principle" as a defense for defying the expectations of the electorate, and they may be justified in so doing. If politicians slavishly obeyed the wishes of the moment of purely local or individual interests, consensus on issues of more general concern would be more than difficult, and regionalism (or pure self-interest) would make national issues impossible to deal with. (Does this sound familiar?)

The proposed Independent solution would minimize this conflict. By its platform approach, and the requirement of its candidates' public support for it, this would tend to ensure that, at the local level, the voters themselves are, by their vote, in agreement with what and how their representatives will be pursuing issues of broader impact. Does this say that representatives have no latitude in how they represent voters? Yes, in those areas of the proposed platform, it does. What about "principle"? That's already been decided when the representative signed on to support the platform as an Independent. By his or her election, it implies explicit agreement between a majority of voters and the responsibility of the candidate.

Trust and loyalty are two sides of the same coin. If you ask for the voters' trust come election time, then they have the right to expect your loyalty in the meantime. If the party or cause or movement that promised you, the voter, something and then did not fulfill that commitment, then the party, including all of the individuals representing it, should be held responsible for that lack of loyalty at the next election.

Someone is going to scoff at all this, smile condescendingly, and point out the obvious: The author here is evidently naïve and doesn't know that elections are not really about specific issues and not about educating the electorate. Today, elections are all about connecting emotionally with the voters; with getting them "comfortable" with the candidate, not the party; with overpowering them with slogans, generalized and ambiguously persuasive "positions," and faux-facts, innuendos, and suggestions about how bad it will be if the other candidate wins. Such facts, innuendos, and suggestions are generated by a professional information politics machine that the electorate in general has no hand in fashioning and is not expected to fathom. Voters are expected to accept it because it comes from authoritative source. "*Trust us!*" We are on *your* side!"; "*We*, not *them*, know what is best for you. Trust us at the polls; you need us in Washington to *fight* for *your* interests; we're *your* kind of people."

Current political wisdom certainly supports this approach, and its apparent success is difficult to refute. But it needs to change if representative government is to continue to be considered, in the eyes of at least most of the people, effective; anything more than mock democracy, a series of individual popularity contests. Just consider the trend line regarding confidence in government: In 2006 those expressing a great deal or quite a lot of confidence in the presidency was 52 percent and 30 percent for the U.S. Congress. Current opinion polls (June, 2008) have it at only 26 percent for the presidency and 12 percent for Congress. In the case of the Congress, this represents the worst rating the Gallup Organization has recorded for any institution in the thirty-five years of measuring the question of confidence.

"Loyalty," to re-cite the earlier paraphrase from William Grieder's 1992 exposé on the betrayal of American democracy *Who Will Tell the People*, "is another word that has fallen into disuse in politics—the other side of trust." Also, to paraphrase Greider, "Given the almost overwhelming complexity of governing today, elected officials, supposedly professional or not, unless they are very sophisticated, are not much better equipped than average citizens to judge between special-interest threats and the popular sense of the right thing to do." So much for the purported benefits to the voting public of ruling elites. A purpose of Independents is to tether the ruling elites more to the will of those who elect them, in the tradeoff between trust and loyalty.

This point leads us right back to the critical issue of a difference in outcome, of Balance in our democracy.

A Rightful Balance in Society

We said earlier that the concept of Balance, as Independents define it, is important. I said, in fact, that a better Balance in American society is the object of producing a different outcome, the goal of an Independent political option. So just what are we talking about here?

Balance, per se, is obviously not a new or revolutionary concept. However, in the sense used here, a rightful Balance (with a capital B) is somewhat different from the usual connotations. It's not so much a matter of an equilibrium, a quid pro quo, or even of fairness; it is a concept of what is *necessary* for a healthy, prosperous, and respectful society. It is akin to the description of what emerged in the final plan of the Constitutional Convention in the summer of 1787: an appropriate distribution, or balance, of interests. A complex society such as ours needs a high degree of Balance if it is to be healthy, happy, prosperous, respectful, and secure. As applicable to our society, a necessary and rightful Balance is generally defined as follows:

> A rightful Balance exists when all parties involved recognize and carry out their responsibilities to the system that supports their way of life—their existence, in effect. In our country, that system revolves around a democratic form of representative government and, basically, a free capitalistic form of private enterprise. The main protagonists in our system today are the private capitalistic economic sector (business) and government.

Only business and government? What about us, the people? Just where do we fit in here? Well as you would expect, very prominently. After all, in the end, it is, as I said at the beginning, all about us. And of course it is people who fill the roles in both business (private) and government (public) interests. But it's more than just that.

While it may sound a bit like Government 101, we the voting public are ultimately the key to the success of the system. We can make it or break it. While this is not always clearly evident, it is the truth. Ultimately, we have the power. Where? At the ballot box, of course. Ultimately, that's where the real power lies in a true (functioning) political democracy, and that is the reason, *the sole reason,* that protecting the effectiveness of the ballot box is so vital.*

The problem is getting us, the public, to use this power on a consistent and responsible basis. That can often be difficult under present election and campaign practices and conditions. (Recall where we pointed out in Chapter 6 in our discussion of public choice theory how Positivist economic theoreticians specifically spoke of the "rational ignorance" of voters.) At any rate, that's our part in maintaining a rightful Balance in our system. It's never been a breeze to do so. It isn't easy today. Just consider the fact that in national elections over

---

* I suggest you reread this brief paragraph, along with that earlier paragraph in Chapter 4 regarding the function of the political system in our society. In these two brief jottings are found the entire rational for writing this book. This will be further examined in Chapter 12.

the past forty-five years, only about 40 percent of the people voted in nonpresidential years, and just 55 percent voted in presidential years. It's hard to find an excuse for that, given the apparent dissatisfaction of so many with government (especially in November 2006), unless voters feel that no matter what the outcome, (*there's that term again!*) things won't change. Despite the trend, I consider such a fatalistic view of possible outcomes unacceptable, if the principles of democracy are followed and if genuine choice is available. Chapter 12 will have more to say about following the rules and principles of our democracy in connection with the ballot box.

Some will argue with me on this power-to-the-people point, so to speak. How, they ask, can you say that the people have any influence, especially in this day and age of powerful lobbies and well funded special-interest groups? My reply to them is, "Bingo!" You've hit the answer squarely on the head: special-interest group. That's the answer. Think about it: Just what is a special-interest group? It's a group of like-minded individuals banding together to promote their own agenda and lobbying for it, isn't it? No, you say, you're wrong on this. Just consider special-interest groups today. They are considered by most as a major cause of our political problems, and if that's the case, how can they possibly be a part of the solution to the same problem?

Well, I have to agree, to a point. The problem in considering the proper influence of special-interest groups—and there should be a place for them at the political table—is being able to see the forest for the trees. Even though early in our history as a democracy James Madison cautioned us in the Federalist Paper Number 10 about the possible negative effects of pressure groups, the problem is not that special-interest groups are bad, per se. The problem is that we (the voting public) have allowed narrowly focused (factional) special-interest groups, and/or groups of artificial entities, to gain an abnormally large influence over the major issues in our country that are subject to government attention. The result is imbalance. This is tantamount to government by the minority.

The resolution to this shortcoming the system is tolerating—giving in to factional, lobbying special-interest groups—is to recognize that the ultimate and biggest interest group in our society is the American voter, as a unity, and that this ultimate interest group goes to the polls every two years to make itself heard; to express either its satisfaction or lack thereof with those who are supposed to represent its interest through government. The composition of that group, along with its breadth and its size, is critical to a necessary and rightful Balance.

So, with this explanation of the peoples' role, let's refine our definition of Balance a bit more precisely:

> In our country, Balance exists when (1) the private capitalistic economic sector (business) feels it's able to pursue its aims with a minimum amount of outside interference; (2) when government, in its role as representative of the people, feels that the results of capitalism, in the broadest sense, are distributed equitably enough among the people, and (3) the people, through their voice at the ballot box, concur with the government's assessment. When all this happens, America is a healthy, happy, prosperous nation. America is in an acceptable, necessary, and rightful Balance.

This sounds nice, but is such equilibrium, such a balance of interests, ever reached and sustained for any period of time? Probably not. But that's not the key issue. It's the goal, the better tomorrow we strive for. And as long as this Balance is generally perceived as acceptable for the moment and that we as a country are moving in the right direction—which is toward it—most of us are inclined to go with the flow and continue working toward this perfect if unreachable goal. Why? Largely because of self-interest. Because we've been led to believe that in so doing we stand to see our personal, social, and economic fortunes improve and our country prosper: prosperity we should all be entitled to share—some more than others, certainly, but generally enough to go around.

So bottom line here, looking at the profile and purpose of an Independent voter, here is what we see:

They may represent a wide range of personal and demographic attributes. Independents probably do resemble the descriptions we saw when discussing Independent political activist groups around the country earlier: As individuals, they adhere to a broad range of ideological and political views. They may be conservatives, they may be liberals; they may be young, they may be older. They may represent "the middle"; they may not. They may be sectarian or they may be secular; they may congregate more in the West and Southwest; they may be anywhere along the economic ladder; they may be "political leaners," they may not. But one thing seems certain: *They are dissatisfied!* Probably not all by the same thing or things, but bottom line, they want to see *a change in outcome,* an improvement in Balance, as we have described it here, and they do not believe that the existing political choices of Democratic or Republican representation are either willing or capable of producing that change. In this sense, the scholars who concluded in their book *The Myth of the Independent Voter* got it wrong. Independents do have something in common, something huge in common: the desire for a different outcome.

Our existing parties are by now mature, entrenched interests, if you will, which appear to be ever more partisan in the way they approach governing. But the contradiction in this is that, though they may represent opposing ends of the political ideological spectrum, in our society Balance and/or the direction toward Balance appears unaffected by whichever of them is at the moment in political control of government. This reflects the antithesis of governing for all of the people most of the time or most of the people all of the time. As everyone knows, the parties themselves only represent minorities, clear minorities, of the American people.* They both resemble governing elites who, between them, have done (and continue doing) their best to see that they perpetuate their duopolistic, power-sharing economic and political control of America for purposes that a minority may see as worthy but that a majority of Americans arguably do not. This perception, conscious or unconscious, has to have major significance as more and more voters register as Independents. At this point, it represents only an impotent protest, conscious or unconscious, against the existing two-party political system by a large—the largest—bloc of Americans registered to vote.

---

*   The Parties themselves, not necessarily their general sub-ideological back-drop they profess to champion, i.e. Liberalism or Conservatism.

The fact is the preponderance of these unhappy conservatives and liberals *have no practical political option.* In view of the evidence here, the conclusion regarding the myth of the Independent voter, that many, perhaps most, are really closet Democrats or Republicans, reflects primarily the fact that these unhappy conservatives and liberals *have no practical political option.* Existing third parties come nowhere near providing options, given their own ideological or single-purpose orientations. No one has offered Independents a practical (read challenging) third political choice. And the existing duopoly has done its best to block any third political force from access to the electorate by means of those difficult-to-overcome structural barriers.

No one, until now, has suggested an Independent political option (solution) to the problem of correcting America's imbalance. No one has recognized or been able to successfully communicate the need, not for a bipartisan approach to governing, but for a nonpartisan approach to governing—a condition that has not existed since shortly after the inception of our republic. As trusting citizens, we naturally want to assume our government governs for all of the people most of the time or most of the people all of the time. That "trust" appears to be fading. With political parties as partisan as they appear today, such governance is unlikely. If the party approach to governing in accordance with ideological positions happens to satisfy others, so be it. But it is not what parties actively set out to accomplish. It is simply a collateral benefit, if you will.

While there has long been recognition of the need to protect minorities from majority abuse, one of the cardinal rules in a democracy is that the majority has the ultimate legitimate right to decide the affairs of government through their preference at the polls. But to form a majority (if only at election times), both parties need Independents to side with them. That does not make them true majorities. The problem is, once election time has passed, these "swing" (Independent) votes count for little in the halls of government. What we end up with is rule by a minority, imposed on the majority, for primarily a minority interest, by either party. Somehow, doesn't that sound like the world upside down?

Independents, by their very existence, seem then to suggest or create purpose in response to this situation:

- Politics needs to clean up its act. Independents can help.
- The link between trust and loyalty is losing credibility. Independents can help.
- Our society is out of Balance. Independents can help.

To Independents, democracy that seems to produce an unacceptable political outcome of minority rule, of unacceptable Balance, is *the* problem. So what to do about it? How can it be corrected? When the problem becomes too severe, recall that Freud prescribed psychotherapy; Marx prescribed revolution. Are they the only alternatives?

Hardly.

Chapter 10

An Independent Political Option

If all the people registering as Independent voters are, as we suspect, not happy with the ways of governing today, why can't they do something about it? Perhaps they can. After all, they represent a plurality of people registered to vote. Perhaps there is an Independent approach to realizing a different outcome. Let's look at the possibilities.

First, the concept of an Independent political option merits a bit of expansion before we proceed too much further. Given the common misconception that Independents are somewhere left of conservatives and right of liberals, some might read such an option as a middle of the road approach. That's not necessarily the case. Nor can it be considered centrist in the usual connotation. An Independent option is not just about pleasing the center (whatever that means). It is not an average. It's not necessarily a compromise. An Independent option is an attempt to promote greater tangible Balance, as previously defined.

For a brief spell, I penned a weekly Internet-based commentary titled *The American Family Gazette,* promoting Independents as a third (Balancing) force in American national politics. I received comments on occasion that these views on the potential of Independents as a means toward achieving Balance was a formula for stalemate; it was unworkable fence straddling in American politics. One assumes such well-meant criticism was from clearly partisan folks. Nonetheless, they made a point: To accomplish something—anything—you have to take a position. This seems especially true in politics. But such positioning does not necessarily have to be toward one extreme or the other to be workable. Likewise, it probably won't be in the "center," because in a bipolar environment, that pleases very few; *that's* fence straddling. As such, an Independent solution does not represent a centrist philosophy, centrism being defined here as promoting moderate policies that tend toward the middle ground (compromise) between the political extremes.

An Independent solution is not conceived as occupying a position or location on the present political spectrum but as a potential "force." Think of it as a defined threat, if you will, or as a catalyst between two extreme elements that under normal conditions will not combine or work together. As such, it might either (1) induce those normally favoring more ideological (partisan) solutions to issues to respond to their concerns, or (2) compete with them directly for the right to govern. In the first instance, its influence (threat) is catalytic. In the second instance, its influence (threat) is competitive: a formalized electoral alternative to the two major parties.

When you have a one-dimensional political spectrum of left-right politics, you have (only) one acceptable side to an argument—yours or theirs. Unless the weight of power between you is significantly in favor of one or the other, what do you have? Right: You most often have stalemate. This is especially true where ideological/philosophical issues are at stake—which is the usual case. Unless there is political compromise (horse trading) or political intimidation (arm twisting), nothing happens. Issues in need of resolution remain unresolved on the table, with each side blaming the other. What has this actually accomplished? Kudos, perhaps; defense of "ideals," and perhaps some succor for alpha-type personalities. But aside from such bragging rights, nothing, absolutely nothing gets done to resolve the issue(s). More often than not, stalemate is what results from severely partisan politics.

An Independent option is viewed as a strategy for overcoming this. So how do we go about accomplishing this, and what is our premise for doing so? At this point our premise for proposing such an option has been demonstrated with some degree of probability, to wit:

A. Independents now equal or exceed the number of voters who openly support either the conservative Republican or the liberal Democratic parties. Either party must capture a significant portion of this Independent vote to win elections. Nonetheless, their governing policies continue to reflect primarily, if not exclusively, the partisan nature of their ideologies.

B. Such bipolar ideological approach to governing makes resolution of any number of issues of significance to all Americans difficult to achieve, exactly for the reason of partisan bias highlighted above.

C. Voter expressions of political independence no doubt represent for some a dissatisfaction or disillusionment with either party's performance in governing. Just what percent of Independents hold such feelings is not at all clear, as many continue to regularly vote for one party or the other much of the time. A primary reason for such continued if reluctant loyalty to these parties may be the current absence of any practical political alternatives.

Given these circumstances, it would seem that what we have at present is a proverbial Mexican standoff: a significant and willing, possibly even eager, desire for change confronted by a significant and recalcitrant power-structure unwilling to allow such challenge, practically if not legally. No one has been successful in challenging these parties, certainly not in the past century. What makes me believe that an Independent movement might be different?

It might be different if such a movement demonstrated to the voting public that its political agenda was both broad as well as different, that it didn't represent just a different shade of the same old political fabric. It might be different if it offered the voters a clearly different deal; if it offered at least most Americans a different vision of governing. And it might be different due to the perceived state of affairs in government. We have on many occasions herein highlighted the degree of apparent political dissatisfaction evident in America today. An Independent movement might be different if, as we hypothesize, enough Americans want a different outcome to make it different.

Considering the likelihood that at least one, possibly more than one, of these reasons why an Independent movement might succeed, based on the premises, it seems worthwhile to consider how Independents might go about accomplishing that. There appear to be at least two, possibly three, options to examine.

The first and most apparent option is to go the traditional third-party route; to develop an Independent slate of candidates and attempt to be recognized and to qualify for the ballot in all fifty states. While third-party movements have been somewhat successful in highlighting dissatisfaction with existing economic and social conditions, they have most often either been too narrowly focused on certain issues to capture the larger American political wave, or else their major platform issues have tended to be co-opted by one or the other of the two major parties, stealing their thunder and, in effect, their reason for being. I'm thinking specifically of the Populist movement of the early 1900s, much of whose platform was subsequently adopted by the Democrats and incorporated into the New Deal of the 1930s. So, while a third party is an option, historically third parties do not do well in American politics. Still, it's not inconceivable that a third-party movement with a clearly differentiated and electorally broad platform under today's conditions could break this mold.

The second option would be a fusion approach of some sort. Traditional electoral fusion is an arrangement where two or more political parties support a common candidate, pooling the votes for those candidates. Fusion was once common in the United States but is now commonly practiced only in New York State, although it is also allowed by law in Connecticut, Delaware, Idaho, Mississippi, South Carolina, and Vermont. In several other states, fusion is legal when primary elections are won by write-in candidates.

In New York State, fusion is still common. New York Mayor Michael Bloomberg was a fusion candidate, supported by both Republicans and Independents. Rightly or wrongly, the New York Independents like to point to their success in helping electing him to demonstrate the "power" of the Independent vote. What did Independents get out of this? Hope eternal! As one influential New York Independent reportedly remarked, "... we went more for him than he went for us. But he was reaching out to try and make something new happen." The best we can say here is that these Independents, by their support of a Republican candidate, helped get him elected rather than someone whom they perceived as less favorable to their cause elected. However, this is little more than an example of achieving the least unfavorable result. It really doesn't move Independents much closer to an independent political option.

This may still represent a partial victory for many Independents, as a fusion candidate (or party) may more closely represent their political positions and preferences than any other. But to reiterate, it does not really offer Independents a real political option. (They could have voted for the candidate anyway.) What it possibly does indicate is the magnitude and, in a specific instance, the preference of such an Independent vote, to the degree that such vote is in fact directable, which today is highly questionable. To that degree, it may indicate to the political power structure some benefit to consider and even accommodate some of the political views of Independents in their overall political activities. Maybe.

The fusion approach still requires Independents to qualify as a party on state ballots. The major difference between this and the traditional third-party approach is there is little or no need to develop a separate platform or run an Independent slate of candidates. The intent here is to "co-brand" candidates as a combination major party and Independent party pick and try and horse-trade with the major party for some political and policy concessions in return for throwing their support behind one party's candidate or the other. Fusion may achieve some of the objectives and goals of an organized Independent movement, possibly shaping one or the other or possibly both major party platforms, as the Populists did in the last century. It does little, however, to ameliorate the partisan character of present-day politics. And because current state laws limit the ability to go the fusion route, it does not seem like a good near-term option in any but a few states. Still, there could be that exception as it applies to write-in candidates.

A third approach would be to eschew consideration of Independents as an official third political party for that of being simply a major but centrally directed political force—a lobby, in effect. To a degree, this is what the fusion route implies at the state level, e.g., the ability to influence the outcome of elections. But as we have seen, electoral fusion is only permitted in seven states and a few others if primary elections are won by write-in candidates. Furthermore, in a legal ruling that was a blow to advocates of electoral fusion, the Supreme Court, by a 6-3 margin, in 1997 rejected the argument that fusion was a right protected by the First Amendment's freedom of association clause. Thus, under existing conditions it seems unlikely to be adopted by other states.

Ignoring the fusion aspects for the moment, the latter approach of developing the presently amorphous Independently registered voting population into some form of a coherent, and centrally directed political influence to challenge the two parties seems to offer some possibilities. One possibility would be a centrally managed interest group that operated along the lines of a "shadow government," promulgating its own proposed "legislation" to address public affairs. These positions would be made readily available to the public for comparison with what is coming out of Washington, D.C. Obviously, there could be howls about "second-guessing," about being divisive, but notwithstanding, it has some potential.

Another possibility is something along the lines of the present Consumers Union organization, which compares products and services and publicly rates them in their widely available magazine, *Consumer Reports*. A voter-friendly political equivalent might work to get things started. It is at least consistent with the concept expressed above that an Independent solution is not conceived so much as occupying a position or location on the present political spectrum as it is a "force"—a defined threat, if you will, or catalyst between two extreme elements that under normal conditions will not combine or work together. If successful, it might even evolve into something more formally electoral.

So, our Independent political options appear to be, practically speaking, two: (1) a nonelectoral "shadow government"; an organized, active, and visible interest group if you will, possibly in the organizational form of a "think tank." This would pursue the catalyst line of thinking. I can see considerable merit in this approach. (2) A direct electoral challenge to the existing duopoly in the form of an Independent political party. This would pursue the competitive line of thinking.

Action-wise, the latter is a much less conservative approach than the first option. At the same time, the latter approach (direct competition) is the option that should most convince the existing power structure to mend their narrow, ideologically partisan ways sufficiently to move America more in the direction of Balance—the Independent political objective.

I said earlier, in Chapter 8, that "until some credible potential challenge is formulated, then articulated and promoted ... the existing duopoly is going to continue to ignore those [Independent movements] and their calls for change or reform. They are toothless." Considering this as we move forward, we will be thinking "credible potential challenge"; we will be thinking, "new paradigm." We will be thinking "third party."

With this option as our goal, let's consider how we might go about it.

Chapter 11

The Superstructure: How It Fits Together

Now we need to construct a purpose-specific superstructure that will support a unified Independent movement along the lines determined: a formal political party. The key features of this have already been expressed: A common political ideology around which Independents can coalesces (the "what") and a platform (the "how") to accomplish the objective of returning greater Balance to our society. The "why" of all this, should one's memory need refreshing, is to produce a different outcome—one that will restore a greater Balance in our society. Based on these two building blocks alone, Independents can construct and then project to voters their proposed solution to this critical issue pressing on our society.

The Independent Political Ideology: The Greatest Good for the Greatest Number

In dealing with the term "ideology," we need to be clear in our use of it. Recall from Chapter 4 that an ideology is a belief system. It represents values accepted as fact, or truth, by those who hold to it. We pointed out that to some degree, a political ideology includes all of those views relevant to our society's socialization system, social stratification system, and economic system, and stressed that the political system is the deciding factor in the kind of society we shall live in. If there are features within society we are not happy with, it is largely to the political system we must look to try to correct them.

However, we also pointed out that it seems to many that it is precisely conflicting political ideologies that all too often hinder the political system from being what it is intended to be, that mechanism for correction. In this sense, the system is, as that gentleman from Texas said in 1992, "broken." Thus we are badly out of Balance. The system needs to be fixed. But if it is the case that competing or conflicting ideologies can be blamed for this condition, and Independents introduce yet a third ideology (in addition to the existing conservative and liberal views), will this just further complicate the existing political system difficulties? Hopefully not. It shouldn't, if we get it right, if we understand that the Independent political ideology is designed to govern in a manner that neutralizes, or at least minimizes, the antithetical nature of the present seemingly incompatible one-dimensional, left-right ideological view of governing. And that is to govern for all of the people at least most of the time and most of the people all of the time. That is, in an Independent view (our ideology), the proper purpose of government. So with this qualification, in an effort to "get it right," let's consider an Independent philosophy.

Broadly speaking, philosophy is the rational investigation of the truths and principles of being, knowledge, or conduct. That's too far-reaching. Here we limit our use of this term to the sense of conduct, as a system of principles for guidance in practical (political) affairs. This philosophy is to govern on the basis of what will provide the greatest good (happiness, or perhaps better stated, satisfaction) for the greatest number. It's that simple. That is how Independents would conduct affairs.

Nonetheless, some are going to question, philosophically, if this greatest good is also right and proper? Here we will encounter philosophical disagreement. By "right," in their challenge, they will mean that which is morally or ethically proper. "Right" in our meaning is that which is good or just. These are subjective terms. What is good, what is just, what is morally or ethically proper? These represent personal beliefs most of us define in accordance with our ideologies, which are largely based upon our comprehensive philosophies (our beliefs of truths and principles of being, knowledge, or conduct). Recall that we defined an ideology as a value or belief system accepted as fact or truth by those who hold to it. It provides the believer with a picture of the world both as it is and as it should be, in accordance with those beliefs. Ideology organizes the tremendous complexity of the world into something fairly simple and understandable.

Based upon its philosophy (the greatest good for the greatest number), the Independent's political ideology is to govern to the degree possible on a personally unbiased approach (conservatively or liberally) to decision making. It is based primarily upon the utilitarian principle, the greatest good for the greatest number. This is a nonpartisan (not bipartisan) approach to dealing with issues. It strives to govern for all of the people most of the time and at least most of the people all of the time. Such acts undertaken by Independents to produce this result are not undertaken (philosophically) based upon any "right thing to do" morally or ethically, according to left-right ideologies as the origin of either intention, motivation, or preferred outcome of the act, but on the basis that the end result that the act produces is consistent with the professed Independent objective. Said simply, it is not ideological motives behind acts that count, it is the results that acts produce that count. In politics it defines the proper results of actions, much as the English radical Jeremy Bentham did wherein the objective of democracy represents the greatest good (happiness) for the greatest number. Independents recognize that you cannot please all of the people all of the time, but they adhere to the philosophically based ideology that it is representative government's responsibility to try to fairly and consistently represent (at least) most of the people all of the time and all of the people at least most of the time. This is the antithesis to the direction the existing two major parties appear to be heading in, as both become increasingly more ideologically partisan.

What is right, true or proper, philosophically, always remains open to challenge, but Independents see no requirement to justify their ideological position any further than has been openly presented here. It is a position put forth to accomplish specific objectives, as also openly put forth. To the degree it accomplishes this, it is useful and proper.

To the degree that few may eventually agree with either its manner or agenda, it will not be. But at the very least, it will provide expanded choice.

Utilitarianism

Politically, we have determined that a utilitarian philosophy best serves the rational and ethical needs in aiming to achieve a different outcome. But what exactly does that mean? We briefly highlighted what this means in Chapter 9. Based upon what we referred to as a broadly utilitarian philosophy, Independents translate the slogan that "meaning is use" into "it is representative government's responsibility to try and fairly and consistently represent (at least) most of the people all of the time and all of the people at least most of the time."

But is such a statement anything more than trying to do the right thing? If it isn't, then can't everyone claim to be pursuing utilitarian ends? Sure they can. Therein lies the reason why clarification is necessary. So, fasten your seatbelts while we take a quick metaphorical dash to arrive at our destination: utilitarianism as a complete and proper political approach to achieving a different outcome in America. Always keep in mind that the different outcome we seek is an improvement in Balance, and, as pointed out in Chapter 4, the means to do so is political.

First, we need to be clear on our understanding of the term "utility" before we can correctly incorporate it as the basis of our philosophy. We said that anyone can claim to be using a utilitarian approach, if it means simply doing the right thing—or the right thing from their particular view point. Today we see and hear these terms—utility, utilitarian, utilitarianism —widely employed. So widely in fact that their meanings are too variable to have a great deal of significance in the political sense, i.e., like "motherhood" and "apple pie." Who isn't for those concepts? In addition, over time, the term "utility" has taken on expanded meaning.

In its traditional sense, "utility" simply means usefulness. We use this sense of the term on which to base the principle of a utilitarian ideology: That which is conducive to the happiness, in the sense of good or of satisfaction, of the greatest number of people is useful. However, today, the term has gradually moved away from this general sense to its current, more specific meaning in social science. Its more familiar technical use and application today is in economics, decision theory, and game theory, where its cogent meaning is that which leads someone to choose one thing over another: a basic unit of desirability or preference. Most traditions of ethical thought recognize more variable and worthwhile goals to life than simply satisfying an arbitrary sequence of preferences, usually quantitative. Furthermore, when used as a technical term, utility has no normative connotations. For example, "utility furniture" may be contrasted with "beautiful furniture," but maximizing utility is the same as maximizing beauty, if beauty is what you want to maximize.

So, to clarify: utility in the political sense for Independents means usefulness. And as its root has morphed in use and meaning, so has the term "utilitarian." A bit of historical background is helpful here, so keep your seatbelt on for a bit longer.

Utilitarianism is basically an ethical theory, usually credited to Jeremy Bentham and advanced by James and J. S. Mill, Henry Sidgwick, and others, that claims to answer all questions of what to do, what to admire, or how to live in terms of maximizing utility. Utility, in the general sense that these gentlemen used it, meant (then as now) usefulness. The most famous definition of utilitarianism equates it with the belief that that action is best which procures the greatest happiness for the greatest number.

Generally the philosophy has drifted off in two different directions, which can be called economic and broad utilitarianism. Economic utilitarianism replaces happiness (the good) as the central concept with the extent to which individuals get what they choose, or what they would choose (preference, as indicated above), if they had a choice. Thus proponents of economic utilitarianism claim it is able to develop a precise theory based on real and hypothetical choice and to allocate (monetary) values to outcomes; it generates such political and administrative applications as cost-benefit analysis. In this sense, economic utilitarianism uses different concepts from those of its founders.

Broad utilitarianism, as it has been developed by moral philosophers, is more in keeping with the spirit of those founders, insofar as it tends to eschew precise calculations in favor of more general judgment that allows more qualitative evaluation of its actions.* There is a problem about rules. Strictly, a utilitarian should acknowledge that "rules are made to be broken," and calculate each individual act of obedience and disobedience on its consequences. But we are liable to be happier if at least some rules are obeyed habitually and generally. The doctrine of "rule utilitarianism" suggests that we should always obey the rule that, if always obeyed, would have better consequences than any other rule, always obeyed.

Arguably, however, this latter cannot be called utilitarianism at all, its insistence on strict adherence to rules having crossed a philosophical boundary into neo-Kantianism. But for Independents, we take the risk and state that to a large degree we obey one rule that, if always obeyed, would have better consequences than any other rule, which is to (at least) represent all of the people most of the time and most of the people at least all of the time.

However, even broad utilitarianism has boundaries. The limits of what constitute utilitarianism can be delineated by three conditions, individually necessary and collectively sufficient to define it as a distinct form of political philosophy. Utilitarianism is necessarily:

1. *Consequentualist:* It judges, evaluates, and proposes actions according to their consequences and not according to conformance with ideological rules, whether derived from reason, revealed religion, or the human condition.

2. *Aggregative:* It sums benefits for a population. This can be a small population or the global population. It does not allow any individual claims or rights (special interests) to be wholly immune from inclusion in the aggregate sum.

3. *Sensualist:* What is aggregated must be reducible to the feelings of well- and ill-being of the population it is dealing with.

Seatbelts off.

---

*   Although originally Bentham believed he could quantitatively calculate a "felicific calculus" of the units of pleasure derived from his utilitarian approach.

It should be clear now just what Independents mean when they say they would govern on a utilitarian basis, "tailored" perhaps to accommodate a utilitarian based ideology, i.e., that conceptual scheme with a practical application. That conceptual doctrine is utilitarianism. The practical application is to represent, at least, most of the people all of the time and most of the people at least all of the time, the result of which is to provide the greatest happiness to the largest number of citizens in America.

How would it be "tailored"?

America is a country governed by the rule of law, from the Constitution on down. Independents' actions would fall within such rules, the criticism of rule utilitarianism notwithstanding. In this sense, the observation that, for pure utilitarians, rules were meant to be broken is ignored. Said differently, the prophesized political *tsunami* represents an evolutionary change, not a revolutionary change.

Utilitarianism is aggregative. In addition to the traditional sense of this term as spelled out above, it also means that the changes Independents would bring about are additive, in the sense that it is not progress if a change is provided by one hand and simultaneously cancelled with the other hand. To wit: It probably isn't utilitarian if it's a zero-sum game.

What is aggregated in this philosophy must be reducible to the feelings of well- and ill-being in the population—happiness, or the lack thereof. This question of the sensuality of the actions of Independents' rule, on both the individual and the community as a whole, will be clearly and directly made known from time to time (aggregated) by the vote of those directly concerned, the American people.

In a neoclassic economic sense, utility means to extract maximum personal benefit from any situation. This view of utility is rationalistic, materialistic, and totally self-serving; it's a selfish view for personal decision making that is currently being questioned by some. In the larger political sense we are dealing with here, the theory of utility deals not only with quantity (how much good) but with quality (of the good) as well. It is not, as some have characterized it, a cold impersonal calculation devoid of feeling or morals; rather it's an approach to issues that attempts to take out of the decision-equation the preferences of any one particular minority, or combinations of minorities, that may be the decision makers for a particular outcome, other than what will produce the greatest good for the greatest number. Importantly, that standard of the good an action produces is not the standard of the one taking the action, but the greatest amount of good altogether. As for those who contend that utilitarianism has no moral quality, I believe John Stuart Mill addressed this issue quite adequately when he said:

> "...what the assailants of utilitarianism seldom have the justice to acknowledge, that the happiness (Good) which forms the utilitarian standard of what is right in conduct, is not the agent's own happiness, but that of all concerned. As between his own happiness and that of others, utilitarianism requires him to be as strictly impartial as a disinterested and benevolent spectator. In the golden rule of Jesus of Nazareth, we read the complete spirit of the ethics of utility. To do as you would be done by, and to love your neighbor as yourself, constitute the ideal perfection of utilitarian morality. As the means of making the nearest approach to this ideal, utility would enjoin, first, that laws and social arrangements should place the happiness (Good), or (as speaking practically it may be called) the interest, of every individual, as nearly as possible in harmony with the interest of the whole; and secondly, that education and opinion, which have so vast a power over human character, should so use that power as to establish in the mind of every individual an indissoluble association between his own happiness and the good of the whole; especially between his own happiness and the practice of such modes of conduct, negative and positive, as regard for the universal happiness (Good) prescribes; so that not only he may be unable to conceive the possibility of happiness (Good) to himself, consistently with conduct opposed to the general good, but also that a direct impulse to promote the general good may be in every individual one of the habitual motives of action, and the sentiments connected therewith may fill a large and prominent place

in every human being's sentient existence." (*Utilitarianism*, by John Stuart Mill (1863), Chapter 2)

Like achieving Balance, such a realization of the "impulse to promote the general good in every individual as a habitual motive of action" may be an unattainable goal in the real world. But like Balance, so long as the direction those governing is moving toward it, that probably suffices and should produce fertile ground to govern in such a utilitarian manner. Therefore, for our purposes, this standard of utilitarianism, this ethical guide for decision making, would seem an adequate political philosophy to include as part of our superstructure.

Unity of Purpose: The Independent Political Platform

How do we present the Independent option to the voter? By unity of approach to action. By building a platform of issue planks that demonstrates exactly what Independents will focus on, and why and how—exactly—they will approach solving each particular plank, or issue. This does not on the surface sound revolutionary. (To some it may not even sound politically desirable.) All parties have platforms on which they intend to run, or campaign. However, some ask if any Americans believe party platforms have been important documents for holding government accountable anytime in the past thirty years? If they haven't been, they should be, because it is via its platform that a party communicates and explains exactly, or not, what it considers important and what it will focus on, if its representatives are elected.

That's the theory. The reality falls considerably short of that, and has for some time. This again amplifies the fact that more and more voters are offered individual candidates to consider come election time, not committed party programs or specific governing platforms. This tends to make politics very subjective rather than objective. The last time I actually tried to read a Republican or Democratic platform—in 2000, I think—it ran to over one hundred pages. It had so much in it in an attempt to placate all factions of its membership, and then some; it tended to treat the issues so generally as not to restrict itself, nor to offend anyone, that the end result was pretty uninformative; a pretty good example, perhaps, of "yada, yada, yada." Also, as would be expected, their platforms were primarily partisan, intended for their supporters and sympathizers, highlighting how they would do things "their way." Even if the draftees believed they were creating a document of significance to their cause, it was only germane to the party itself, not to the voters in general. Another example of the choir singing to itself.

An Independent platform must reflect the following:

1. Its utilitarian philosophy, i.e., not intentionally partisan

2. A voter-oriented issue focus

3. Clear presentation

4. Be brief and understandable

5. Be publicly accepted and campaigned on by any and all certified Independent candidates
(The meaning of "certified" will be clarified in Chapter 12, under the section on elections.)

For Independents, the platform does not represent just a broad ideological backdrop to a candidate's individual political agenda; it *is* the candidates' agenda. For any candidate to run as a certified Independent political candidate for office, such candidate must first publicly declare his or her acceptance of and commitment to work to achieve all the planks in an Independent platform, as put forth by the Independent leadership, in both form and understanding. That is, there needs to be a *unity of purpose* (beyond simply getting elected) and a commitment by all involved. The leadership of the movement must support its candidates, and those candidates must be committed to the movement's goals and objectives. As naive as this may sound in today's political environment, where the electoral focus is on the individual candidate, it may be a welcome change for the voter disillusioned with the politics of the day and the resulting government it produces. Off the top of my head, I can't recall a single instance in history when change was successfully brought about without a unity of purpose among those involved in the effort.

While the present two parties admittedly each have unity of purpose, it is in each instance, quite aside from either gaining power or staying in power, to govern in a manner and purpose favorable to or compatible with their political ideology. We have seen that neither party is a majority party. Each commands but a minority following of the American voter's ideological preference. And as the number of Independents grows, those minorities—especially those with what is described as a "weak" tie to the party—continue to shrink. As such, party unity of purpose falls well short of what America must want in a government: a commitment to govern for (at least) all of the people most of the time and most of the people all of the time. That is not their goal. Their goal is to obtain political power and then govern in a manner that is, by all evidence, narrowly self-serving; one that furthers their particular minority vision of the manner and direction in which the country should be directed. The only unity of purpose of the two parties broader than their own special partisan ideological interests is a common interest in preventing—to their detriment— a third political option for leading America develop.

It seems reasonable (even if currently politically unorthodox) to expect that by demonstrating a unity of purpose—and hence commitment—among the movement and those campaigning to implement the Independent agenda, as well as by being open, up front, and clear with the voters, that Independents can demonstrate to many Americans how and why they can expect a different outcome by supporting them rather than the other two parties. Here is our platform. Here is what we believe is necessary to accomplish to make a difference in outcome in governing America. Here is how government should attempt, and Independents would attempt, to govern for (at least) all of the people most of the time and most of the people all of the time. This is how we will govern to try and rebalance our country, economically and socially.

That is why Independents view the platform as so critical in their approach to voters. It is their proposed formula for governing, laid out for all to see. It is their considered approach to producing a different outcome in government. It is their avenue to governing for all of the people as often as they can. As such, their candidates must as well be committed to the platform and their commitment made explicitly to—and seen by—the voters. Plain and simple; no smoke or mirrors— not a lot of wiggle room come the next election.

To reiterate, Independents believe purpose trumps personality, and this is why: unity and commitment. If there is not clear commitment to the voters on the part of the candidate, how can there be commitment on the part of the movement? If there is not clear and public commitment to the planks of the platform by the candidate, how can there be unity within the movement? The whole purpose of the movement is to propose to the voter governmental actions that are conducive to producing a different outcome from what has come to be expected from the Democrats or Republicans. The voter is being asked to vote for the platform when he or she goes to the polls, not the individual candidate. Does this mean that the candidates are unimportant? In a sense, yes, it does; but only in a narrow sense. Obviously, people judge people, and any candidate is going to be judged on image; character, personality, professionalism, commitment, and ability to convey a message. To a large degree, the candidates reflect the movement behind them. To this degree, the candidate is important. But it is the message, the platform that the candidate campaigns on, that is of primary importance. In this sense, it is the candidate's purpose rather than his personality that is important. The goal, to achieve the agenda, would be to elect Independents, not one specific Independent over another, all else being equal.

Vision—A Bigger Picture

Independents thus have an internal philosophy, and we have an electoral platform format. Good. Is that enough? Don't we need someone or something that is responsible for "organizing" the effort; someone or something to define the issues and propose our utilitarian approach to solving them? Don't we need a larger vision of where we believe we should be leading the country? What is our scheme for America's future, and how is this to be decided? Who is responsible for framing this before the American voting public? Just what is our national purpose? I mean, isn't a national purpose what government should pursue?

In their book *The Plan*, Congressman Rahn Emanuel and Bruce Reed, editor of the Democratic Leadership Council magazine *Blue Print*, speak of "a politics of national purpose." Their comment is that if your leaders aren't challenging you to do your part, they aren't doing theirs. But just what does this mean? Is it just a more obtuse way of saying our political leaders should summon Americans to think about the world from a broader perspective than how a given issue affects them directly? Or is it simply a sophistic attempt to refocus people away from tough here-at-home issues that need addressing, which our partisan politicians either can't or won't get resolved? But Messrs Emanuel and Reed's admonition begs the question, is it proper for our political leadership, speaking to people as citizens, to ask them to participate in something that, according to these leaders of the moment, has or involves a larger "national purpose" than their own self-interest? What if such larger picture appears to run directly counter to their apparent and perhaps immediate self-interest? (Perhaps globalization, for example.)

Yes, it probably is proper, if in fact such larger national purpose can be demonstrated to be in the genuine interest of at least most of the people. (Again, globalization, perhaps.) This follows the democratic principle of majority rule. But as we have seen, both parties that currently share governing have dramatically different views of what might be called a national purpose, or at least profess to have. Furthermore, both represent clear minorities of American voters. Representing primarily partisan interests, what they, respectively, hold out as representing a larger national purpose is questionably in the interest of at least all of the people most of the time or most of the people all of the time. Their agendas, by design, put forth policies that promote their particular ideological ends, not necessarily what will be the best for the most.

Independents, while certainly conscious of the potential benefits of fostering a longer-term national purpose, believe that polarization has yielded a kind of electoral stasis, with both parties (and the coalitions within them) staying remarkably united, scratching and clawing to hold on to political power once they have it. Thus their pursuit of any greater national purpose would seem more in the political interest of the pursuit and maintenance of power than in any greater national interest. This of course is justified by identifying their interest with a national interest. In the words of the Independent view of the greatest good for the greatest number, such partisan visions are, in effect, primarily in the interest of those proposing it. That is not in keeping with utilitarian principles as expressed here.

This is not to say that Independents holding the reins of government would have no national vision. But Independent leadership would eschew political rhetoric that exhorts voters to think beyond their personal situations in the cause of some envisioned grandiose national scheme, or purpose, or destiny, with one specific exception: to direct the country on a path of political action that will promote greater Balance, as has been described. To that end, Independents' hold that there are no greater issues than those that effect our citizens directly and personally. This is not a purposeful policy of ignoring or sidestepping any bigger purposes than the self-interest of our citizens. It is more a belief that in promoting their grandiose visions of national purpose, or national destiny, or whatever you wish to term it, our traditional political leadership has focused government attention and resources on such esoteric ends at the expense of the more mundane— perhaps—issues that do directly affect the self-interest of the majority of Americans. I cite taxes, social and economic security, the effects of globalization, health care, immigration, education, a crumbling national infrastructure, national defense, and a near- and long-term foreign policy that is based upon national interest, in the broadest contexts, as specific examples.

Independents perceive the need to resolve these self-interest issues on a priority basis, not just debate them from ideological extremes. It's basically "Be sure you have taken care of your own before you set off to take care of others." On a partisan, or even a supposedly bipartisan basis, this simply isn't happening. Whether it's the system, a mentality, or the people involved, it really doesn't matter. These are problems, and they need fixing, not just talking about. Our present two parties, independently or in concert, have demonstrated they are not up to this task.

Now, back to the original question: As a movement, how will/ should Independents (1) frame such a program, and (2), who is to be responsible for doing so? In addition, we have indicated that certified Independent candidates for office have agreed to support the Independent platform; to make it in fact their political platform. Who does the certifying?

Initially at least, those who are proposing this approach as an alternative political option will by necessity have to be responsible for its development and presentation to the voting public. They will likewise be responsible for certifying candidates supporting the agenda. The philosophic guideline is developed. The platform format has been laid out. The political aim and objective of the Independent agenda is clarified. All that is left to consider is who and how these are brought together and presented to the voting public.

A traditional grassroots hierarchical organization starting at the local level and continuing up through a national organization does not seem either necessary or desirable under contemporary conditions. Media and voter communications are no longer primarily local. We have seen what television and now the Internet have done to transform how candidates give and voters get their political and campaign information. As it is at primarily the national (and state) level that Independents should have the most leverage, the organization needs to be tailored to meet these conditions. Those who buy into this agenda already know what they want to accomplish. By definition, they are focused on the objective. To this end, a central directing body needs to be such as to have tactical discipline and the ability to make those involved and responsible for carrying out the objective accountable. You can do this best within a smaller rather than a larger deliberative body. As with any effective, successful management group, it must rely upon its marketplace for the information it needs to act. It must make decisions clearly, consistently, and decisively. It cannot define the elephant by some broad yet narrowly internal consensus of the well-meaning, but blind. Here, new tools, such as the Internet, will certainly play a role.

Therefore, an Independent leadership needs to be more than autocratic but less than democratic in its tactical approach to managing this process. It must be both disciplined as well as in touch with America. Guided by its philosophy and employing its platform format, it will from time to time set the priorities for the agenda to follow. Once set, it will broadly publicize it and accept applications from potential candidates for certification. Orientation meetings will be held with such candidates, where give and take may occur and a meeting of minds either occurs or doesn't. Where it does not, there is no certified Independent candidate, no support from the movement. If there is not acceptance and public commitment on the part of the candidate, he is not certified. Likewise, once certified, there must be a commitment on the part of the Independent governing oversight group to publicly endorse and support the candidate in all possible ways.

Exactly who the individuals for such an Independent oversight board are or will be or how they are to be chosen and for how long, with exactly what responsibilities, is an open issue. Only time, and to what degree, if any, interest in this alternative develops, will tell. On such matters, rules about rule making (constitutions, if you prefer) are obviously necessary *a priori,* and agreement thereon, as on any democratic basis of rule making, must be greater than majority rule, if less than the rule of unanimity, for practical reasons. Obviously, such individuals, like potential candidates for office, must first and foremost be committed to the objective of the Independent agenda: a difference in outcome leading to an improvement in Balance. This has been established and is not open to debate or change. What is open to debate is the specific planks of the platform to further the goal, which is better Balance in American society, and which is politically served best by a government that governs for all of the people most of the time or at least, most of the people all of the time, over time.

Whether such an Independent agenda is more or less attractive than what the Democrats or Republicans, or others, offer come election times, it is the voters who have both the right and the obligation to determine this by their voice at the polls. It shouldn't take long for this to be determined.

This Independent leadership structure sounds rather elitist in concept. Is it? In truth, it probably is. And that should (and no doubt will) give cause for concern to some. As indicated, a limited number of committed individuals would decide both the issues that need to be addressed and the manner, the "how," as well as who receives the blessing of this cadre, its certification and subsequent backing for candidates as its representatives. That, in and of itself, does not sound very democratic. But if a movement or a party (or almost any organization) is to have unity of purpose and focus on its objectives, it's the only approach with an acceptable probability of success. A key to success here is the degree that the understanding of utilitarianism, as defined herein, is maintained and practiced as the guiding principle. This could be easier said than done.

And if you scratch the surface of the existing major parties today, you find an interesting phenomenon in this context, which may well be indicative of some of their problems. The parties not infrequently approach individuals to run because they believe they could be successful candidates. We also see where he parties may find themselves with candidates not necessarily of their preference winning office under their banner. The result is representation under a banner of either Republican or Democratic ideology that is seldom either focused or united in representing anything except either (1) themselves individually or (2) the party itself. This alone should partially explain the apparent disunity the public perceives when either party governs. Somehow, the larger public seems left out of the mix.

Therefore, lacking convincing evidence to the contrary, Independents accept the reality that government is in practice confined to elites; that, following a maxim from Hume, "ought" implies "can." In other words, there is no point in saying that government ought to be more controlled by the people if in practice it cannot be. This takes us back to the issue of American democracy in practice in Chapter 4 and the critical issue of the importance of the sanctity of the ballot box highlighted in Chapter 9, and which will be reiterated yet again in Chapter 12.

Many Independents are Independents, we have asserted, because of a perception that the present two parties see their primary objective as an internal one of power as opposed to good governing; where their efforts are directed primarily at attacking and defeating their political opponents, not governing for the country at large. That, if what they accomplish for themselves in this effort also happens to benefit others, well, that's at best a collateral benefit. To this degree, the normative argument put forth by pluralists that competition between elites is a major means of protecting citizen involvement and individual rights may only be the case in a very limited sense. The evidence of the anti-pluralists that the only thing of interest to our two-party elites today is staying in office seems persuasive. To that end, the argument of competition as a necessary and sufficient protection does not guarantee effective government or one apparently concerned with either Independent concept: Balance or a utilitarian concept of the greatest good for the greatest number.

Thus Independents concede the fact—and accept the label—that they would represent just one more group of "elites" competing for office. But, we would stress, we bring increased competition and increased political goods to the political marketplace: more options and, we believe, expanded choice, a different purpose as put forth herein. Expanded voter-choice, which in itself represents a greater voice in governing, becomes not just A or B, but A, B, or C. And to reiterate, because more and more voters are apparently indicating a declining satisfaction with either the A or B option, one would certainly think that increased competition in the political arena will be positively considered and then adopted by those finding fault with the present limited choice.

Yale University professor Ian Shapiro in his 2003 book *The State of Democratic Theory* contrasts his view of democracy with Rousseau's assumption that democracy's task is to express a general will that reflects the common good. Instead, according to Shapiro, democracy is better thought of as a means of managing power relationships so as to minimize domination. He goes on to discuss domination, pointing out that it can in some social and political instances be both normal and expected (the military, for example). Shapiro's conception of domination is one resulting from the illegitimate exercise of power. The point Shapiro makes in his discussion of dominance that Independents would highlight is the following:

> "…I do agreed that domination can result from a person's or a group's shaping agendas, constraining options and in the limiting case, influencing people's preferences and desires."

Independents would propose it is exactly this enumeration of dominating characteristics that describes the actions and motives of both existing parties in their intramural battles to hold on to political power, both individually and collectively. More voter choice and new competition aimed at the existing duopoly is the avenue to better government, as we have described it. My reading of professor Shapiro's presentation, both on this point of domination and elsewhere in his book, would certainly seem to validate our Independent political agenda: More competition offering wider choice leads to better government, or at least offers that possibility.

But...What About Duverger's Law?

Well, yes, Duverger's law is certainly an issue. But upon reflection, it probably isn't a "show-stopper" for Independents to move ahead politically. As a matter of fact, given the apparent current voter dissatisfaction (81 percent believing the USA is on the wrong track!), Duverger's law might well prove *supportive* of an Independent political option.

Duverger himself did not regard his principle as absolute. Instead, he suggested that single-member district plurality (SMDP) representation would act to delay the emergence of a new political force and would accelerate the elimination of a weakening force. In other words, if there is instability within the political system, SMDP and FPTP voting may postpone correction, but when such correction gets underway may well favor it.

The significant emergence of Independents may very well represent evidence of instability in our political system—obviously, I believe it does. There is not even a close race between the Democrats or Republican parties representing anything like a clear majority of Americans. Admittedly—by everyone—both need a coalition with Independents to win elections. However, once they've won, both proceed as minority governments, in effect. This implied coalition is developed simply for electoral convenience and nothing more. That's why Independents are referred to as "swing voters." They have no political option of their own. No one really represents their political preferences. Under current conditions, they are reduced to choosing the least objectionable option come each and every election, sometimes in the Republican position, sometimes in the Democratic. They are politically homeless. Some 38 percent to 40 percent of America's voters today are not inclined to consider themselves supporters of one or the other of the only two political options available.

Putting this all together, the evidence for political instability, even if only circumstantial, seems compelling:

- Some 81 percent of Americans believe America is on the wrong track (even considering the somewhat difficult period we were/are experiencing in 2008 when this latest poll was conducted).

- Some 76 percent of Americans believe that our two-party system has either (a) real problems or (b) is seriously broken.

- Some 68 percent of Americans describe their degree of confidence in Congress to pass meaningful legislation to deal with issues of corruption as "not much" to "none at all."

- And, to my way of thinking, the most significant fact: some 38 percent to 40 percent of voters, or at least a potentially significant portion of them, feel they have no practical, positive political option at present but to vote for one or the other of the existing parties, like it or not.

Add to these the above observation that "domination can result from … a group's shaping agendas, constraining options, and, in the limiting case, influencing people's preferences and desires." It seems obvious that what we have currently is a two-party domination constraining options solely for their own benefit. In economics this is referred to as an anti-trust issue, and we don't allow it. Why do we allow it politically? Our legal system has been sympathetic to this duopolistic arrangement for good and understandable reasons (in the main), and as we have indicated that is unlikely to change. It probably doesn't have to in order to accomplish our objective here. Maurice Duverger's law concerning the effects of such a situation may well be enough to start moving this mountain.

Part Three

As stressed, an Independent political option is defined by the agenda it puts forward to the voting public. This is done through its platform. The platform dictates not only what but how. It's not only the explicit contract between the electorate and the Independent movement, the platform is the explicit contract between Independents that might represent the movement in government and the movement itself. It represents the unity of purpose of all concerned: party, candidate, and voter.

Means Versus Ends

There's an old English expression about what's right and what's not right: If something is right, it's described as being "cricket." If wrong, "not being very cricket." The expression implies following rules or acting fairly. Over time—a great deal of time—civilized societies have developed and then institutionalized both written and unwritten rules and norms and attitudes about what is and what isn't "cricket."

The basic rules regulating the relationships between our government and those it is intended to govern for are set out clearly in our Constitution. They represent the means to an end. They are, however, a starting point, a framework if you will, delineating certain boundaries within which government may legitimately act.

Unfortunately, these "means," these constitutional rules, apply to governing, not to ideological political movements that compete for the legitimate right to govern. As the right to govern carries with it significant power and authority to those holding the reins of government, it's understandable that the goal of governing is pursued vigorously and aggressively by differing factions in their power-seeking self-interest.

So what; that's politics, isn't it? So, bad habits are hard to break. It matters not if multiple factions are competing against each other for the legitimate right to direct government, as some authority would have us believe, if their motives are the same: power and manipulation for their own sake. The term "dirty politics" is not uncommon. That translates, for too many involved in the political process, to the ends justifying the means. That's not particularly "cricket."

The political attitude toward "dirty politics" to achieve ends risks being carried over from the battle for the right to direct government to the process of governing, once in power. The result, as I have highlighted on numerous occasions along the way here, is an ongoing, never-ending political "war" between and among these competing ideological factions that produces less than satisfactory government results for what looks like an increasing number of America's voters. The result: Independents.

Still, Independents—non-Democrats or Republicans—understand that we will have to compete with these existing movements for the legitimate right to direct government. Will our means to do so be any different from theirs? Will our goals in holding the reins of government be any different from theirs? Yes, and yes. How will the voter be able to tell? By our commitments going in and our results come election time; e.g., their trust and our loyalty to such trust.

In this section we outline some of those critical issues of how Independents would work toward this end. What follows are some examples of (A) those issues and (B) their proposed solutions. The examples are by no means exhaustive; nor, with a single exception, is one more important in the Independent agenda than the others. That exception is special-interest influence in our electoral system; i.e. campaign and electoral reforms.

Two classes of issues are highlighted. The first are examples of issues most feel not only need attention (of which they get a lot) but resolution (of which they get little). They spell out how Independents (or at least this Independent) believe such issues can best be resolved to serve the greatest good for the greatest number. Taxes and Social Security are examples. Conflicting ideologies represent the primary problem in issue resolution.

Matters that are of primary and direct importance to the subject of Balance in our society comprise the other class of issues. Absent addressing and then resolving basic questions inherent in these issues, such as those surrounding the ballot box and the responsibility of capitalism in society—is it our servant or our master, or something else—the question of a necessary and proper Balance will remain purposefully clouded and obscured. Special-interest political influence and working-poverty questions are examples.

Reform is not a term I particularly like. It has been overused and abused in the political arena by everybody who wants change— often just to conform to their particular desire. That may result in "correction" or it may not. Nonetheless, when the term is used in the connotation of amending conduct and/or to mean the improvement of what is wrong, corrupt, or unsatisfactory, reform is about as clearly understood a term as we can use.

These are examples of issues that, if resolved along the lines proposed, will make a difference in outcome; they ought to produce an improvement in Balance, as we have described it. If enough voters— those presently calling themselves Independents and others with doubts—agree, then perhaps we will have the opportunity to at least test-drive this approach.

In our final chapter we consider much of what we have found reason to question in the context of what we advocate. The conclusion and final message to you, the reader, is not about Independents, per se. We believe we have made our case in this regard. Instead, we come full circle, back to a concern highlighted in the Introduction and referred to several times throughout this presentation. We described it there not as the problem, but more a possible result of the problem. Balance is the problem. The issue is the proper role of government in society and the potential threat to government's continuing ability to fulfill this role, given both the present state of Balance and the direction our country appears to be heading—in our opinion, away from Balance. We rely heavily on some voices from the past to show us the direction forward.

Chapter 12

An Independent's View of the Propriety (or Impropriety) of Special-Interest Influences on Government

Now I want to cover an issue that has perplexed government, in one form or another, almost since its inception. It's an issue covered by James Madison in The Federalist Papers #10, wherein he advocates a republican form of government over a pure democracy. It's the issue of faction, which he defines as "... a number of citizens, whether amounting to a majority or minority of the whole, who are united and actuated by some common impulse of passion, or of interest ..." Today we call this a special-interest group. Madison goes on to point out that due to human nature, the causes of faction cannot be removed and that relief is only to be sought in the means of controlling its effects. To paraphrase his language, you can't stop people from wanting certain advantages over others, so you must limit or control their ability to gain such advantage to the detriment of others.

Madison was primarily concerned about the appropriate form of (popular) government to best handle this problem, a republic or a pure democracy. His preference was for a republican form of government, for the good reasons spelled out in this federalist paper. He posited that, "… by delegating government to a relatively small number of citizens elected by the rest … the public views by passing them through the medium of a chosen body of citizens, whose wisdom may best discern the true interests of their country and whose patriotism and love of justice will be least likely to sacrifice it to temporary or partial consideration, that under such a regulation it may well happen that the public voice, pronounced by the representatives of the people, will be more consonant to the public good than if pronounced by the people themselves, convened for the purpose." One may question whether or not those lofty qualities he attributed to elected representatives have—if they ever truly existed—survived to the present. On this point he does recognize that representative government is not a guarantee of good government; not without its risks: "Men of factious tempers, of local prejudices, or of sinister designs, may, by intrigue, by corruption, or by other means, first obtain the suffrages, and then betray the interests of the people." Keep his counsel in mind as we now fast-forward a little over two hundred years and apply it to the present-day issue of faction; i.e., special interests.

This a key issue with Independents. It is an issue of the proper, or improper, influence by special-interest elements in our politics. Chapter 4 noted that "The political system is that segment of society that draws together or integrates all the others. Within the political system decisions are made that are binding upon the whole of society." That makes special interests a key issue with Independents, as it should for everyone, as we've stressed repeatedly. Addressing it is basic to attempts to make a difference in outcome. It is, specifically, the issue of the demand for money in politics generally, and of how we finance our elections particularly. In no uncertain terms, it is a most difficult one to deal with. But also in no uncertain terms it is the most critical that must be dealt with in the pursuit of rebalancing our democracy.

Why is this? Because as everyone recognizes, money is power in American politics. Unchecked influx of money equals unchecked power by those who have it to use. Ergo, if you have financial clout, you have power in our political system today, directly and indirectly. If you lack such clout, you don't. As such, it has always had the potential, and lately that potential has been largely freed from constraint such that money in politics has become the most significant contributor to corrupting balance in our society today. Money has always been important in politics, and it is impractical to believe that you can take it out of politics. You can't; you don't have to.

What is called for is to (1) define more clearly those who are constitutionally authorized to participate in and/or influence the nature, direction, or outcomes of our electoral activities; (2) deny the relatively few among us who have lots of money and are willing to spend it to achieve their special ends from preferential (tax) treatment that encourages its spending in this manner; and (3) reinforce the concept that politicians are, at least so far, constitutionally elected by the voters of their political district, whom they represent and are primarily responsible to. Their party allegiance comes second and the voices, causes, agendas, and special interests of others third. Today, most people would probably say the inverse is largely the rule.

Spending on elections by outside political and nonpolitical organizations is on the rise. In total, groups on both ideological sides are expecting to spend more than $1 billion dollars to "influence" the 2008 presidential and congressional elections, according to a *Wall Street Journal* analysis. That's more money than ever. Overall, the 2008 national elections could cost more than $6 billion dollars. Most of this spending will come from the candidates themselves and the national parties. If you doubted either the need for money in politics, or its potential for influence, these numbers should dispel any such doubts.

This area is a major (*major*) issue with Independents, because, as things are currently perceived to operate in the national political arena it is considered an open secret that money is narrowing the focus of government's attention; it is a very visible ideological affront to the Independent understanding of what representative democracy is supposed to deliver, e.g., the greatest good for the greatest number. To paraphrase Bill Greider, we should not tolerate that the quality of our democracy be a measure of the contentment of any minority, but rather how the political system meets the needs of those who lack personal advantage or political clout, which is usually the majority. Today, Independents would give those holding the political reins in government an "F" in this aspect. We need a different outcome.

But while many bemoan this issue, despite talk about the need to correct it—almost ad nauseam, it seems—and the piecemeal efforts in this direction, little has been done to definitively correct matters. And why do you suppose that is? My guess is that it is an addiction. Like for any addict, it is difficult to "kick the habit," and politics and politicians are addicted to money. They "have to have it" if they are to survive in office. It is a fact of political life. Money is to electoral politics what lifeblood is to the human body. Therefore, though the system as a whole may recognize the corrupting influence of the power of money, may agree that this needs to change, may agree that it puts the majority of the electorate at a disadvantage, few if any of those making up the system are willing to put their futures as elected politicians on the line by trying to "kick the habit." And you can hardly blame them. In today's environment, for all but a very few it could be tantamount to political suicide.

While there may, from time to time, be rumblings toward addressing problems in this area of an unchecked influence of money, or the benefits thereof, any self-introspection within government is usually precipitated by some rather public scandal, which elected officials are forced to acknowledge and then projecting an appearance of dealing with. But it seems that the power of money has the muscle to override any real attempts to deal with it. Now this observation may seem like nothing more than sour grapes or cynicism. But consider that around the time of this writing, Washington was going through the motions of addressing such an issue. Congress (both houses) was working on "lobbying reform" legislation in the wake of the lobbyist Jack Abramoff revelations. Let me quote what the magazine *The Economist* (5/20/06) concluded from what it had seen of this effort, and then reconsider my statement. I hasten to add that the views of this magazine are simply views of this magazine, but note also that you do see their comments from time to time reprinted on editorial/opinion pages of newspapers around the country, which may say something of the consideration others give to its opinions:

> "Members of the second-oldest profession in Washington, DC, did not need to worryabout the "lobbying reform" bill that passed the House early in May. It is a toothless

sham. The Senate's version of the bill, passed at the end of March, is a bit less lax, but not much ... Even the premise of the reform is illusory ... Congress claimed to want to regulate the everyday practice of lobbying. It hardly tried ... As for campaign finance reform, forget it ..."And for the sake of humor if nothing else, I feel compelled to include *The Economist's* concluding word on this matter: "There is agreement at least on one thing: a mandatory ethics-training course for registered lobbyist and House employees. Congressmen themselves are 'encouraged' to attend. As long as it does not conflict with lunch plans, of course."

If the issue here was not so serious and the public-pretense by our representatives to address it so pitiful, the situation would be laughable. But it is, so it's not.

What would Independents offer in this area that we can't seem to get from the existing regime(s)? First of all, they would clearly present the problem and then focus on the cause, not just the symptoms. The problem generally is one of equal political representation, or at least as equal representation as can realistically be expected in a vertical pluralistic society such as ours. Independents support the demand that our government(s) represent (at least) all of the people most of the time, and most of the people all of the time. That's the general problem.

The specific problem: a decreasing feeling on the part of office-holders of political dependency on, with a resulting attitude of a reduced sense of obligation (loyalty) to, the majority of people they purport to represent, no matter what their slogans and bylines come election times. That seems fairly clear. Independents define three major causes driving the problem. Part of this is due to incumbency. Part of it is due to the very short terms in the case of House members, who must stand for reelection every twenty-four months. Part of it is due to the ability of both individuals and political parties to solicit and collect money for political purpose from almost anyone, almost anywhere—practically, if not legally. But note that all three causes revolve one way or another around the issue of money—its availability and/or its requirement.

Incumbents will in almost all cases be able to raise more money for political purposes than challengers simply because they are incumbents. They are already a part of the system and have access.

In the case of House members, facing an election every twenty-four months, this in this day and age, is the equivalent of perennially campaigning to raise funds. (Recall Representative Murphy's comments in Chapter 6.) No matter what they are doing or involved with in Washington, they have to view such activities and each political decision, as a plus or minus for the "upcoming election" and act accordingly.

Because individual politicians and parties can raise campaign funds from so many sources, both directly and indirectly, political districting has diminished meaning or significance. Many in politics raise as much, if not more, from non-district sources than in-district sources. One recent study found that today's typical congressional candidate now receives more than two-thirds of all individual donations from people outside the contested district. In 18 percent of all congressional districts, candidates receive almost all of their personal checks from beyond the boundaries of the area they are seeking to represent. So what? So follow the money. There you will locate points of obligation equally as strong, if not stronger, than to the constitutionally represented voters. If nothing more, we have permitted a system here that requires loyalty to two masters. That, as history has demonstrated, usually means one loses out in such a struggle over loyalty. Follow the money, and as often as not, you will detect the true winners and losers. The problem is, as those involved in gathering the money realize this, they make it as difficult as possible to "follow the money:" more trees for politicians to hide behind in the political forest.

Thus, Independents narrow the causes above down to one conclusive factor: *the cost of politics.* Money, the demand and need for money, is only the apparent symptom of this cause. Most Americans would not find this a startling revelation. The resulting symptom, as defined, produces the expected outcome of unequal political influence, which, as pointed out, creates the general problem of equal political representation. And unless one subscribes to the theory of might makes right, a virtuous goal is to minimize such unequal influence where possible. Equality, like Balance, is difficult to achieve. But when it gets so obviously out of whack, it does need correcting, to the degree practically possible. Areas of concern encompass both lobbying and elections. Both need attention, but here we want to address the specific case of elections.

Independents would promote the following three-prong approach:

A. Redefine the terms of House members from the present two years to four years

B. Limit those entitled to have a say in or influence either the issues or the electoral process itself, directly or indirectly, to those constitutionally entitled to vote.

C. Reduce the cost of politics through revising election ground rules. Independents would recommend a three-step approach covering (1) Primary elections; (2) General elections and (3) political party funds and funding.

The basic argument for extending the term limit for elected representatives from two years has been spelled out.

The question of who is constitutionally sanctioned to vote is not generally in dispute (see Section 2 of the Fourteenth Amendment, itself subsequently amended for age and sex). The issue of just who is entitled to have a say in or influence either the issues or the electoral process itself apparently is. Natural persons of a certain age, who hold citizenship in the United States, are properly registered for voting purposes, and are (most often) not convicted felons, are eligible voters. Artificial entities authorized under state or federal charter and created for legal convenience, sometimes referred to as corporate persons, are not sanctioned to vote. By extension, natural persons, and we would selectively included groups and/or associations of natural persons, are eligible to have a say in or influence the issues and/or the electoral process itself through their direct and indirect active participation. And also, by extension, artificial entities, their subsidiaries and affiliates, as well as their employees, officers, and/or directors, acting directly or indirectly on behalf of such entities, are not.

While this constitutional description of the right to vote continues to this day, the reality of the political arena is somewhat different from the technical presentation. The economic—and hence political—power of corporations, as well as the necessary functions of the State, has grown beyond anything imaginable by our founding fathers. In reality, the single separate citizen, while retaining his narrow and technical advantage of casting a ballot, no longer has the power and independence in the populace envisioned when the allocation and protection of rights and checks and balances of the Constitution were being considered. Gradually, our society has evolved largely into one of organization(s); its conflicts are largely between organizations and between organizations and individuals collectively, not between separate individuals. In this sense, of course, government is an organization. In a recent example noted in the *Wall Street Journal*— "Why airlines are picking a fight with business jets," we have the Air Transport Association in conflict with the National Business Aviation Association over $10 billion a year in taxes and fees. Both protagonists are artificial entities that themselves represent primarily other artificial entities, arguing (lobbying) for the other(s) to assume more of the cost. It would appear that, if only unconsciously, to compensate for this rearrangement in the de facto power in the political arena, these artificial persons are increasingly being offered the powers and protections originally exclusively envisioned for natural persons.

Over the years there has been an increasing tendency to convey upon artificial (corporate) entities certain constitutional rights conferred upon or reserved for natural persons. These include: Section 1 of the Fourteenth Amendment, equal protection under the law; protection under the Fifth Amendment (self-incrimination); Seventh Amendment rights to a jury trial; Fourth Amendment protection against unlawful search and seizure (specifically in one case—would you believe—requiring the government to obtain a search warrant for a safety inspection on corporate property); and First Amendment rights of free speech, or free expression. Are these proper conveyances? If such artificial entities, created for legal convenience, are to have any value in their creation when appearing before the courts in cases of law that concern their purpose and/or operation, they probably are. But what are their limitations, if any? Where are the boundaries such that we recognize these legal entities for what they are, not necessarily for what they want? Pushing their boundaries farther and farther out has been, in the mind of this Independent, a major contributor to the imbalance in our country as a whole. This has created, or at least exacerbated, the view that government is not governing for (at least) all of the people most of the time, or most of the people all of the time, unless of course you recognize these artificial entities as "citizens."

Recognizing that organizations are increasingly important participants (currently treated as denizens, in the British sense perhaps, but not, I emphasize, as citizens—as clearly highlighted in Section 1 of the Fourteenth Amendment) in American society and as such are by their power attempting to manipulate the political arena to their particular benefit, what is to be done here to restore some semblance of Balance? Restoration seems a must, but at what level? Individual citizens must continue to have a meaningful place at the political table. Why? Because this and in reality this alone translates into attention to the particular needs, rights, and freedoms of citizens in the halls of government, which is a very, very extensive and busy organization itself in this day and age. And that should come as no surprise to anyone. Obviously, we can't simply ignore organizations politically. But again, if the concept of necessary Balance presented here has any validity, the collective influence of these organizations needs to be counterbalanced, for just those reasons Madison spelled out in Federalist Paper Number 10.

The view that what might have been good for General Motors would also have been good for America at one point (a variety of the trickle-down theory) is a questionable philosophic approach under today's conditions. Some argument might be made for the validity of a "trickle-down" approach. But economically, the timing and the uncertainty as well as the eventual distribution of such perceived benefits, not to mention a perceived if not actual political favoritism inherent in such a philosophy, makes it unacceptable today. Likewise, unabashed egalitarianism is not a solution. Those appear to represent the extremes of possibilities, what we have today in the ideologies of our two-party politics. But as pointed out earlier, an Independent solution is not necessarily a middle-road centrist position of trying to please and appease enough to retain political advantage. Furthermore, attempting a truly centrist approach almost guarantees that the least moderate of your persuasion will either (1) force your policies more in their direction or (2) abandon you (or your faction) for someone more ideologically faithful. Centrism is thus an illusion in our present political system, employed for campaign purposes only. Anyone who truly and philosophically considers himself or herself a centrist is a borderline Independent. But as Independents presently have nowhere to go, politically speaking, the default description today is a "centrist." But I digress.

The interest and motivation of this broad but narrowly focused economic special-interest group of artificial legal entities (business) is at once in common as a group (profits) and at the same time potentially if not actually at odds with the interests of the broadest interest-group, the individual (and collective) constitutionally empowered voters. Where? Almost everywhere. Specifically in wages, taxation, working conditions, commercial practices, environmental issues, safety requirements, government spending, international rules and regulations and others. These are potential conflicts of major proportions, which in most cases are decided by government, the mediator/regulator between citizens and the economic sector. Someone once said, and I agree, that the business of the legislator is to produce harmony between public and private interests. How government (ultimately) decides these issues depends upon whom we elect to represent us in government, and this is achieved primarily through elections. Issues of concern and importance to all and candidates standing for office are, as constitutionally provided, supposed to be decided by and elected by *people*, i.e., by citizens.

If artificial persons continue to receive increased access to the same menu of constitutional rights and guarantees as natural persons, then do we need to recognize a new classification of citizens? Aren't we applying the same laws to them as we do to individuals? Do we need to allow them the right to vote as well (kind of like super-delegates)? While this may at first appear absurd, is it really? If we now allow artificial persons, through interpreted rights provided to the rest of us under the Constitution, to increasingly influence the policies of government and the politics of our democracy through the power of money, then by reason of such financial clout and power, they have largely trumped the democratic power of the ballot box reserved for people. The ultimate outcome of the direction we are heading is a most unbalanced position. But apparently, neither Democrats nor Republicans believe this is the case. If they do acknowledge a problem here, apparently they do not believe it has gotten out of hand—all of us would like to believe we can control our addictions—at least not far enough out of hand to require effective corrective as opposed to cosmetic steps. So, do we let them all the way into our political process? Understand, however, that once we do, America will no longer enjoy a true representative democracy, or as Rousseau would describe us, an elective aristocracy. America will run the risk of becoming a corporate tyranny, even if ritually the ballot box and the Congress are retained. This controversy and debate over the issue of "corporate citizenship/personhood" is long-standing. And capitalism's pockets are deep enough that it can afford to sustain the pursuit of adapting the rules to its advantage.

No one, of course, expects the world to come to this. But it could.* In order to assure that it doesn't, concrete steps must be taken. What needs to be recognized, legally, is that these entities are not "persons" for the purpose of participating in or in that which surrounds our electoral processes. This Independent's view is that they have no inherent fundamental or "inalienable rights of life, liberty or the pursuit of happiness," as one business apologist recently appeared to imply, writing in *Capitalism Magazine.* Corporations are special-purpose creations of the various states; their existence can be terminated, voluntarily by the entity itself or involuntarily by the state, or bought or sold to others.

They do not merit protection under the Constitution except in the narrow sense having to do with the purpose for which they legally exist, to engage in an enterprise. Political lobbying for favorable treatment and conditions under which they operate may or may not be a legitimate undertaking. If so, it should probably be limited to an industry-wide application through trade associations as opposed to individual entities. An interesting concept, but that is all I have to say concerning it here.

---

*   Recall journalist Robert Kaplan's purported observation in the introduction: "The US is evolving into a corporate oligarchy that merely wears the trappings of democracy."

The legal determination that money is synonymous with freedom of speech is a key element contributing to the potential political corrosion stemming from organizations. Many would challenge this association. The Supreme Court itself has not been unanimous on it. Other areas of our civic and political life do not follow this logic but are governed by the principles of fairness, due process, and equality before the law. It has been pointed out, for instance, that lawyers arguing before the Supreme Court are each given a half-hour to sum up their case. If money equaled speech, some have argued, they should be able to pay for more time to make their case, i.e., freedom of speech. Nonetheless, a close scrutiny of the First Amendment wording, coupled with the argument put forth for it by those who successfully challenged Buckley *v.* Valeo, arguing that virtually all meaningful political (campaign) communications in the modern setting involve the expenditure of money e.g., *the cost of politics,* lends support (agree with it or not) for the Court's ruling: the recognition that the cost of politics demands the ability to spend money.

But how much money, and from what sources? An Independent would argue, as does the Court, that arbitrary limits on spending might be potentially restrictive of speech under current political circumstances. The Court also argues at the same time that unqualified contributions—both as to how much and from what sources—for political purposes can be potentially corrupting to representative democracy, and thus may be—and should be—"reasonably" qualified. The concept that those who have more money are entitled to more speech is a potentially dangerous one in a liberal representative democracy. (It is the opinion of this Independent that that is not exactly what the Court meant to convey, but the practical effect of their ruling implies it.) It leads invariably to catering to the priorities and desires of such sources, be they good, bad, or indifferent to the system as a whole. By extension, allowing political contributions directly to candidates by out-of-district sources leads to the same results, to the detriment of those whom the representative is supposed to primarily represent. While Independents both recognize and acknowledge the importance of (corporate) organizations in our society today, they do not support efforts for the preferential treatment that this broad special-interest group today demands from government through the shoveling of money, and what money buys, into the troughs of politicians, directly or indirectly.

As a counter to this, the Independent proposal for how artificial entities are authorized to participate in or influence our electoral process would be as follows. For the purpose of funding campaigns, we make the process a three-step situation covering primary elections, general elections, and political party funds

Primary Elections: A. Any qualified person can run for office in the primaries. B. It is up to the individuals running in primaries to develop their own organization and raise their own funds to conduct their district primary campaigns. C. Only monies collected from approved (legal) sources originating within the candidate's district can be accepted and spent on the campaign. Campaign funds cannot be transferred. Funds raised in one district are not transferable to other districts. D. All candidates (including judges) running for the same office under the same party banner must participate in a minimum of two (2) issues-focused debates, publicized and publicly available, prior to Election Day: One to cover primarily local issues and one to cover primarily national issues. Debates for judges may be based upon other criteria. E. Political parties may certify but not endorse specific candidates nor contribute funding to Primary candidates, directly or indirectly.

General Elections: A. The Primary Election winner for his or her party's nomination becomes the party's candidate in the General Election. B. The party may contribute funding toward its candidate's general election campaign to the degree and amount it deems desirable, in addition to whatever funds the candidate and his local district organization have raised for his campaign from authorized donors within the candidate's district. No outside district funds other than from the party may be accepted and used.* No single donor or controlled group of donors can contribute more than "X" amount per candidate (limits are open to discussion). C. All candidates (including judges) running as their party's candidate in general elections must participate in a minimum of two (2) issue-focused publicized and publicly available debates prior

---

*   *In the 1990s, an Oregon regulation in this connection was deemed a restriction of speech.

to election day, in the same format as indicated for primary election purposes. In the cases of national office candidates, the two debates would (separately) cover national issues and international issues.

Political Party Funds: The only legal sources of financing for political campaign purposes shall be (1) contributions raised directly or by others on the behalf of a candidate within his or her own political district and (2) funds contributed to the candidate's campaign directly by his or her political party. No party financing shall be available to any candidate in primary election campaigns (before, in effect, he or she is the party's candidate). The political parties shall receive funds for campaign financing purposes—including so-called public services purposes—only from the (particular) state or federal government and on the following basis.

The federal government shall contribute, out of general funds, $X per voter voting in the primary elections, allocated to each party on the basis of voter political party totals for that preliminary election. If states choose to follow a similar system, each state shall determine its own per voter campaign financing amount to be allocated and the basis for such allocation, within its boundaries, for state office. It is recommended, however, that a system compatible with that proposed for federal campaign financing be considered.

Both state and national election funds, based upon preliminary primary election returns, shall be made available in whole or part to the party recipients within ten (10) working days of the primaries, with all funding due within thirty (30) days of the primary, provided, however, that no funds, based upon this paragraph, need be disbursed to the parties sooner than 150 days prior to the scheduled general election.

Such government-provided funds must be used for direct candidate campaign spending purposes only, and the parties will make an accounting therefore within ninety days of the general elections. Unused funds, if any, will be returned to the source of the funds within thirty days from such an accounting.

From this it is clear that there is little, if any, provision for artificial persons, aside from political parties, to influence elections through the use of money, and the source of money for the parties for campaign financing purposes is clearly indicated. While it may be both unwise and impractical to attempt to deny artificial entities access to government to lobby for their particular agenda(s), it is (a la James Madison's position) both practical and wise to restrict their future influence in our election process. If the American people truly have both the clear obligation as well as the privilege to be responsible for the election of their representatives, then they have little legitimate claim to complain if representatives don't perform in Washington as they promised they would. Next election, this can, and should, be corrected.

Does this approach, under present laws, leave open the ability of artificial entities to influence the elections through issue advocacy and/or "public service" advertising? Possibly. I would agree that it would be difficult to plug such loopholes completely, and it's probably not in everyone's best interest to do so. There is no doubt that from time to time these entities raise legitimate issues for consideration, especially as they impact the business environment. I believe our judiciary must be of a mind to control possible back-door intervention through a pragmatic and constitutionally supportable rendering of law (The Congress, of course must give us appropriate laws). The existing concept of commercial speech, which the courts have viewed in a more restricted light than political speech, must be further defined to make our electoral system effective, defined such that artificial entities are recognized for what they are, not what they necessarily want.

A funding approach where the parties themselves are responsible for the amount available to spend on their own behalf come election time, and that depends upon their performance and voter support at the ballot box seems a lot more likely to make both them and their candidates more responsible to the general interest as opposed to special interests. That should go far in improving Balance in America.

We need a different outcome.

Chapter 13

An Independent Tax Solution

There are three basic principles of sound taxation: It should be simple, neutral (not distort the economy) and fair. In 1996 the National Commission on Economic Growth and Tax Reform—the Kemp Commission—concluded the following:

> "The income tax system is impossibly complex, outrageously expensive, overly intrusive, economically destructive, and manifestly unfair."

Now, to my way of thinking, that conclusion certainly sounds at odds with what we might describe as a sound system of taxation.* Nonetheless, as is the case with the present state of our political system, that conclusion would not be news to most Americans.

The Commission did point out that significant progress on capital gain tax relief, dividend tax relief, and some modest improvements in

---

*   *In all, the American Institute of Certified Public Accountants lists ten widely recognized indicators of good tax policy, most of which the Income Tax Code appears to fail.

individual income tax rates and business expensing and depreciation had been made. The Commission nonetheless opined that the tax code continues to tax income multiple times and penalizes work, savings, investing, and entrepreneurial risk-taking. Aside from this "tinkering," nothing of significance has been done with our income-tax system as a result of the Kemp Commission report. We continue to be taxed under a system deemed by a government-constituted commission to be expensive, intrusive, economically destructive, and unfair.

There is presently a government initiative afoot to (once again) "reform" our individual income-tax policy. According to the Government Accountability Office, "streamlining, simplification, and additional reforms are desirable." From the government's perspective, the issue here is primarily one of income sufficiency. As the Comptroller General put it in his August 3, 2006, testimony before the Senate Committee on Finance, "The debate about the fundamental design of the tax system is occurring at a time when the nation also faces a large and growing structural budget deficit, as under current [tax] policy, the gap between revenues and spending will widen over the next few decades." Translation: Government wants more money from taxes.

While the fiscal needs of government certainly cannot be minimized, and herein they are not, the following argument outlines why we need to largely discard the individual income tax for something (a) better for the American public (a greater good for the largest number), and at the same time (b) that remains sufficient for basic governmental purposes; i.e., the top point of view is taxpayer-oriented, not government-oriented.

Personal Taxes

Here are some specifics on how an Independent political solution might approach the issues of personal taxation. Following this, we'll consider business taxes.

Why is a change desirable? Well, from the Kemp Commission's conclusion, as well as from experience, this would seem self-evident; perhaps it's not. The most obvious answer is that the majority of Americans, up and down the economic ladder, don't seem to approve of the present income tax system very much. They don't view it as particularly fair. Those on the lower rungs perceive the richer are favorably treated; others that they are, in effect, overtaxed.*

Philosophically, having some part of what you work to earn, your wages and salary earnings withheld from you and sent directly to government instead is a bit like being in servitude, where servitude is defined as a right possessed by one with respect to another's property, for some purpose. Whether or not that is in fact the case, it doesn't seem like it should be. Government, most believe, exists to protect private property rights and serve its people; the people don't exist to serve and support government, which seems to many largely the case today. Those are certainly good if perhaps not sufficient reasons to consider a change.

Another reason is the formidable complexity of the income tax itself. The present system has generated a growing antagonism between the people and government. For too many, it's become almost me-against-them when it comes to paying taxes. There ought to be a better, fairer, less antagonistic way to accomplish the primary financing of government than we have now: one that is less costly both to the taxpayer and to the government; that is simple and generally viewed as fair, in both how much is paid and how it is collected; that is less subject to manipulation to either favor or penalize.

The different, desirable outcome is: (1) an improvement (simplification) in the manner in which people pay their personal taxes, and (2) an improvement in the attitude people (and maybe even government) have about the fairness of the taxpaying system, up and down the economic ladder, as well as one much less susceptible to political manipulation. Such an outcome, if nothing more, addresses itself to eliminating an expressed dissatisfaction of the electorate and is responsive to the concerns of (at least) most of the people.

As to how much is to be paid in taxes, two, admittedly oversimplified, options seem available: a top-down approach and a bottom-up approach.

---

* We do not intend to go into the merits of either argument. It is an ideologically subjective issue that leads nowhere. Likewise, we will not debate the issue that, as a whole, Americans pay less in taxes or tax rates than in other developed countries. Our focus is not on relative issues but rather on our own tax system that just about everyone can find fault with.

In the top-down approach, government calculates what it is going to spend and then raises the taxes and/or borrows to support that spending. The bottom-up approach says "Here is the amount of money we taxpayers, as the beneficiaries of government, feel we want and can generally afford to spend on the privilege of being governed." Government must (generally) operate within what that contribution allows. I think it prudent that the characterization attributed to Calvin Coolidge in this context should be kept in mind: governments are continuing concerns. They have to keep going in good times and in bad and therefore need a margin of safety. If taxes and debt are established at high levels—all the people can bear—when times are good, there will be certain disaster when times are bad. Coolidge presided, of course, in pre-Keynesian times. Today, government simply keeps the country in hock, borrowing to support its voracious fiscal appetite.

Independents will favor the latter, perhaps rather radical-sounding approach, for several reasons, aside from Mr. Coolidge's. First it allows for a separation of powers: The people get to say how much will be spent and allow the government, through their representatives, to determine the spending priorities. Secondly, it's a discipline for both not to expect more than the electorate has determined can be afforded. In this sense, it reflects the belief in human nature that when you are spending other peoples' money, restraint is improbable. It also reflects the principle that it is not only fiduciarily imprudent, but also financially unsupportable, to continually spend in excess of what you earn; and what government earns is primarily what its taxpayers will contribute. Finally, it provides, at least conceptually, a built-in brake on just how much and how fast government can grow itself (although some recent investigation has questioned the results of this approach). If this latter suggests a preference for limited government, as this might be defined by the necessities of a changing society and a globalizing world, it's not disputed. So, having determined *how* we establish the cost of being governed (bottom-up), the next issue is the form in which the money is raised.

Currently, and for much of the past one hundred years, the preponderance of government revenues has been raised through income-type taxes, both personal and business. Less than 10 percent of national budget receipts are in other forms (9.5 percent in 2000 and 6.1 percent estimated for 2007). At some point in our history the income tax must have made sense, if for no other reason than we (1) have it and (2) it has to this point continued to be tolerated. However, Independents would declare that in its evolved form it has outlived its fiscal and non-fiscal useful and purposeful life. Given the long and widespread criticism, both professional and lay, of the income tax code, its (continually growing) complexity, its technicality, and, some would say, a certain ability to manipulate it, it seems somehow redundant here to need to justify almost any criticism of it. Much hand wringing, complaining, and studying of and making recommendations concerning the income-tax system has been an ongoing exercise for as long as I can remember. All that activity seems to have accomplished is, one will assume in good faith, to perpetuate a tax code of horrendous complexity that is continually revised, modified, added to, expanded, and technically made into a guarantee of lifelong job security for bureaucrats and tax accountants. Currently the Code contains some 66,000 pages of often incomprehensible tax laws to comply with, supporting some 526 separate forms to be filled out. Is it any wonder then that in 2005 six out of every ten taxpayers needed the help of a trained professional to complete their returns? That was hardly its intention. So, under the assumption that everyone, or at least most of the people, would like to see this situation corrected—and this means remedied, not just further papered over—let us propose what an Independent political solution might offer to change the outcome.

To begin with, the first (bottom-up) issue is: How much do the people say they should have to pay for the privilege of being governed? Twenty-five percent (25 percent) of our earned incomes. Most people, when asked not too long ago, seemed to feel that's a "fair" proportion to pay in taxes. That, for an Independent, would be sufficient reason to try and work with that figure. Note that this 25 percent needs to cover *all levies*, including taxes on earned income, withholding taxes for Social Security, and state and local taxes. Keeping about the same proportions as at present, that would suggest a federal effective overall tax-rate of about 16.5 percent and about 8.5 percent for state and local taxes. In actual fact, for many Americans today, we may not be too far from those figures.

How we ought to pay our taxes needs to change. All Americans, be they individuals or corporate entities, should have the opportunity to legally earn however much they can, or want to (that's the American dream!), most all without regards for the tax consequences. Today, many individual and business decisions are subject, at least in part and/or in theory, to income-tax considerations. This is the issue of tax neutrality: These tax-influenced considerations can involve work and employment practices, investment, savings, and jobs, i.e. distort the economy.

A big part of the solution is to stop taxing salaries and wages—earned income—as well as business profits. Let's look first at individuals.

Americans (and especially their politicians) tend to describe approaches to taxation as either "progressive"—that's good— or "regressive"—that's bad. That's it! Americans have this inherited mindset regarding taxes. This is a bias that has been ingrained and perpetuated by social outlook and disseminated by political preference. As mentioned, politically, liberals are perceived to tend toward promoting "progressive"—that's good—methods of taxation, political conservatives toward "regressive"—that's bad—alternatives. Again, an oversimplification, but basically descriptive.

For reasons that purportedly have to do with "equality," "fairness," and "ability to pay," we tax people (and business) on the basis of the more you earn, the more you ought to pay. We call this progressive taxation, and tax rates on higher "brackets" of taxable income increase accordingly, from 10 percent to about 35 percent of that income today. Lower rates (5 percent and 15 percent, depending on taxable income) apply to long-term capital gains and dividend income. We have, generally, been led to believe this is a fair and equitable way to tax. Fairness and equality are important characteristics for us.

A tax on income at a flat (single) rate for all or some part of income up to a certain amount, such as the levy for Social Security, is a tax that is regressive. It represents a higher percentage of a lower earnings total than on that of a higher earner. We've been led to believe this is an unfair way to tax. However, if our elected representatives really believe this theory, then one has to ask why a regressive tax approach is now the heaviest tax burden on average taxpayers, e.g., the Social Security levy. It would be considered an unfair tax, wouldn't it? Yes, but … (In the upcoming chapter on Social Security, we will question just whether or not the Social Security levy is a tax in the general sense, and if it is, should it be?)

We inquired earlier whether or not there are any alternatives to a liberal-conservative political spectrum. We need to ask here if there isn't any alternative to a one dimensional, bipolar concept of a progressive to regressive tax system. Independents would say that there is; that there has to be. But to arrive at it, to even consider it, one must be willing to shed the predisposed mind-set of liberal (progressive) versus conservative (regressive) partisan thinking. Here is where the Independent's utilitarian political philosophy is preferable to the otherwise partisan approach.

The Independent approach is not motivated by a progressive/liberal ideology of making taxes more progressive, or by a conservative approach of making them more regressive, or by the oft-heard argument that the tax system must first and foremost promote savings for investment and growth, or support the under-class, etc., etc. Consistent with Independent philosophy, the goal is to restructure the tax system such that it represents an equitable, simple, transparent, reasonably affordable, and revenue sufficient base that does not penalize economic growth, personal incentive, or individual limitation. Such a system provides the greatest overall benefits for the greatest number of people. It would be consistent with the three primary principles of sound taxation: simplicity, fairness, and neutrality. From whose viewpoint? Ultimately, from both the tax payer's' viewpoint as well as Government's viewpoint. It needs to be a win-win arrangement.

The considered recommendation for improving the tax burden, as well as the tax preparation and paying burden, on individuals is as follows:

A. Generally (but not totally): Shift the tax base away from earnings from salary and wages to consumption, in a manner that retains the general intent of an ability-to-pay approach.

Independents recommend the most equitable way to correct the present unpopular, and perceived as unfair, income-tax approach is shifting the primary tax base from income to consumption. Actually, it works out to a tax on consumption (primarily) and on unearned income (secondarily). Practically, analysis indicates this could be less regressive overall than our current personal earnings taxation package (income plus withholdings). Conceptually this sounds like the Savings and Investment Tax (SIT) proposal by the 2005 presidential tax commission. But our proposal is less concerned with business, capital formation, or savings (more on this below); here it is purely taxpayer oriented.

Why not a flat tax? Because (1) that's still a tax on income, and (2) the cost and bureaucracy to administer it probably wouldn't be any smaller than what we waste now. Given the nature of politics, no matter what income-based tax replacement scheme the experts come up with and we trusting average Americans sign-off on, you have to assume (if only from experience) that government, in its self-assumed wisdom and under political pressure, will want to keep fooling with it to maximize and/or minimize some faction's special interest or some perceived social benefit. We have gone past the need for or the desirability of using the tax code as a carrot and stick.

To gain the maximum acceptance, the tax system needs to be de-politicized to the degree possible. In this connection, using consumption as the tax base may not be absolutely perfect, but it should be a significant and noticeable improvement over the use of income taxes, be they intended to be progressive or flat. Consumption taxes are also considered simpler and more conducive to economic growth.

B. Recognize that basic living costs (expenditures) should be exempt from the consumption tax, for everyone. This amounts to a standard deduction from taxes for all Americans.

The Independent's consumption tax would be a simple national retail sales tax at the point of final sale (or service). It would be a *graduated tax,* ranging from 5 percent to about 20 percent. The tax rate would be dependent upon product and, to some degree, price. To be a fair system, it has to consider who has how much to spend and for what. Certain purchases are basics to living, and those you don't tax. That's not only fair, it's morally incorrect to do so—even today in (many of) our state and local sales tax systems, certain basics are not taxed. Just extend this philosophy to the national level.

Not a value added tax (VAT). While most consumption tax schemes we see are of the VAT type, VAT systems create a paper bureaucracy not unlike that for administering income taxes, as it works its way through the commercial system. That's to be avoided if possible. Simplification as well as cost reductions for all involved in paying and collecting taxes are major goals in any change.

> C. Other purchases (nonbasics) would be taxable on a sliding scale related primarily to price, but in some instances to the item category. This represents built-in progressivity.

This question will certainly come up: "Where and how do you draw the line between a basic necessity and a creature comfort, so to speak?" First of all, Independents give credit for common sense. Overall, what's a basic necessity shouldn't take a rocket scientist to figure out. And you don't have to "draw a line." There are shades of gray between black and white, and you can have a progressive sales tax on consumption dealing with this issue (see above). For example: basic groceries you don't tax. Basic clothes you don't tax. Basic health care you don't tax. Basic accommodations or transportation you don't tax. Free education is available now through secondary schooling, and higher (up to four years) education you don't tax.[*]

Some other changes would go hand-in-hand with a switch to a consumption tax base. Independents believe in the concept of fair-share when it comes to financing government. Therefore, the issue of unearned income must be considered. We must also recognize that all people consume the basics of life pretty much at the same (quantitative if not qualitative) level most of the time. For those at the

---

[*] Author's note: I go more deeply into the details of this proposed shift to taxing consumption and its effects upon both the taxpayer and the government including the mathematics in substantial detail in my book, *The Delicate Illusion*. These are obviously necessary to substantiate that such a taxing system will both reduce and simplify the tax burden on individuals and be revenue-sufficient for government's basic role.

lower end of the economic ladder, however, those basics take up the preponderance of their earnings, and they are left with little disposable income. Unfortunately, from a tax point of view, not much changes for them. As with the current income-tax system, they will pay little or no taxes, but they will have little extra to spend or to save. However, for these Americans, taxes are not today, nor will they be tomorrow, the problem. Insufficient earnings or earnings power is their problem, and an Independent political option addresses this concern under separate topics, including the working poor, the subject of Chapter 15.

That is how we handle earning from labor (wages and salaries). How about individual income from capital? As income from either source is still income, and both sources are significant, income from capital has to be considered as well.

D. Tax unearned income at some flat—or progressive—rate.

These so-called unearned-income items, such as dividends, interest, royalties, rents, etc. would be subject to a federal tax withheld (where practical) at the source. How much? About twenty percent, if on a flat-rate basis.

Capital gains are kind of a class by themselves. Other than for the tax code, it is questionable whether these are earnings, yet for many of the better-off, capital gains can represent a significant portion of their income. Capital gains/losses are really profit or loss on an investment, taxed currently as if they were earnings. As for most taxpayers, these items are not a significant portion of their total incomes, Independents would only tax such gains (or allow offsetting such losses) for people earning over a minimum income threshold. How much? $200,000 sounds like a reasonably fair threshold to consider.

E. High income earners would be subject to an additional tax on income in excess of a predetermined level

And finally, for the richer among us, we need to balance the boat by asking them to pay a reasonable rate of tax on incomes over a determined level. For starters, let's say $400,000. Currently, at that level, we are talking about a very small percentage of total taxpayers. (Consider that in 2005, families earning $150,000 a year represented just 7.7 percent of American households. And for the record, $1,000,000 tax returns in 2005 represented just 0.15 percent of taxpayers.) We would propose a flat tax on income above a certain level, probably about $400,000 (income, that is, that hasn't already been subject to tax). A progressive tax in this area would not be out of the question.

Independents wouldn't consider this "soaking the rich," by any stretch of the imagination. We consider and justify it as a fair way to balance the tax burden. It maintains a degree of progressivity in the system, at least on a relative basis. It is a proper civic responsibility to pay a fair share of their incomes as much in proportion to average taxpayers as is justifiable. Fair? Well, fair, yes, even admitting that fair is in the eye of the beholder, or in this case the taxpayer.

A quick perusal of Annex II at the end of this chapter shows that the projected results certainly look "fair" (and fairly progressive) and support the benefit projected to all income-earners in this proposed tax rearrangement. Furthermore, it supports a policy of balancing tax burdens between earnings from labor and earnings from capital. Independents would argue that there is no basic reason to discriminate, in so far as the tax burden each should carry, between these sources of income. Independents would also agree that neither should be taxed more than once. Running the numbers also indicates it should be almost revenue-neutral for government budget purposes.

Business Taxes

Let's look now at a possible corporate tax policy.

Independents believe in the benefits of a generally free-market approach. However, free market does not always or necessarily mean an unregulated market. Why not? Because free market can too often be equated with *caveat emptor,* which equates to unfair market. Independents recognize that left entirely to itself, capitalism as totally self-serving. Thus, regulation to some degree is in line with the Independents' philosophy of responsibility for maintaining Balance (… when government in its role as representative of the people feels that the results of capitalism are distributed equitably enough among the people …).

In the area of taxation, government has over the years become increasingly intrusive into the business practices of Business in a desire to get its tax entitlement out of Business. It has enacted all sorts of tax laws, regulations, guidelines, and other intervening measures to try and ensure that, from the sales-revenue level down to the taxable-income line, business has not "fudged" for taxpaying purposes. In a system of taxing income, that's understandable. But business, small to multinational, spends considerable time, talent, and money to comply with (or try to avoid) these regulations. In effect, in many areas, from pricing to customer development, marketing, costing, and accounting, government says what firms can and can't do for tax purposes. The end result is, as we know, two sets of books: one for the government and one for everyone else. That's not necessarily bad, but it is a burden, self-inflicted or not, that business has to endure. Independents believe it's neither necessary nor desirable.

Independents believe that the tax issue needs to be taken out of how Business runs its business. Again, it's an issue of tax neutrality; taxes should not distort the economy. There are numerous considerations of how to properly, legally, and ethically run a business, most of them appropriate, but Independents do not think taxes is one of them. That does not mean that the results of the capitalistic system should not contribute, through taxation, a fair share of the cost of government. Most would agree that this sector benefits considerably from government. It means however, that for tax purposes Independents would redefine "the taxable results" of capitalism from profits to sales and revenues. With this basic philosophy, here is a proposed business tax approach.

A. Tax business at the net sales, or net revenue, line in a manner that results in approximate tax equivalency to the reasonable tax burden determined from time to time by government under the current system.

Again, the goal is to reduce both tax complexity and cost. Taxing business at this level should all but eliminate governments meddling into how Business runs its business or defines its profits. Other governmental or nongovernmental institutions or agencies may have some input and/

or regulation in these matters, but we are speaking about taxes only here. The value represented by sales or revenues should be substantially simpler and more transparent to calculate than a concept of income before tax, under current law.

  B. Continue to tax business on global sales and revenues, allowing for foreign tax liabilities to avoid double taxation.

  C. Tax certain categories of foreign-source domestic sales and revenues at a rate (meaningfully) higher than the domestic-source tax rate.

This "plank" merits a bit of further clarification. The motivation for this might on the surface appear to encourage as many jobs as possible here in the USA. This could well be an effect. However, the underlying philosophy here is more fundamental. It is reflective of the Independent philosophy of Balance: that it is government's responsibility to see that "the results of capitalism, in the broadest sense, are distributed equitably enough among the people." (See Chapter 9.)

Would or should this be considered "protectionist" or anti–free trade in either nature or intent? Independents would say not, in both instances. In fact, Independents would claim it recognizes and even encourages free trade. However, at the same time it recognizes that there are societal and economic considerations—costs—as well as benefits to free trade—to globalization, as our professional class is want to position this issue.

Over the past several decades, America, its communities and its workers, have seen entire industries "outsourced" abroad. This reflected capitalism's efforts to both maximize profitability as well as, in many instances, remain domestically competitive with imported competition that benefited in free trade due to relative favorable factors of production—less expensive land, labor, or capital or some combination of all three. This may also include tax considerations. It is difficult to fault Business for pursuing such opportunities (or defenses). Who wouldn't, considering the alternatives?

But what of those social and economic consequences we mentioned? They are real, they are tangible, and they are personal. Who pays, or ought to pay, for those? So far, it doesn't appear capitalism has been asked to absorb these costs to any significant degree. Why not? Isn't it capitalism that has and continues to benefit from these moves? There may be realities to face here, as well as two sides to the story, and there may be benefits, as claimed, in all this. But that does not negate the costs that capitalism's actions leave to be considered. As it has played out to date, it seems a very unbalanced situation.

You may ask, is outsourcing to Taiwan or Brazil any different than business moving from California to Georgia? Absolutely! While dislocation (and costs) occurs locally when a company moves, much like a move abroad, the gain in the domestic destination creates an equivalent amount of jobs, revenues, and taxes that were lost in the domestic relocation. Nationally, it's a zero-sum situation. Not so in a move to a foreign country. We lose.

Consistent with supporting free trade, Independents hold that business should be free to conduct its affairs and operations as it sees in its best interests. However, to the degree such conduct is at someone else's expense, it is to Business we should look to shoulder at least a major portion of such cost, not to the rest of us through government. Support and promote our economic community? Absolutely. Subsidize it? Questionably. Our federal government needs to (1) properly recognize the problem and then (2) adequately and fairly define the rules of the game to compensate for the problem. Just as we recognized some time ago that unregulated domestic capitalism was not workable, the same needs to be recognized for globalized capitalism. One size does not properly fit all. There should be no objection to the concept of "fair trade" overlapping "free trade."

Until this marriage of fair with free can be worked out globally, here is how Independents define the rules of the game:

> "Certain categories of foreign-source domestic sales" represents the following: Products acquired, directly or indirectly, from countries considered (as variously classified) less-developed and which are for direct or eventual (consumer) sale/resale in America.

What about for products for which there is little or no availability of domestic source alternatives? Petroleum, rubber, and other basic resources come immediately to mind. Certainly a consideration, but no basic conflict. Imported raw materials necessary for domestic manufacture or production do not fit the definition of "foreign source goods for (consumer) sale/resale in America." And for those products at the intermediary or finished level for sale/resale in America for which no domestic substitute exists or is practically possible (pineapples, bananas, coffee, coconut—Hawaii considered), obviously these are the exceptions that must be reconciled to the rule.

D. End deferment of paying U.S. taxes on foreign-source taxable items.

E. Provide meaningful (50 percent less?) tax incentives for U.S. exports

The last provision can't be done, the experts will say. Look what happened when we tried to do this (Off-shore international sales subsidiaries) and the World Trade Organization (WTO) ruled it an illegal (by prior agreement) subsidy of domestic business, or something to that effect, after European countries challenged it. Our answer is that where there is a will, there is a way. Independents, while strongly in favor of expanding global trade, do not feel globalization in all its manifestations to be a holy grail, so to speak. This is the subject of an entirely separate discussion, but for now, and for taxes, I will limit it to this. Such policy is consistent with the philosophy that if you allow your competitors to always set the rules and you agree to play by them, you may be at a significant disadvantage. Not that there should not be rules, and not that once agreed upon, you should not have to abide by them; it's more that before agreeing to such rules you take a long, hard look at what they are liable to mean to you, with "you" being most of the people all of the time and all of the people at least most of the time.

Again, this is not an example of traditional economic protectionism. It is a realization that the world has evolved and will continue to evolve commercially, socially, and politically. In so doing, government (and business) must look out for the long-term interests of both itself and its people while cooperating with the world community as it moves forward with global integration and cooperation. It is certainly not a balanced position for one segment of society to unduly prosper at largely the expense of another segment. It is government's role here to see that this type of conflict, while perhaps somewhat inevitable, is minimized in both its duration and in its consequence for all parties involved.

Finally a word must be added as to how the above proposed consumption tax would be applied to business.

Business is in some sense as much of a consumer as it is a producer. To that degree, it should be subject to consumption taxes like everyone else. Without delving into details, generally what business acquires for use in the production cycle and that comprises a component of the direct cost of the goods it sells should not be taxable to business when acquiring it. What business consumes in the operation of its business, as well as what business acquires that is capitalized and depreciated or otherwise written off over time, should be subject to the consumption tax. Similarly, goods destined for ultimate retail sales would not be taxed as they progress through the wholesale/distribution network. Company sales represented by exports would be assessed at a lower rate than other sales, as suggested.

What will these recommended tax modifications hope to achieve? The major objective is that they jointly work in the direction of promoting greater Balance as described herein. A subsidiary benefit is that through greater simplicity, transparency, reduced compliance costs, business flexibility, and a broader tax base they will accomplish multiple goals. The first is to restore the peoples' faith, through transparency, in the equity and appropriateness of everybody's tax burdens; second, to ease and simplify the tax-paying procedure; third, to enhance compliance for all involved; fourth, to give at least semblance of some degree of taxpayer control over how (through spending decisions) he or she pays taxes; and fifth, to provide, without increasing the tax burden, sufficient government revenues from the tax system by increasing the tax base and by facilitating tax compliance (largely in the latter case by increasing tax compliance). Official sources estimate there is presently a significant "net tax gap," which is the difference between the tax that should have been collected and what was, or will be, actually paid. This "gap" is estimated at about $290 billion a year (2001 figure), most of which is attributed to the individual income tax. It results from underreporting income, under-paying the tax, and/or failing, altogether or on time, to file a tax return. This "gap" amounts to approximately 20 percent of what the individual income tax should have yielded to the government. To say the least, it represents a significant inefficiency in the system, for which no small responsibility might be attributed to the complexity of the system itself. The proposed tax rearrangement should significantly shrink this tax gap, if not eliminate it altogether, which is probably too much to realistically expect.

Parenthetically, while Congress of late has been made more aware of the magnitude of this "tax gap" and has mandated that efforts be made to shrink it, Treasury Secretary Henry Paulson said in April 2007 that trying to close the gap can't be done without " ... Draconian and painful requirements on all taxpayers." He suggested Congress not look upon these theoretically available funds (which could possibly grow to as much as $3 trillion or more over the next decade) as a honey pot that they can use to fund favored programs or to shrink the deficit. This is, if nothing else, a further argument for changing the income tax system.

And a final thought on tax system objectives and design to lay to rest, or at least to repose, the popularly held economic theory that the tax system needs to be designed to favorably promote saving (for investment purposes). First of all, savings represents a use of discretionary income. If you don't have much of that, you can't opt to save much, no matter how attractive it might appear, which is yet another example of the expression "should implies can" (or perhaps just an example of rational intuition).

Currently, an argument can be made that government has skewed the tax system heavily in favor of the economic sector. Corporate taxes are at or near lows as a percent of Gross Domestic Product (GDP) over at least the past forty-five years and are projected to decline further. Individual income taxes—actually down since 2000—are projected to increase as a percent of GDP over the coming ten years, such that by 2015 the relationships as percentages of GDP will be -17 percent for business taxes, and +46 percent for individual taxes. This might otherwise be an acceptable way to promote policies of economic growth if, repeat if, the results of that growth are in the end "equitably enough distributed among the people," which today we can see by growing income disparity is not the case. Government has allowed, either directly or by default, through its policies and actions the incremental benefits of economic growth to be distributed very narrowly among business, its senior managers, and the investing sector of our economy. This concentration of income distribution questionably benefits the goal of Balance and represents, at best, acceptance of a "trickle down" economic approach that is unacceptable to Independents based on its current results.

This is not to say that savings and investment tax issues can be ignored; obviously they can't be. However, in the open economic model we live in today, the relevant issues to consider here are (1) how competitive our business and investment tax conditions are internationally and (2) how is public spending contributing to or detracting from national savings. We also need to consider how compatible the current practices of both business and government are on savings.

This considers not only the form of income distribution. It also questions both business and government practices and attitudes toward savings: Business heavily promotes consumption—and finances it, while government promotes savings—then borrows it for current spending (consumption). These policies do not, on the surface, seem like a team pulling in the direction of savings for investment and growth. Thus it seems inequitable to look to earned income to provide the resources to support all this public and private economic activity, savings-wise.

And in the end, in the real world, the tax system design itself probably has little or no effect on the aggregate savings rate. (Again, it is ultimately the level of income, not the tax rate, that allows for savings.) To borrow a line from a specialist in public finance at the U.S. Congressional Research Service, "… the offsetting nature of income and substitution effects reduces the chances that changes to the tax system alone will increase savings."

Enough said. We need a different outcome.

ANNEX II

Proposed Taxes Versus Current Taxes: An Example
(Example figures are for a family of four)

	A	B	C	D	E	F
1) Income from Wages & Salaries	$24,000	$34,076	$75,000	$150,000	$320,000	$400,000
2) Dividend/ Rents/Royalties Income	0	30	3,000	5,000	12,000	18,000
3) Interest Income	100	180	600	1,000	1,200	3,600
4) Capital Gains	0	0	1,000	2,400	3,600	6,500
TOTAL INCOME	$24,100	$34,286	$79,600	$158,400	$336,800	$428,100
Less Basics Spending	$15,300	$15,300	$15,300	$ 15,300	$15,300	$15,300
Less Savings & Investments	400	600	5,000	12,000	44,000	80,000
Assumed Spending (Disposable)	$ 8,400	$18,386	$59,300	$131,100	$277,500	$332,800
Assumed Consumption Tax Rate	7.5%	10%	12.5%	16%	20%	20%
Consumption Taxes Paid	$630	$1,839	$7,417	$20,976	$55,500	$66,560
Taxes on Unearned Income	20	42	720	1,200	3,360	5,620
Tax on Excess Earned Income	0	0	0	0	7,360	25,620
TOTAL TAXES PAID	$650	$1,881	$8,137	$22,176	$66,220	$97,800

Taxes Paid: % of Gross Income	2.7%	5.5%	10.2%	14%	19.7%	22.8%
Taxes Paid: % of Disp. Income	7.7%	10.2%	13.7%	16.9%	23.9%	29.4%
Current Basis Taxes Paid	$ 1,133	$ 2,702	$16,128	$ 40,420	$ 93,248	$117,831
Paid Taxes: % of Gross Income	4.7%	7.8%	20.3%	25.5%	27.8%	27.8%
Change Proposed Vs. Actual	$ -483	$ -821	$ -7,991	$ -18,244	$-27,027	$-20,031

Source: _The Delicate Illusion_, by T.R. Harry (1997), page 127

Authors note: These numbers are pre-the Bush 2002 tax cuts and assume these tax cuts will sunset on or about 2010, as originally enacted

Chapter 14

Social Security

Why is Social Security an issue, and why do we need a different outcome with respect to it? Because, under present provisions, the program is, practically speaking, politically and economically unsustainable because of the potential, some would say the highly probable, negative effects on near-future generations that it is expected to inflict, on both old and young alike.

The issue here is two-fold: Cost and benefit, or, some might argue, purpose and necessity; and still others, responsibility and structure. It is at once a major tax issue and, for lack of a better term, a public/private politically ideological issue. By the former I mean that the average American worker now pays more "taxes" (overall) toward Social Security than any other form of personal taxation. By the latter I mean, who should provide it, just who needs it, and how (or should) you determine need? Currently it's an income supplement (though intended to provide retirement income adequacy), universal for all those who have paid into it for a minimum period of time.

Most are no doubt familiar with the background of Social Security at least in its most common conception as an old-age federal income supplement program. A product of the 1930s depression experience, it was liberal government's effort to provide a financial/economic safety net to help its people during a most difficult time, when incomes and asset values declined significantly. Unemployment, which was at 5.2 percent of the workforce in 1920, climbed to 8.9 percent in 1930 and to 14.6 percent by 1940. Purchasing power in the overall economy was anemic, to say the least. The Social Security program is funded by a withholding tax on wages and earnings. Initially, it was a low tax rate on a relatively modest level of income, with benefits available to all regardless of income. In this sense, it is a regressive form of taxation. The program was funded on a pay-as-you-go basis until the early 1980s, when changes in the funding were instituted.

The payroll taxes collected for Social Security are of course taxes, but they can also be described as contributions to the social insurance system that is Social Security. Hence the name "Federal Insurance Contributions Act." It's a shame that from the beginning, these mandatory payments into the system were not designated as premiums rather than taxes. This might have avoided, or at least made easier, resolution of some of the perceived problems with it today. While Social Security, philosophically, tends to be unpopular with conservatives and favored by liberals, Americans in general today view it as an entitlement from government. Why? Because, in their eyes, they have paid for it, most of their working lives.

The perceived problem with Social Security (SS) as it exists currently is that, over time, the vested interests in the retirement benefits will exceed the funds collected (on a current basis) to pay them. Current estimates for this crossover in receipts versus expenditures is 2017 or 2018. When this occurs, the SS Administration will have to call on the U.S. Treasury to redeem the SS Trust Fund's assets, held in the form of special U.S. government obligations, to meet payment requirements. And where will the government get the money to do this? Well, it has several options: It can print it, borrow it, cut other spending programs to compensate for it, raise taxes to cover it, or combine some of these options. In any case, it is going to be a matter of paying for past services out of current income, and that implies less money available to provide for current government requirements at that time. Most would agree that's not a good scenario, politically, economically, or socially.

This "problem" with Social Security was recognized more than two decades ago. In 1982 a bipartisan presidential commission, chaired by then Republican economist (and now recently retired Federal Reserve Chairman) Alan Greenspan, recommended a number of reforms aimed at insuring the soundness of the retirement system far into the twenty-first century. And according to 2006 projections, there should be sufficient monies coming in and assets in the Trust Fund to cover retirement expenses almost until the year 2042. So while this looks like it is not an imminent problem or issue, that's somewhat misleading. We need to focus on that cash-flow "flip" date of 2017 or 2018. The real issue here is that we need a permanent solution to the problem, not just more delays in its occurrence, which is not in question.

Among the proposed 1982 reforms, the program was to be shifted from its historical pay-as-you-go structure to one that would accumulate surpluses starting immediately and going forward for a number of years: hundreds of billions of dollars collected and set aside for future beneficiaries (note the term, "set aside"). These proposed reforms were promptly enacted into law. While on paper this appeared to solve the near-term solvency question, the immediate result for ordinary wage earners was not good. One may recall that it was during this time (1981) that President Reagan was intent on reducing taxes, purportedly for everybody (bless his heart). The 1981 Economic Recovery Tax Act offered something for everybody, it seemed. The middle class would get relief from income tax bracket creep, and every individual was to get tax rate reductions, over three years. The highest tax rates were significantly reduced, Business' tax rates were also to be reduced and depreciation benefits expanded.

However, the Social Security contribution increase rendered the talk about (net) lower taxes largely irrelevant for the majority of working people. Even considering the Reagan tax cuts, most working people were socked with a tax increase much larger than what they were supposedly given. Congress, by adopting the recommendations of the Greenspan Commission, effectively raised their taxes by roughly $200 billion—more than erasing any gain they might have anticipated from Reagan's income tax reductions. This was among the largest tax increases in history, but it was accomplished without much fuss by increasing the payroll tax collected for Social Security. This "revamping" of the cost for Social Security has been described as "bait and switch on a grand scale." Considering the circumstances, timing, and perhaps the philosophy of conservative Republicans involved (although liberals had a majority in the House when it was passed), an argument could certainly be made for such a conclusion. However, speculation is not the purpose here.

Social Security in 2008, twenty-seven years later, is still a net revenue source for the government (excess of receipts into the fund over current payments out of the fund). In 2004 the retirement fund (OASI) had net contributions of $466,807 million and made benefit payments of $411,148 million. (The Trust Fund has increased from about $24,566 million in 1980 to $1,452,550 million at the end of 2004, thanks largely to those 1982 changes.) As long as the "cash flow" here is positive and finds its way automatically into the coffers of government for current spending purposes, it is unlikely that our representatives are going to be eager to change this arrangement. However, the crossover in receipts versus expenditures is not that far in the future—only some nine to ten years, if not sooner. Then, or soon before then, it is going to be a very different story. But Independents believe this by all accounts obvious approaching train wreck can be avoided. Independents propose a nonideological resolution; one with a high degree of probability of avoiding this fiscal train wreck. It would do so in a manner that (1) maintains the originally intended purpose of Social Security for older folks; (2) minimizes the fiscal impact when we see government needing to spend more on benefits going out than contributions coming in, and (3) keeps the program where most Americans appear to want it, which is in the hands of government, not the private capital sector.

Here is what is recommended:

A. Maintain (or more accurately resurrect) the philosophy that Social Security is primarily an income adequacy program, a safety net, not an income maintenance program.

Social Security needs to be recognized not as an entitlement for everyone, but as a guarantee of income adequacy in the form of an insurance program—for everybody—against poverty in old age. It was questionably intended to be the principal income option for most older persons. Nonetheless, millions of older people currently receiving it, as well as people approaching old age, rely on it and should expect to receive it after contributing to it all these years. Government simply cannot break faith with them. However, changes are called for.

B. As with most insurance coverage, recognize that if you
    need it, you should receive it; if you don't need it, then
    you should not receive it.

This obviously implies a means test to determine who needs it and who does not. While this suggestion may at first glance seem unthinkable, I would call to attention that this concept is already imbedded in Social Security in the form of income tax on Social Security payments for people earning in excess of a stipulated amount. That tax payment, when received back by the government, is re-credited to Social Security for future requirements. While such "repayments" currently only amount to about 3 percent of benefits paid, it represented some $13,269 million in 2004. That's a means test, albeit a very liberal one. Therefore, considering a means test in this current discussion is not something revolutionary.

A simple, fair, and transparent means test, the same for all, should be acceptable to (most of) the American people. The argument that "I'm entitled to it because I paid for it" is spurious. Most probably recognize that today none of us has "paid for it." Under current conditions we paid into it, but will, over an average life expectancy, receive much more than we contributed. This amounts to something for nothing and most know that free lunches are rare; someone is going to foot the bill.

Some might be tempted to call Social Security a "Ponzi," or pyramid scheme, and while a parallel might be drawn, it would be a stretch to reach such a conclusion. The point is that those currently collecting are getting a lot more than they paid for it. The concern of younger workers is that they are paying pretty handsomely into it, but will there be anything there for them when they reach retirement? It's a fair question. The answer should be "yes," but under current arrangements that may well be contingent upon future generations' continued willingness to support an ever-heavier tax burden to do so. And in fairness and in recognition of just how much today's working public is contributing to this program, and depending upon the individual's life expectancy, at current incomes subject to the current tax rate, more and more Americans are starting to "pay for it." An Independent would deem it prudent to take necessary short-term action to avoid such a confrontation long-term; e.g., make a difference in outcome.

What is a simple, fair, and transparent means test? I would reiterate the above: If you need it, you should receive it. If you do not need it, you should not receive it, or at least not receive it until your financial circumstances have changed such that you do need it. Most would probably question whether a person with a retirement income of $100,000 or more a year "needs" Social Security benefits. As far back as 1993, for example, 453,833 retired peoples with incomes in excess of this collected Social Security retirement benefits; that cost(s) Social Security about $6.6 billion a year. The same estimate for 1998 was 1,432,600 people at a cost to Social Security of about $20.6 billion, or about 5.5 percent of all benefits paid a year. Independents believe that *only* if you define Social Security retirement benefits as an income maintenance program as opposed to an income adequacy (safety net) do such people merit it. If you accept this means-test-approach, then all that is required is to define "need." The following is suggested:

You need Social Security retirement income if, including it, you earn the median U.S. income for a family of your size, or less. You do not need Social Security retirement income if, including it, your income is equal to or greater than one and two-thirds (167 percent) of the median income for a family of your size. If you earn at least the median income, but less than one and two-thirds times the median income (167 percent), considering Social Security income benefits, you should be entitled to receive some (graduated) percent of Social Security retirement income benefits.

How complicated or obfuscated is that? Even the math is simple. See Annex II at the end of this chapter for an example. And finally, it should be reiterated that the fact that some peoples' Social Security is subject to income tax implies a means test already.

How about the claim that "I'm entitled to it, because I paid for it"? As indicated, Independents understand the mentality after this period of time, and, as pointed out, more and more people are going to be paying for it. Nonetheless, that's still a spurious argument for most today. Under current actuarial and funding assumptions, few have paid for it, no matter what your local politicians have been telling you.

If you are like most working Americans, you have also paid some amount, year after year after year, for health care insurance coverage that in many instances provides protection against major medical situations. How many of us look forward to collecting under these policies (after all, we've paid for them)? Right? On the other hand, thank your lucky stars that it is available in the event that you *do* need it. To be a long-term viable program, one that we can afford to make good on not only today but fifty or sixty years from now, Social Security, whether provided by government or via private institutions, needs to be viewed in the same way: Thank God I have it if I ever need it. It's a financial *safety net*.

Correcting the concept of what Social Security retirement income benefits are intended for is half the battle. The other half is a two-part issue that has to do with the way in which Social Security receipts are applied and how government accounts for and presents the program. Taking the latter first:

Currently, Social Security is an "off-budget" item in the unified federal budgeting process. This is somewhat of a technical term that we don't have to go into great detail for our purposes here. Briefly, from the beginning of the program, its transactions were reported by administrations as a separate function in the budget. This is sometimes described by saying that it was "off-budget." In 1968 a change in the budget presentation put Social Security and all other "trust funds" in a "unified budget." This is likewise sometimes described by saying that Social Security was placed "on-budget." In the changes made to Social Security in 1982/1983, it was again taken "off-budget," which is its official budget presentation today.

But the fiddling with the off-budget, on-budget, off-budget presentations never really changed or affected the fact that Social Security was and is visibly present in the government's budget numbers. Actually, those involved in budget matters often produce two sets of numbers, one without Social Security included in the budget totals and one with it included. Thus the program is still frequently treated as though it were part of the unified federal budget even though, technically, it no longer is.

So, while Social Security today is "off-budget," it still appears in the general annual operating numbers of the government. There we see the receipts and the expenditures for Social Security. However, U.S. Government accounting methods are, if not unique, somewhat opaque. The numbers may or may not be netted, inflated by, or minimized due to what for most would be termed in-house or "inter-company" transactions. Such transactions, when considered, are for purely internal accountability purposes and do not affect or reflect the final result of "doing business," or of governing. U.S. accounts are of course unaudited except by internal auditors. Because of this, there may be some support for looking at the numbers presented and arriving at differing conclusions.

Being "off-budget" or "on-budget," yet (whichever way) still included in the numbers—even if only as a line-item entry—gives these accounts a visibility that is at once good and bad. The good part is it keeps this issue in front of the legislators as a significant contributor to both the revenues and expenses of the federal government. The bad part is it keeps this issue in front of the legislators as a significant contributor to both the revenues and expenses of the federal government. The bad outweighs the good: As these programs are overall (still) totally self-funding, it tends to represent a burden on total government spending that is not merited. The comments of the Comptroller General of the United States before the Committee on Finance of the U.S. Senate regarding taxes on August 3, 2006, support this assertion. The argument not infrequently heard from politicians in Washington that "entitlements eat up so large a part of government revenues" is, like the general public's view of Social Security retirement benefits, spurious, in this case. It may be politically convenient, but it is, with the possible exception of the Supplementary Medical Insurance Trust Fund (Medicare SMI), spurious. Summary figures presented for 2004 in the U.S. Budget Receipts and Outlays report put out by the Congressional Budget Office (in millions) show net receipts of $689,359; net outlays, $530,206, producing a surplus (unaccounted for) of $159,153.

Presently, Social Security contributions received by the Treasury are transferred to Social Security by book-entry accounting. But any unexpended amounts must, by law, be invested in interest-bearing U.S. Government securities. The net effect of this over the past twenty-plus years (at least) has been to provide significant amounts of (excess) Social Security contributions to the government general current account spending needs. In other words, what is collected by Social Security contributions and not returned as benefits in the current year, or spent on administrative expenditures, is available to the government for spending currently as it may determine.

Is this bad? No, not bad, but it does means that these earmarked funds are, effectively, no longer available to pay for future Social Security benefits. The funds have been spent elsewhere. What Social Security has instead is interest bearing U.S. Government securities evidencing the borrowing of them by government, same as any other U.S. borrowings to finance its current cash requirements. In this case, this is simply money that government owes itself; it is no more than an inter-agency transaction, say those defending the practice. And this is true. But in another very real sense this is an external debt obligation: this is money government collected for a specific purpose and will owe it to its (future) senior citizens. This is questionably "setting those funds aside" for future beneficiaries, which was the declared intent in the 1982 funding reform.

The problem comes home to roost when Social Security has to pay these benefits out of its trust fund, built up by past (largely post-1982 reforms) and present contributions. That trust fund in 2008 is in excess of one trillion dollars. To reiterate, this is projected to occur in just another eight to ten years. On the books, this is a significant cache of liquidity to honor its Social Security obligations, probably through mid-century at least. In reality, however, these are IOUs that can only be honored by raising new cash (you can't pay retirements with IOUs). How, we have already pointed out: future borrowings (consider the existing U.S. government debt), increased taxes, reduced future government programs, printing more money, or reductions in the program's benefits. None of these are going to be very politically, socially, or even economically palatable. We need to start now to change the outcome.

To avoid, or at least significantly mitigate, this impending liquidity scenario, Independents would propose the following:

A. All receipts destined for Social Security programs be credited to the Agency

B. Receipts in excess of current benefits payments and administrative expenses to be available to the Social Security Administration to be invested by it in the highest grade marketable revenue and/or asset backed obligations of federal, state, county, and/or municipal obligations

The intention here is obvious: to truly make Social Security as independently self-funding as possible. How? By investing currently excess Social Security assets in a form and manner that they represent a return, a cash flow that is independent of future needs to either raise federal taxes, cut other federal programs, or further increase the national debt. This approach, in effect, restructures on a sounder financial basis what some would describe as the questionable application of increased contributions substantially raised due to the 1982 reforms. A collateral benefit would be to provide a significant pool of funds available to our state, county, and municipal entities for public investment purposes. That's a pretty good use of taxpayer monies, and pretty close to home as well. It is also an example of properly using "savings for investment purposes."

C. Excess Social Security contributions should only be available to the U.S. Treasury for non-Social Security expenditures for the purpose of paying down the national debt on a short-term basis, say for maturities of two years, or less, and limited to some agreed percent of the total Social Security Administration investment pool

Given the fungibility of cash and the ongoing refinancing of our national debt in the markets, this may be difficult to police, but it should be mandated. Why? Because (theoretically) this frees up debt capacity for repaying such borrowings in the future that (again theoretically) would not detract from borrowing needs for other then-current requirements.

These actions—certainly non-revolutionary insofar as sound funding for an insurance/annuity activity—will initially deprive the

Treasury of a source of funding for current general spending. However, it's questionable whether these contributions should have been used for such purpose in the first place. If my understanding is correct, the (huge) 1982 increase in contributions was to protect (fund) Social Security, not (at least publicly) serve as an offset to the Reagan income tax reductions. Nonetheless, that seems to have been the practical effect here. Our representatives voted for the increase in contributions to (we were assured) protect Social Security. They then approved of spending them for other purposes as fast as they could be collected, substituting them in Social Security with IOUs. Most nonpolitical financial managers would be fired for such irresponsibility. Our children and grandchildren are liable to pay a steep price for this expediency. This Independent solution should help alleviate this.

Admittedly this implies a "hit" to the current government revenues, to the extent these excess contribution funds are denied for current general usage. How should this be compensated for? Some among us would suggest that estimated $290 billion "tax gap" highlighted in Chapter 13 is a possibility, with a modified tax system as proposed. Others might propose a reexamination of current spending priorities (which implies a reexamination of national priorities). Defense spending is a huge "big-tent" category that may well yield savings. Independents, strong advocates of national defense in the broadest terms, believe it could be a prime target to cover much of the resulting fiscal "hole" created by this proposed change in the use of Social Security funds, even in today's world. But at the sake of being redundant, I reiterate this would require a serious reexamination of national priorities.

Another possibility: Eliminating the tax expenditure need for an Earned Income Tax Credit and/or a Child Tax Credit (note I said the "need for," not the benefit of), which together represent about $81 billion a year. Possibly on some of the more egregious pork spending, now days referred to more politically correctly as "earmarks," that are routinely demanded by members of Congress. That's another thought. But probably few if any cuts on many already appearingly "starved" domestic social or infrastructure programs. That's an Independent thought.

And finally, to reiterate, Independents believe it would be beneficial to remove Social Security completely from the current operating budget numbers, for at least two reasons. First, while continuing as a general obligation of the Government, it is (or should be once revised) to function as a pure retirement income adequacy (insurance) program and not an income maintenance (pension) scheme: a largely self-financing, long-term program; one that ought not impact, nor be impacted by, short-term or variable annual government fiscal considerations (possibly short of real war). Secondly, once removed from the annual budget development process, it denies politicians the straw man of "how much of taxes are eaten up by Social Security entitlements," and therefore are not available for current spending programs, etc, etc., etc.

That simply does not appear, from the numbers, to be the case. These programs on a current basis, if you can believe the numbers, pay for themselves, at least so far. Removing Social Security is just one less tree politicians can hide behind. Independents favor fewer trees in the political forest. It promotes improved public visibility.

On the surface at least, this approach seems likely to pass muster with Government Accounting Office's (GAO) analytic framework for assessing proposals for restructure of Social Security.

- The extent to which a proposal achieves sustainable solvency and how it would affect the economy and the federal budget

- The relative balance struck between the goals of individual equity and income adequacy, and

- How readily a proposal could be implemented, administered, and explained to the public.

The urgency implied in this recommendation is summed up best in testimony to Congress by the Comptroller General of the United States in early 2003: "Taking action now on Social Security would not only promote increased budgetary flexibility in the future and stronger economic growth but would also make less dramatic action necessary than if we wait." This position was reiterated in August 2006 testimony regarding taxes by the Comptroller General David Walker.

We need a different outcome.

Annex II

Example: Social Security retirement payments based upon "need," as defined

Gross Income/yr Before Social Security	Social Security Retirement Supplement	Percent of Allowable	Total Income After Social Security	After Social Security Income as Percent of Median Income
$32,874, or less	$11,460*	100%	$44,334**	=< 100%
$38,874	$ 9,741	85%	$48,615	110%
$44,874	$8,280	72%	$53,154	120%
$50,874	$7,038	61%	$57,912	131%
$56,874	$5,982	52%	$62,856	142%
$62,874	$5,085	44%	$67,959	153%
$68,874	$4,322	38%	$73,176	165%
$73,860***	0	0	$73,860	167%

Example for conceptual illustrative purposes only

*Average retired worker benefit for 2004 (Source: Statistical Abstract of the USA, 2006)

**Median household income, 2004 (Source: Ibid.)

*** 166 percent of 2004 Median household income (Source: Ibid.)

Chapter 15

Working Poverty: A Minimum Wage Issue

The United States has for many years had a mandated minimum wage, which is the lowest amount employers (with a few exceptions) may pay employees for an hour of labor. It was instituted in 1938 under the Fair Labor Standards Act. Both the federal government and the individual states are entitled to set a minimum wage. When the two differ, the higher wage rate applies. As of January 2007, thirty-one states (including the District of Colombia) had a higher minimum wage than the federal wage, while only one state (Kansas) had a lower one. Four states had no state minimum wage, while fifteen had one identical to the federal wage.

Like most other issues contemporary government deals with, the issue of whether or not we should insist on a minimum level of compensation for individual work performed in the marketplace—a so-called minimum wage—is strongly influenced by conservative and liberal ideologies. Such influence is purportedly supported, in both cases of course, by economic theory.

The economic argument against a minimum wage mandate is that it results in a reduced demand for workers and a resulting increase in unemployment, especially involving just the low-paid worker who a minimum wage is supposed to help. That's in theory. And in theory, the logic is difficult to refute. In the real world, however, the direct relationship has been difficult to verify.

Economic theory clearly in favor of a minimum wage policy, within a market-driven capitalistic system, is difficult to find. Therefore, in most instances, those favoring one do so by pointing out the weakness of the theory against it. Generally, under "real world" conditions, this has not been difficult to do. Why not? Primarily because (1) those who oppose such a policy have not been especially successful in accurately documenting its effect in real world situations; (2) while proponents, acknowledging the theory of the argument against it, highlight that economics (and most economists) has a single-minded-drive toward "efficiency," steamrolling everything in its path toward that objective. We have pointed out elsewhere that capitalism (based as it is on free market economics) is perfectly compatible with slavery, while democracy is not. Here is a prime example. Theoretically, and in some practical senses, capitalism would pay the lowest wage possible in its drive for profits, whether or not such wage represented a living or supporting wage or whether or not it even reflected the value received for the effort. "That is not our concern," would say the capitalists (or economists). "If the worker is willing to work for the amount we offer, then that must reflect a fair market wage. That is all that concerns us."

That argument may, in some situations, be a fair one. In many, it probably isn't, because it tends to overlook or assume several issues in any employment market. For example:

1. The relative bargaining position of the employee and the employer in the market may strongly favor one or the other.

2. Both parties have perfect information.

3. Workers and employers have many options to choose from.

4. Workers can enter or leave the market, or change jobs, or get fired without incurring loss.

Historically those offering employment in most local markets have had an advantage, especially when only one or a few employment opportunities and limited mobility were the case. Whoever was the dominant employer would tend to "set the hiring wage," and the other local business would key their salaries to that. Obviously, that tended to depress wages. The same circumstances can occur today.

Historically a symbiotic relationship has existed between what we refer to here as Capital (employers) and Labor (employees). Each relies upon the other to meet their goals. This relationship continues today. Nonetheless, the free market between Capital and Labor is, at base, antagonistic: Each would like to maximize its benefit in any agreement. In general, Capital would like to minimize its cost to hire Labor, and Labor would like to be paid as much as it can negotiate. The further up the employment ladder one climbs, the more room for negotiations is available. At the minimum-wage level we are speaking about, it practically does not exist.

By 1956 the minimum federal wage was $1.00 per hour; by 1968, $1.60. By 1978, it was $2.65, and by 1998 it was $5.15, where it remained until July 2007. It is scheduled to increase by $0.70 a year between 2007 and 2009 to $7.25 per hour. In nominal dollar terms, the minimum wage appears to have been an effective tool, protecting low-income workers' purchasing power during the years from its inception through probably the 1960s. Since then, one could reasonably question that conclusion.

In real purchasing power terms based upon current dollars (2007 dollars), the minimum wage has declined rather dramatically. As an example, in current dollar terms, the minimum wage was worth about $9.00 an hour in 1969; in 1979, about $8.50; in 1989 about $5.80; today its nominal value is $5.15. How, and more importantly, why, has this deterioration been allowed to occur? Is the minimum wage for some reason believed unnecessary under recent past and current economic conditions? Has the minimum wage, and the floor-level poverty-protection it was designed for, been superseded by some other equally or more effective work-related anti-poverty tool? Questionably.

One obvious reason for this erosion of value of the minimum wage is inflation. In 1996, the minimum wage was increased from $4.45 (set five years earlier in 1991) to $4.75 and then to $5.15 in 1997, where it remained until mid-2007—ten years. Price inflation increased over 28 percent during this same period. The federal minimum wage is not indexed, or adjusted, to offset inflation, such as Social Security and some other government payments are. Does one need to inquire if, and if so how much, our elected government representatives' salaries were "adjusted for inflation" during this same period?

If this measure of what is supposed to be a "fair wage" under the Fair Labor Standards Act is in fact being handled properly by our representatives in D.C., then the obvious conclusion is that until the mid-1990s at least, Congress believed that Business was overpaying lower wage employees. What other conclusion could be drawn from leaving the minimum wage at the same nominal level while the cost of living for these workers (as well as the rest of us) was rising at an average annual rate of about 2.5 percent a year (1995–2004 figures) for *ten years*! If that is not the right answer, then the answer must be that the minimum wage as a first line of defense against working poverty had been superseded. This is a possibility, but before we look at that question, a look at the composition of government during the period under discussion, between 1997 and 2007, merits our attention.

During this latest period of federal minimum wage stagnation, with just one exception (the 107th Congress elected in 2001), conservatives controlled both houses of Congress, while either a conservative or a centrist (business-friendly) liberal was in the White House. Historically speaking, our leading conservative political party—Republican—has not been known for its labor-leaning tendencies. Might this go a long way to explaining such wage-rate stagnation? Politically speaking, lower-wage-earning populations have not been a major part of the conservative voting base.

Interestingly, however, this same inquiry into which party was running the show in D.C. indicates that during the previous period of federal minimum wage stagnation, from about 1981 through 1990, the "party of labor"—Democrats—controlled at least one house of Congress continuously, while conservatives controlled the other (the Senate) for most of this period. However, from 1987 to 1993, Congress was controlled by Democrats. During those seven years, the federal minimum wage was increased from $3.35 to $3.80 in 1990 and to $4.25 in April, 1991. It remained there until five years later, when it was increased to $4.75 in 1996; then it went to $5.15 in 1997, where it would remain for the next *ten years*.

Based upon fairly recent history, an argument could be made that neither of our two major political parties either (1) championed the objective of keeping America's lower-wage workers out of poverty, no matter their protestation to the contrary, or else, (2) that neither of them considered it Business's responsibility to pay a "fair wage" to a small but nevertheless significant portion of America's workers. This fault finding is mitigated to some degree, because, as has already been highlighted, a majority of the states established minimum wages significantly higher than the federal mandate. In those thirty states, plus the District of Colombia, these higher, if still sub-poverty, rates are in effect, and many are indexed to inflation.

This failing on the part of our federal lawmakers is still further mitigated by the fact that Business itself for the most part offers hourly wage rates usually above at least the federal level, even where not mandated, in many locales. Businesses know, apparently, that minimum compensation is simply not enough to attract needed workers. This is not viewed as benevolence on their part as much as it is as a condition of employment reality.

Poverty

What does being poor mean? Well, probably a number of things, few if any being very positive. Statistically, it means earning less than the set dollar amount that the U.S. Government calculates is required as a minimum for basic personal and/or family support. It assesses pre-tax cash income against a number of thresholds, based primarily on food spending. In this sense, it is a normative concept. The fact that people can work (full-time it is assumed) and still be "poor" is a reality. In this sense, poverty is a real concept or condition. It exists. But our question here is need it exist? Not should it, which implies a value judgment, but need it, which implies the question of whether or not it is avoidable.

Government must believe that working poverty need not exist. Why not? Because (a) it not only established the minimum wage to try and eliminate or at least minimize the economic and social effects of it, but (b) legislation that provides a menu of direct and indirect financial (welfare) measures to minimize poverty, or at least poverty's negative effects upon individuals and families. Just consider a few of the more common programs: the Earned Income Tax Credit (EITC), food stamps, Aid to Parents With Dependent Children, Title Eight housing support, and Medicaid. Many of these programs, either alone or in combination, have been successful in either reducing the crushing effects of poverty or of lifting working people and families out of poverty. Considering this, the answer to the question, is poverty for the working poor unavoidable has to be no, it isn't unavoidable.

Having thus answered the question of necessity, the question of responsibility remains. Poverty exists, that's a demonstrated fact. So the next question has to be, What part of society do we make responsible for minimizing working poverty in a socially liberal, free, and equal society with a generally free-market-oriented economic sector? While there is demonstrably a benevolence (charity) effort within our private sector, there is clearly enough historical data to show that we assume it is government that most people look to as a provider of last resort, and increasingly so. Is this a proper function of government? Is this a proper claim on government for those seeking such support? While a thought-provoking question, we aren't going to pursue such line of inquiry much further here because it leads us right into the area of ideology. Ideologies, again, are normative, comprehensive doctrines, and we have said that poverty is an actuality, so there can be no adequate resolution that those of opposing political ideologies can mutually agree on. We simply look for a solution that ought to be in the best interests of at least most of the people, all of the time.

There are at least two major areas of poverty to consider: (1) poverty due to an inability or unwillingness to work and (2), poverty resulting from a capitalist inability or unwillingness to pay all who are willing and able to work at a sufficient level of compensation to enjoy (and I use that word "enjoy" purposely) a standard of living at least at—and hopefully above—what is calculated, objectively as well as independently it is presumed, as a poverty threshold. In the first instance, we must again consider two categories: those unable to work and those considered unwilling to work. Those unable to work, for whatever reasons, are still members of society, even if not fully contributing members. In the instance of not knowing such individuals, it's easy to say they are not "my" problem. If, however, they are part of your family or circle of acquaintance, it is less easy.

We know them; they are real to us; we sympathize with their plight. But know them or not, as a group such people, as well as those who assume primary responsibility for them, may in many instances merit the economic and/or social support of the community. Just remember, it can happen to anybody, any time. In the case of those unwilling to work to support themselves, the solution is less apparent. If they won't take responsibility for themselves, why should others? Do we need to resurrect the old English poorhouse concept? At this point, as the latter is beyond the scope of our argument here, I leave this particular issue unaddressed.

In the second category of the "working poor," for Independents, the issue is clear and uncomplicated: A primary objective of work is to earn a living, whether one is the employer or the employee. It is not to provide one's services and skills to another, no matter how basic or low-level they may be, and then to be taken economic or financial advantage of. If an employer is unable to offer employment at a level of compensation that reasonable people objectively and independently calculate is necessary to support oneself at or above a level of poverty, then such employer has a questionable economic basis to hire employees. He apparently can't afford to pay them and also make an acceptable income for himself. And a federally (or state) mandated minimum wage rate that permits this is unacceptable. It is a subsidy to capitalism, both big and small enterprise, that either keeps businesses afloat that could not otherwise compete successfully in the marketplace or else permits the owners of these businesses to employ "sweatshop labor" to their own enrichment. Either way, it is an unacceptable government policy.

If as a society we were experiencing a marginally profitable economic period for whatever reasons, then a temporary subsidy in the form of a low minimum wage, greater tax benefits, or other indirect supports might well be in the interest of at least most of the people until such structural conditions had improved. However, by almost any reasonable measure, our business sector is not only competitive and financially healthy, it is robust, and capital is rewarding not only itself but its upper levels of managers lavishly, according to many public financial reports. Everyone? No, but enough to lay to rest the idea that business, viable business, cannot afford to pay its workers—

all of them—compensation allowing at least an above-poverty-level wage. For example, in the year 2006, profits stood at 12 percent of gross domestic product, the highest level since the 1960s, 33 percent above the historical average of 9 percent. There seems little, if any, justification for business to cry "poverty."*

Independents support an effective minimum wage policy that puts the burden (responsibility) for eliminating working poverty on the system that benefits most directly from the employment pool: business. This is the sector we look to in order to provide society's economic opportunities and well-being; placing responsibility with business, or more generally capitalism, is in the interests of at least most of the people all of the time, including those at the helm of capitalism, for several reasons.

First, it goes directly to the issue of Balance as we have described it ("… wherein government believes the results of capitalism, in the broadest context, are equitably enough distributed among the people …"). Government has (objectively and independently, we will assume) determined what it costs its citizens in our economy today to support a family unit, whether that unit represents one person or a larger family, at what is described as a standard of living above poverty level. This is both very important and very revealing. It is important in that some responsible and impartial agency in our democratic society has established a base line representing a minimum adequate standard of living. This is not necessarily a "good" standard of living, whether on a relative or absolute standard, but one that will provide at least the basics for living with a minimum of hardship.

It is revealing in that this base line establishes, on what we take as an objective and disinterested basis, what that family unit needs to earn

---

* These comments may appear outdated, or in conflict with an apparent descent into "recession" that not only our economy but much of the developed world appears to be facing toward the end of 2008. One might argue that the excesses causing the present situation are to some large degree self-inflected. In any case, a cyclical business downturn does not change either the above picture of the results of capitalism in America or the argument that capitalism can afford to pay its workers a level of compensation consistent with a minimum acceptable standard of living. A depressed economic environment may well mean reduced levels of compensation for all, but the "pain" involved, even if only relatively, should be prorated, and not just by those at the bottom of the economic ladder.

in the marketplace, in one form or another, to support itself, thereby achieving at least what has been determined as a minimum acceptable standard of living.

If capitalism—business—or some parts of it is unable or unwilling to pay workers a wage that provides an above-poverty-level existence, then one of two conclusions is evident: Either (1) capitalism expects the rest of society to contribute to the support of this segment of workers (welfare), or (2) it is tacitly eliminating a segment of society as potential customers for many of its products and services. As the second alternative seems unintended (or at least illogical), then we must assume that capitalism believes it is acceptable to transfer some portion of the cost of labor to the rest of society to bear, for its benefit. This, in the view of Independents, is highly unlikely to be in the interest of most of the people even some of the time.

A direct example of this cost-of-labor-burden shift from business to the rest of society to support low wage earners is the Federal Earned Income Tax Credit, the so called EITC. This program today receives pretty solid bipartisan support. However, in the eyes of at least this Independent, it is a major—if not *the* major—reason we have seen our federal minimum wage policy stagnate. It bears looking at here.

The Earned Income Tax Credit

A bit of background.** Since its inception in 1975, the Earned Income Tax Credit (EITC) has become a robust and, most would claim, largely successful component of America's labor and antipoverty policy. It is the nation's largest public antipoverty program for working families.

Originally proposed as a bonus program for the poor who were willing to work, it evolved into a more modest focus on reducing the regressive effects of rising payroll taxes. In 1975, 6.2 million families claimed $1.5 billion in credits. The credit was made permanent in 1978 and in 1986 was expanded significantly as a part of a major federal tax law overhaul. In 1993, Congress doubled the size of the EITC to try

---

** This background summary on the EITC is in the main extracted from a February 2006 Brookings Institution research paper, *"The Earned Income Tax Credit at Age 30: What we know."*

and ensure that a minimum-wage worker could support him or herself and family with full-time work.

The 1986 tax law indexed the EITC for inflation, protecting against erosion in the credit's real value. Indexing, combined with expansion in eligibility, led to phenomenal growth in the program's size. By 1996, the EITC exceeded total federal and state Aid to Families with Dependent Children (AFDC) payments, and it surpassed the Food Stamp program in 1998. In 2003, 19.3 million families received $34.4 billion from the EITC. It is expected to pay out about $41 billion by 2008. The requirements that the taxpayer must have been a U.S. citizen or a resident alien for the full year and that the taxpayer, spouse, and all qualifying children have valid Social Security numbers affects many immigrants.

What sets the EITC apart from many other tax code provisions is its refundability. The amount of the credit for which a taxpayer is eligible is determined independently from the amount of income tax owed. If a taxpayer's family has an income tax liability, the amount of the EITC for which he or she qualifies reduces that tax. Any amount left over once tax liability is reduced to zero is returned to the taxpayer as a part of a tax refund. If there is no tax liability at all, he or she may receive the entire EITC as a refund—along with any taxes withheld. This refundability allows low-income workers who miss out on the benefits of most tax credits and deductions to take full advantage of the incentives offered through the EITC. A number of states have now established EITCs for their residents along the lines of the federal program, but most provide more limited tax relief.

Spending for the federal EITC has grown dramatically, from $8.7 billion in 1990 to $34.4 billion in 2003 (in 2003 dollars). In 2003, approximately 88 percent of EITC dollars were refunded, a little over $30 billion. The majority of EITC dollars are paid to families with at least two children. Note the following: The EITC benefits more "moderate-income families" than traditional government benefit programs, such as cash welfare or food stamps. In 2002, 26 percent of EITC payments went to households with adjusted gross incomes under $10,000, 53 percent went to households with incomes between $10,000 and $20,000, and 21 percent was paid to relatively higher-income families.

Based on data from the 1996 Panel Study of Income Dynamics, 13 percent of U.S. households that year were eligible for the federal EITC. That's not the same thing as the number of households under the federal poverty line. The EITC-eligible population overlaps with, but is distinct from, the population defined as poor. The average household income of those eligible for the EITC is about 125 percent of the federal poverty level. About one-third of households with incomes below the poverty line do not have children and fail the age-test for the credit for workers without a qualifying child. (Most are believed elderly.) Nearly as many meet the qualifying child or age tests but do not have earnings. Altogether, only about 35 percent of households in poverty are eligible for the EITC. The median income of EITC recipients increased from $10,808 in 1990 to $15,400 in 1999. This was only about 9 percent higher in constant dollars; much of the increase reflects the indexing of the EITC for inflation. Many EITC filers are self-employed, roughly 21 percent in tax year 2003.

What have been the impacts of the EITC? Researchers have devoted a great deal of attention to analyzing the effects of the credit on measures of income, work, family formation, and household or community expenditure patterns. A number of claims are made.

- The EITC has lifted 4.4 million people in low-income, working families out of poverty.

- From 1995–1999, the EITC reduced the overall poverty rate by 1.5 percentage points, even though only about one-third of poor households qualify for the credit.

- Expansions of the EITC have proved critical for enabling low-wage workers to support themselves and their families without falling below the poverty line. In the first year (1975) of the credit, the combination of the credit and full-time, year-round work at the minimum wage provided an income $107 above the federal poverty level for a family of three. In 1986, the same combination of wages and the credit would have left the same family $1,511 *below* the poverty line.

- Increases in the credit in the early 1990s reversed this, however, so that minimum wage work plus the EITC

provided $1,154 more than the poverty level for a family
of three in 1995. Also however, because the minimum
wage had not increased since 1997, by 2005 the same
family would have fallen $1,000 short of the poverty
threshold (again).

Does the existence of the EITC affect worker wages? Because the credit
is an earnings supplement, the EITC could theoretically lead employers
to reduce wages if they find they can pay less and still fill jobs. There is
no *strong* evidence that the EITC has depressed wage rates *significantly*
(author's emphasis). One study reportedly found that a 10 percent
increase in a state EITC was associated with a 4 percent drop in the
wages of high school dropouts and a 2 percent decline in wages for those
with only a high school diploma. A 2005 study concluded, however,
that expansions to the EITC during the 1990s had *little apparent effect*
on hourly wages near the bottom of the wage distribution scale.

Who can argue that the EITC does not represents a direct subsidy
to capitalism? Other programs in support of low-wage earners and
the unemployed that are considered necessary to achieve at least the
minimum standard of living deemed acceptable are the Food Stamp
program, housing vouchers, cash assistance (TANF), child care aid,
and medical care payments. In many instances, these noncapitalism-
provided "support" payments to low income workers are far greater
than workers are paid in wages by the system that uses them in pursuit
of its goal, profit. It is tempting to define this as exploitation.

It is a truism to say that so long as this situation exists, the results
of a profitable capitalism are not equitably enough distributed among
the people. Business may counter by pointing out that they pay taxes
on their profits in support of these government programs. This is
dismissed by pointing out that (a) their taxes are not "earmarked,"
or dedicated, funds, and (b), while these government subsidies to
capitalism have increased, business' taxes as a percent of total federal
taxes paid decreased between 1990 and 2004.

A second reason Independents support a meaningful minimum
wage policy is the potential societal, as opposed to the purely economic,
impact. A family unit in which the breadwinner, or in many cases
the breadwinners (both parents), are forced by economic necessity to

spend most of each day, every day, away from their families and each other in pursuit of even a marginal livelihood tends over time to be dysfunctional and a further potential burden on the local society in general. Such family units tend to perpetuate a cycle of poverty that is difficult to break. This, again, is hardly in the best interests of at least most of the people all of the time. External institutions, such as schools, are more depended upon for "raising children" than was ever intended. Parental responsibilities, by necessity, too often slip; all the issues with latch-key kids and teenagers growing up are exacerbated in families in these conditions. Does that mean the kids always grow up badly? Certainly not, but in too many instances the odds for success that most of us take for granted will be against them. Capitalism would tend to say that this is not their problem. Independents say it is as much their problem as for the rest of society.

Thirdly, we have highlighted the nonearned financial support that low-wage earners require just to get by. Currently, most receive this primarily from local, state, or federal government. This is a drain on our public resources. While, as indicated, there may always be some portion of our society that simply can't economically make it on its own, to the degree that those that can work are paid a sustaining wage for their work will free-up public resources for more productive and desirable alternative uses (or, alternatively, allow lower taxes). This would seem to be in the interest of at least most of the people at least most of the time. I use the example of the Federal Income tax Credit as an example of imbalance: Today, this public "wage supplement" is second only to Social Security, which is self-funding, in its annual cost to the federal government, and its effect on seriously poor workers, as highlighted above, is debatable.

Having laid out the issue(s) here and explained why Independents favor a meaningful minimum wage policy as a part of the overall umbrella of economic opportunity for our citizens, we would be remiss to leave an impression that capitalism, overall, is grievously callous on this issue. In most instances, the concept of a free-market wage scale works. Business has to be competitive in its search for employees, and employees do usually have options in the work place. In reality, according to a Heritage Foundation 2006 analysis of the then approximately 127 million workers in the labor force, only 1.9

million earned the minimum wage. Most (63 percent) were women. More than half (53 percent) were between the ages of sixteen and twenty-four. Many were part-time workers, voluntarily or otherwise.

Still, this perspective on the magnitude of minimum-wage earners only reflects the tip of an iceberg. It overlooks the fact that, according to 2003 figures, a total of 8.6 million individual workers reported incomes of $15,000 or less. Working forty hours a week, 52 weeks a year, $15,000 equals $7.21 per hour. An additional 3.8 million two-person households earned $15,000 or less, as did 1.6 million three-person households. A level of earnings that enables our citizens to enjoy a standard of living that is described by the government as above poverty level is the real issue.

The national poverty rate—the percentage of the population whose income falls below the government's official poverty level, adjusted each year for inflation—was 12.7 percent in 2004, up slightly from 12.5 percent in 2003 but below the 1990 level of 13.5 percent. This translates to about 37 million Americans living "in poverty" in 2004. That number obviously includes many more than just those earning the minimum wage. To a large degree, however, many living in poverty is the result of a stagnant minimum wage.

Now some will contend that poverty in America is a lot less draconian than poverty in less developed countries. Supposedly, nobody starves in America. In a December 2007 editorial piece that focused primarily on purported income inequality, the magazine *The Economist* highlighted the fact that the difference between the very well-off and the poorer among us is not nearly as wide a gulf as it was in years gone by, at least not in relation to the material basics of life we all take for granted today. While there is certainly a difference between a $10,000 SubZero PRO 48 model refrigerator and a $350 economy model, the "lived difference is rather smaller than that between having fresh meat and milk and having none." The article also pointed out that more than 70 percent of Americans below the official poverty line own at least one car, and "the distance between driving a used Hyundai Elantra and a new Jaguar XJ is well nigh undetectable compared with the difference between motoring and hiking through the muck."

In the above sense, Independents agree that while income inequality is on the rise—and *The Economist* concurs with this conclusion in this editorial—the purely "material gap" between the two extremes is not nearly as extreme as it was in years past. But it says little about such matters as income security, proper nutrition, health-care provision, family cohesiveness, and other matters that most today would consider basic quality-of-life issues. Even if we accept poverty as a relative term, considering the wealth of America, it shouldn't exist here, at least not for working Americans. Admittedly the complete elimination of poverty, like achieving perfect Balance, may not be possible in the real world for a variety of reasons, but it ought, like Balance, to be a goal. Efforts ought to be to move toward that goal, not simply tolerate poverty. And there are ways to do this. The first step is to insist that capitalism pay its workers, all its workers, no less than an above-poverty wage.

The Independent Option

Exactly what would Independents propose here? We would propose (1) to end, or significantly reduce, the need for and resulting public cost of the labor subsidy currently paid to business in support of its profitability in the form of an earned income tax credit, along with (2) ending or significantly reducing the economic need to provide additional financial support through many of the existing welfare program now available to the "working poor." If you can and do work, you should not be poor, as poverty is defined from time to time as a level beneath an acceptable minimum standard of living, as is fairly and disinterestedly determined by some acceptable institution (governmental or other). That would be the Independent program.

But, having said that, one must be careful not to throw the baby out with the bath water, so to speak. As mentioned previously, Independents strongly favor free markets. Markets can and usually do serve us well. But to reiterate, free markets are not necessarily markets without any degree of monitoring or direction or even, in instances, regulation, within broad parameters. This is an area where some regulation seems in the interest of most of the people all of the time. So, how do we go about this? Carefully!

Let's look at the experience of others. Several Markets in Europe have experienced negative consequences of mandatory high wages. The result has been greater long-term unemployment than they would prefer. It is true that because this has not been the case here in America, numerous low-wage industries and services exist and expand here in the USA that could not exist or expand in European countries with much higher minimum wages—France, for example. It is also true that higher-paying jobs here have moved to lower wage-rate countries abroad. In Japan, historically it has not been the level of wages that have been a severe drag on business but instead the policy of lifetime employment that has crimped profitability for so many businesses. We can, perhaps, learn from these as well as our own experiences and structure our wage policy to avoid it.

If Independents summarily increase the federal minimum wage significantly—say to about $10.00/hour—will this drive low-wage industries out of business? Possibly, and that could significantly decrease employment opportunities for this sector of the work force. No doubt that would be the first line of argument from such business (and local politicians) in defending lowest wage requirements. On the other hand, and excepting agriculture as a special case for the moment, it is in many cases just such low-wage industries that attract immigrants, both legal and otherwise, and create the need for immigrant workers. If such a minimum wage requirement proved uneconomical to such magnet industries, the effects upon our economy as a whole and our permanent legal workforce would get "rounded off," so to speak. The demands upon the rest of us for income support through government and the social services demands often felt by communities could be reduced. That would certainly seem to be in the interest of at least most of the people, all of the time.

What of the potential job loss and tax reductions to local and federal coffers from the loss of these business and workers' incomes? Independents would reply that if these several government units depended upon the taxation of such exploitative ventures to finance their operations, then they need to give priority to exploring other options. While such action may "tilt" the return on investment decision for potential new entrants and/or expansion in these sectors, it may not. It all depends upon just how profitable they really are to their owner-investors. It is also difficult to believe that all retail establishments, department stores, fast food outlets, and other such consumer services companies would fold up shop and go fishing. Remember that in at least thirty states and the District of Colombia, the minimum wage is already higher, in some significantly higher (and these tend *not* to be the poorer states in America; California: $8.00, Connecticut: $7.65, Massachusetts: $8.00, Michigan: $7.40, New Mexico: $6.75, New York: $7.15, North Carolina: $6.15, for example). Business will cry "Ouch," adjust, and life, and employment, will go on.[*]

No doubt consumers will "eat" a bit of the price increases that these businesses will attempt to pass on. That's okay. It will be selective. Not everyone is going to see prices for their purchases go up (more than they currently do), and competition (which capitalism is always dragging out as in the consumer's benefit, unless of course they are trying to gobble up their competition, and then it is the "economies of scale" that will benefit the customer in the absence or reduction of competition) will tend to mitigate any such price inflation. While there could no doubt be some short-term adjustment in the employment markets, we will continue to have our unemployment safety nets to fall back on. And because not all workers will be terminated in this upward adjustment of wages, those continuing in employment will be an off-setting credit to the government's costs during such a transition period.

To mitigate the overall magnitude of the proposed change in the basic minimum wage, Independents would propose two exceptions to the full-time minimum wage standard. The first is to recognize that a certain ongoing number of people employed at or near minimum wage today are not primary breadwinners. In fact, the Heritage Foundation identifies slightly more than half of the 1.9 million minimum-wage workers as part-time workers, many of whom we can assume are teenagers working not to support themselves or their families but to support their leisure expenses and indulgences. In an effort to encourage jobs for this group, Independents would support a minimum wage about 80 to 85 percent of the full-time standard

---

[*]   An example: McDonald's Corp reported a 27% rise in third-quarter '07 earnings but its U.S. restaurants encountered "head winds" caused by costs for commodities and labor. The fast food company said it has raised prices at its U.S. restaurants about 3.5% this year, partly to offset minimum-wage increases. U.S. restaurant-level profit margins weakened slightly to 18.4% from 19%. Globally, however, operating margins rose to 18.3% from 17.3% at company operated stores (*Wall Street Journal* 10/20/07)

minimum wage for employees nineteen years old or younger, in school at least part-time. For these workers, jobs in the fast food outlets, retail, swimming pools in the summer, babysitting, and other basically seasonal and after-school and weekend employment offer them the opportunity for making pocket money as they take their first steps into the job market. This is not an original concept; it was found in minimum wage legislation in the early 1990s, often referred to as a training or apprentice wage. In fact, as of January 2007, workers under twenty years of age may be paid as little as $4.25 per hour during the first ninety consecutive calendar days of employment. In addition, certain full-time students, student learners, apprentices, and workers with disabilities may be paid less than the minimum wage under special certificates issued by the Department of Labor.

Why nineteen years? Workers this age and under who are in school are assumed to be public-school students. Education is being provided them tuition-free. Those over nineteen and still in school will in most cases be paying for their education; if they have to work during this period, Independents assume that it is in some real sense to support themselves or to assist their families in carrying this burden.

The second exception would be for agriculture, where significant numbers of imported low-wage workers are often necessary for seasonal crop-harvesting work. Where such an imported workforce is used, the minimum wage available to them should represent no less than what they could be expected to earn (for similar work) in their native country, on either an hourly or daily basis, plus an adequate allowance for decent local housing and meals while they are temporarily employed in this country. In lieu of a cash payment, the allowance requirement may be met by the temporary employer providing adequate housing and meals to these workers.

In all instances, where the market for labor merits or demands a premium over and above these minimums—a higher market rate—it becomes a negotiable issue between employer and employee. The minimums proposed for the various sectors represents but a floor. And finally, Independents would propose that the minimum wage levels be linked to a cost of living index, as are consumer costs, on a regular basis, not less than bi-annually.

To Independents, it seems totally unacceptable that business—or any segment thereof—should expect that the rest of society ought to subsidize their labor costs in pursuit of profits. By almost any reasonable measure of success, U.S. business is healthy and doing well at the bottom line. Consider these yardsticks:

	(Dollars in billions)			
	1990	2000	2004	2006
Proprietors' income (non-farm)	$349	$706	$885	$993
Corporate profits after tax*	$292	$553	$885	$1,141
Corporate taxes	$145	$265	$231	$381
Corp tax as percent federal receipts	10.2%	11.2%	11.4%	15.1%
Net dividends paid	$169	$378	$540	$642
Undistributed profits	$123	$175	$343	$499

*With IVA and CCA

Source: U.S. Statistical Abstract 2008, tables 466, 468, 656, 767

If all of the minimum-wage-earners' wages were increased at once to the $10/hr figure, that would put a dent in the combined proprietors' and corporate pre-tax incomes of roughly $21 billion (grossed-up to include the 7.5 percent social insurance cost). As this combined before-income-tax figure totaled, per above, approximately $2,134 billion in 2006, it represents less than a 1 percent incremental cost. If all workers earning less than this $10.00/hr figure were increased to this wage rate, the total cost is estimated to be about $101 billion, or about 5 percent of the combined proprietors' and corporate pre-tax incomes. Business, overall, would seem to have little justification for complaint (except their profit margins will be squeezed a tad). But we know that this labor-cost increase would actually be less than this due to the higher minimum wage rates already in effect in the various states. Politically this may appear a "hot-potato" for politicians and their business community constituents. But economically, it wouldn't appear to be that steep a hill to climb.

In the real world, we know that such a proposed minimum wage hike would affect some businesses more than others. General Electric or Microsoft likely have few minimum wage positions. Local, smaller, and more marginal businesses will obviously feel this increase the most, but in many instances these small businesses compete against larger firms on the basis of lower cost and price. This may make some areas compete on a more level playing field. Some will successfully make it. Some probably won't. Where they don't, it's not unrealistic to believe that such failures will translate into increased business for the others, with the demand for additional workers. That's the free market!

We need to keep a primary goal in mind: to assure that capitalism serves not only itself, but society in general, not the other way around. It's a matter of Balance.

Basic economics tells us that the factors of production are land, labor, and capital. These, in some mix or proportion, are necessary to produce goods and/or services available to us in the marketplace. For each there is a charge, and in the product or service we receive, this represents the cost portion of the price. A further component of price in a free market economy is profit. Cost plus profit equal price. The higher the price and the lower the cost, the greater is the profit. The objective of capitalism, as an economic system, is to maximize profit. This is done through a combination of means. Producers try to produce products (or services) with high demand as efficiently as possible, at the lowest cost. That's the way capitalism works. Nonetheless, it is very debatable whether it is in the interests of most of the people any time to have to subsidize capitalism's profitability, or even its viability, on a case-by-case basis.

We need a different outcome.

Chapter 16

A Conclusion and a Message

Well, what do you think?

After due consideration here, do we Independents still appear—as the political pundits represent us—of no apparent practical or potential political significance after all? Or, on the contrary, have we succeeded in establishing that probable significance, as well as the political potential, of Independents? What about our case for the pressing need for a different outcome? Does our argument for improving Balance in our society ring true? And the suggestion for an Independent political option—does it strike a chord?

Is the political sphere, as we observe it in practice, what we need, what we are happy with (or at least satisfied with, as the devil we know as opposed to the devil we don't) after all? What about the argument that government, as it is now determined in the political arena, governs in the best way (or only way) we can expect, all things considered, in a pluralistic society such as ours? Finally, are we after all happy with the status quo? Questions, questions, questions. What do you think?

And, what about the assertion in Chapter 2 that there is no war being waged on America's middle—or any other—class? If not, then why does it feel, at least a little, like this is the case at times? Why does Robert Kaplan's purported observation, or opinion as I chose to regard it, "*The U.S. is evolving into a corporate oligarchy that merely wears the trappings of democracy,*" highlighted in the Introduction, keep bothering me? I find that especially troubling. It may be true; it may not be; it may be just an excuse; it may be a distraction covering some other dynamic, but it is troubling. Before you render a conclusion on all these issues, let me ask you a question:

Do you know how to catch wild pigs?

You catch wild pigs by finding a suitable place in the woods and putting corn on the ground. The pigs find it and begin to come every day to eat the free corn. When they are used to coming each day, you put a fence down one side of the place where they are used to coming. When they get used to the fence, they begin to eat again. Then you put up another side of the fence. They get used to that and start to eat again. You continue until you have all four sides of the fence up with a gate in the final side. The pigs, which are used to the free corn, start to come through the gate to eat that free corn again. You then slam the gate and catch the whole herd. Suddenly the wild pigs have lost their freedom. They run around and around inside the fence, but they are trapped. Soon they go back to eating the free corn. They become so used to it that they forget how to forage in the woods for themselves, so they accept their situation, their captivity.

A (*very*) conservative friend of mine sent this to me via e-mail. He's very good at sharing parables such as this and other notably slanted writings in support of his preferred political ideology. For him, it illustrates the way "big government," through all its entitlement programs and special-interest goodies, is seducing its citizens into accepting a more socialized society. However, with but a little thought, it is not that big a (theoretical) stretch to see that it applies equally well for those who might sympathize with Mr. Kaplan's concern. Only here it would be big business as opposed to big government that is spreading the corn ($$$) and building the fence (political dependence). Why? To increase its odds in pursuit of its agenda through an ability to influence and/or manipulate varying levels of the electorate and government, tipping that Balance in favor of their interests, to accomplish their objectives.

Consider, if you will, our argument concerning the Earned Income Tax Credit for low income workers. Like the casinos in Nevada (and elsewhere today) capitalism doesn't require a huge advantage to come out ahead; just an edge. You might ask yourself, where is the "corn" of special-interest money leading us? There is no intent, necessarily, to suggest conspiracy here or any kind of organized movement or implied ulterior motive beyond what we see—the desire for "an edge." It is simply happening. We may simply be blundering into a society where we are, through *the trappings of democracy,* slavishly coming under the interests of an economic oligarchy—a self-serving if benign tyranny. And it wouldn't really matter which of the two parties was in power in Washington. They are both addicted to the "corn." Think about it.

If this were the case, it also implies that maybe there *is* a war being waged on America, and from within, even if somewhat unconsciously and possibly even unintentionally. Whatever, the possible result could be the same: We forget how to "forage for ourselves"; we lose at least some of our liberty and freedom(s); we become highly dependent on others to meet our needs. Is that all bad? Well, that depends upon your definition and view of the value of freedom and self-reliance. Many might say those are overvalued in today's world. Are they?

Charles Fried, a well known professor at the Harvard Law School, a former justice of the Supreme Judicial Court of Massachusetts and U.S. solicitor general in the Reagan administration, doesn't think so: In his recent book *Modern Liberty* he cautions, "In modern, liberal, welfare-administrative democracies, the impositions on liberty are likely to be gentle, marginal. But we must be vigilant, recognize them for what they are, or we will lose our grip on what liberty is, coming to confuse it with comfort, a generalized decency, or just democracy itself…"

Our old French ami Alexis de Tocqueville had some insight into this issue well worth considering (and remember, he was writing over 150 years ago). He notes, "… during my stay in the United States that a democratic state of society similar to that found there could lay itself peculiarly open to the establishment of despotism." That no doubt sounds a bit hollow to most of us, inasmuch as we are a political democracy, a country where we the people chose who will govern us, and hence, by implication, how we will (or ought to) be governed. He continues, speaking about the oppressive, terror-based despotism of absolute sovereigns and emperors of antiquity, concluding that if despotism should be established among the democratic nations of "our day," it would probably have a different character. It would be more widespread and milder; it would degrade men rather than torment them. It's worth a closer look at some of his thinking here:

> "Thus I think that the type of oppression which threatens democracies is different from anything there has ever been in the world before ... In the first place, I see an innumerable multitude of men, alike and equal, constantly circling around in pursuit of the petty and banal pleasures with which they glut their souls. Each one of them withdrawn into himself is almost unaware of the fate of the rest. Mankind, for him, consists in his children and his personal friends. Over this kind of men stands an immense, protective power, which is alone responsible for securing their enjoyment and watching over their fate. That power is absolute, thoughtful of detail, orderly, provident, and gentle ... It gladly works for their happiness but wants to be sole agent and judge of it. It provides for their security, foresees and supplies their necessities, facilitates their pleasures, manages their principal concerns, directs their industry ... Thus it daily makes the exercise of free choice less useful and rarer, restricts the activity of free will within a narrower compass, and little by little robs each citizen of the proper use of his own faculties ... It does not break men's will, but softens, bends and guides it; it seldom enjoins, but often inhibits action. It is not at all tyrannical, but it hinders, restrains, enervates, stifles, and stultifies so much that in the end each nation is no more than a flock of timid and hardworking animals with the government as its shepherd ... this brand of orderly, gentle, peaceful slavery ... [could get] itself established even under the shadow of the sovereignty of the people. Our contemporaries are ever a prey to two conflicting passions: they feel the need of guidance, and they long to stay free. Unable to wipe out these two contradictory instincts,

they try to satisfy them both together. Their imagination conceives a government which is unitary, protective, and all-powerful, but elected by the people ... One should never expect a liberal, energetic, and wise government to originate in the votes of a people of servants."

As with any extract from a larger text, there is always the question of quoting out of context. On the whole, however, I believe it is pretty representative of the message of Toqueville's chapter titled "What Sort of Despotism Democratic Nations have to Fear." Tocqueville's concluding thought on this matter is, I think, of special importance for us Independents and what we are about here:

"The vices of those who govern and the weakness of the governed will soon bring it to ruin. Then the people, tired of its representatives and of itself, will either create freer institutions or soon fall back at the feet of a single master."

I for one find that voice from the past somewhat unnerving. This is especially so when considering (1) the issue of Balance and (2) the question of governing for at least all of the people most of the time and most of the people all of the time. To the degree that these two pillars of our society are continuingly undermined, the greater the possibility of a future that Tocqueville prophesized coming to pass. And the danger in all this is that, as a society, we will probably never even recognize that this "war" on our democracy was even occurring. Like the wild pigs analogy, we will simply wander into it, unaware of the end consequences, good, bad, or otherwise, until it's too late.

It's not hard to believe the author of the wild pigs parable might have been reading this chapter of Tocqueville's *Democracy in America*, in which the potential picture he paints is not very pretty or very positive concerning the future. Has history proven Tocqueville wrong here? Some would say it has: this scenario hasn't happened here yet. Others would say it hasn't: it hasn't happened here yet, but it has in other countries, specifically in Germany, Italy, and Russia in the last century. True, those examples did not endure, but they did occur and arguably along the lines broadly outlined by our friend, creating totalitarianism in each country. Have we learned sufficiently from their experiences to avoid the same "slippery slope" from democracy to socialism (or tyranny) to totalitarianism that they experienced? You tell me.

The late economist F. A. Hayek's mid-twentieth century book *The Road to Serfdom* is often held up as a kind of bible by conservatives in support of libertarian principles of political and economic, as well as personal, freedoms. And in many ways it is, if you keep clearly in mind when it was written (1940–1943) and why, specifically, it was written—to counter the English intelligentsia's high regard for continental-style socialism as capitalism's inevitable successor. It reiterates, or is at least sympathetic to, much of what Tocqueville says about potential creeping domination by government. But he points out two significant things about the book in the Preface to the 1976 edition.

First:

> "The reader will probably ask whether ... I am still prepared to defend all the main conclusions of this book, and the answer to this is on the whole affirmative. The most important qualification I must add is that during the interval of time terminology has changed and for this reason what I say in the book may be misunderstood. At the time I wrote, socialism meant unambiguously the nationalization of the means of production and the central economic planning which this made possible and necessary. [Today] socialism has come to mean chiefly the extensive redistribution of incomes through taxation and the institutions of the welfare state. In the latter kind of socialism the effects I discuss in this book are brought about more slowly, indirectly, and imperfectly. I believe the ultimate outcome tends to be very much the same..."

Secondly:

> "It has frequently been alleged that I have contended that any movement in the direction of socialism is bound to lead to totalitarianism. Even though this danger exists, this

is not what the book says. What it contains is a warning that unless we mend the principles of our policy, some very unpleasant consequences will follow which most of those who advocate these policies do not want."

I bring Hayek into the discussion here to make two points: Here we have an authority of much more recent vintage who, for all intents and purposes, seconds the opinion of our Ami, Tocqueville. And at the same time, he clearly asserts that a process put into motion in the direction of "socialism" (or capitalistic tyranny, perhaps), for lack of a better term, is neither inevitable in its consequences nor irreversible. This is a critical point in the consideration of our arguments in this book.

What we have attempted to demonstrate here is that Independents, simply from the fact of not supporting a political party today, may well be sufficient evidence for the case that America is in dire need of achieving a different outcome from government. The reason for this is the search for better Balance in our society, as we have defined it. In effect what this amounts to is heeding Hayek's—and Tocqueville's— warning to "mend the principles of our policies." It acknowledges that if we do not, a slow progression into (some form) of domination by a segment of our society to the detriment of all other segments seems, over time, a real possibility. Mr. Kaplan's observation is one very real possibility.* In this connection you could say that the arguments and proposals in Chapter 12 are exactly what Hayek says are necessary to avoid this unwanted eventual outcome: Mend the principles of our policies toward how we conduct and who we allow to influence our electoral procedures and practices. Obviously, those with a different agenda are not going to accept such actions timidly.

Everyone, it seems, is quick to find fault with politics and government, which are critically important institutions of modern society. Today, this Independent would say there may be good reasons for this. They are the mechanisms that provide cohesiveness for society and, as importantly, are the mechanisms we have for adapting and making changes in society, as we have pointed out. The critical

---

* President Eisenhower, at the end of his second term almost fifty years ago, was very likely implying something similar when he cautioned America against a military-industrial complex.

consideration regarding how politics and government fulfill their roles in society is, in the end, to whom are they responsible; whose ends do they truly serve? Just who, effectively, controls them?

Karl Marx is largely remembered today as a revolutionary prophet of doom for capitalism. Writing primarily in the 1840s to 1860s, he saw in capitalism the seeds of its own eventual collapse. Much of the purely economic (materialistic) analyses he based this premise upon were not only theoretically sound, but have at least in part been validated by history. During much of the twentieth century, capitalism disappeared in Russia and Eastern Europe. In Scandinavia and England, it was partially abandoned. In Germany and Italy, it drifted into fascism.

Indeed, for much of the last century—until quite recently—almost everywhere except in the United States, capitalism was on the defensive. While wars, brute political power, exigencies of fate, and the detrimental effects of revolutionaries all contributed their share, a good argument could be made that capitalism's at least temporary "demise" was largely because of the very reasons Marx foresaw: It broke down.

Why the breakdown? In Europe, partly because it developed the instability Marx said it would. A succession of business crises, compounded by a plague of wars, destroyed the faith of the lower and middle classes in the system. However, that was not the entire answer. America too had its wars and depressions, and yet capitalism continued strong here. Something else spelled the difference between survival and destruction: European capitalism failed not so much for economic as for social reasons.

The Marxist prediction of decay was founded on a conception of capitalism in which it was socially impossible for a government to set wrongs right—intellectually and ideologically impossible. For Marx, it was simply impossible. The dialectic told him that the state was only the political ruling organ of the economic powers. The thought that the state might act as a neutral body, as an impartial third force that might balance (there's that term again) the claims of its conflicting members would have seemed little else but sheer wishful thinking to him.

To some degree, it was just this lack of social (government) flexibility that weakened European capitalism. When all democratic trade unionism was stamped out in Russia under the Tsars, when monopolies and cartels were officially encouraged in England and Germany, the Marxist dialectic looked prescient indeed. As recently as about fifty years ago, some capitalist governments (Greece, Italy, and France, for example) had difficulty collecting taxes they levied on their own business communities. When one looks back (hopefully into the past) at the enormous gulf between rich and poor in Europe and sees the evidence of the indifference of the former for the latter, it's not that difficult to imagine that the psychological stereotypes that Marx cast in his historical drama were all too truly drawn from real life—at least, real life as he both experienced and witnessed it.

For those who might dismiss this argument about European government's "social flexibility" as being an inapplicable historical relic, I would highlight an oblique reference to such mentality in a recent article in *The Economist,* which included the following: "And everywhere … the feeling has grown that the EU and its treaties are elite projects that may please self-serving Eurocrats but are remote from the concerns of ordinary citizens … and it is one the EU's political leaders seem quite unready to deal with."

These very facts provide a clue why capitalism has worked as well as it has here in the United States. Capitalism here has evolved in a land untouched by the dead hand of aristocratic lineage and age-old class attitudes. Hence, we have faced up to the economic problems of capitalism with social attitudes from a less rigid heritage, which allowed us to develop a healthy disrespect for too much power, public or private.

We are a nation in which almost no one thinks of himself or herself as a "proletarian." On the contrary, as we saw in Chapter 2, somewhere around three-quarters of us think of ourselves as "middle-class." Upper-class America may have at times kicked its lower classes around a bit, but it has not despised them. Here we have a government that historically actually prosecutes monopolies, or at least those it has not, with some consideration, sanctioned.

Why, you might ask, this digression into Marxian matters at this late stage? The answer is that it's Marx, of all people, who indirectly provides us with the final "linchpin" to make, actually re-make, the simple but crucially important connection that *government counts,* and that therefore, *politics matters;* that the basic reason why is to provide and maintain Balance in society. That's the difference. Society lacked an effective mechanism for correcting Balance in Europe, and for that lack, both its people and capitalism suffered. We have enjoyed a mechanism for correcting Balance in America, and from that Balance we have benefited; many have prospered, and capitalism has largely succeeded. Our example has been emulated by many, and others are attempting to do so.

The mechanism that makes the difference is obviously not just government, per se. History has demonstrated that it is liberal government that represents at least most of its people all of the time; its philosophy is delivering the greatest good (happiness) to the greatest number. Imperfect as it may be, America has been successful (enough) in this connection ... so far. The danger Independents perceive is that the political leaderships are losing sight of this requirement. It has always been a challenge in a bi-polar ideological environment, but with a "big tent" opportunity on both ideological sides, it has muddled through.

Here, again, are the three key concepts leading to Balance in America:

1. The private capitalistic economic sector (business) feels it is able to pursue its aims with a minimum amount of outside interference.

2. Government, in its role as representative of the people, feels that the results of capitalism, in the broadest sense, are distributed equitably enough among the people.

3. The people, through their voice at the ballot box, concur with government's assessment.

All three requirements are important, and government, as the representative of the people, is the fulcrum. The key issue here is the voice of the people at the ballot box. If, through influence or other muting, that voice is either unable to get through or is ignored once it does, then Balance is jeopardized. Therefore, if we are to enjoy a reasonably balanced society, government counts, politics matters, and just who is authorized, and how, to participate in and/or influence the political process that determines the composition of government needs to be clearly defined. Not only clearly defined, but rigorously observed. This is not a defense of the virtue of government. It is the recognition of the need for it.

That's why I worry about Robert Kaplan's concern, why I worry that my friend's parable of the wild pigs hits too close to home, not necessarily as he perceives it. I worry that other popular "isms" he sends me might also apply here: "A government that takes from Peter to give to Paul can always count on Paul's support." This is a truism. Those who strive to govern are concerned for and about power, and maintaining it. What price are they willing to pay for it? Who is Peter, and who is Paul? Another example: "It's totally democratic [but questionably fair] to have two wolves and one sheep vote on what to have for dinner." Democracy means little without adequate consideration for the rights of minorities. Conversely, a minority, no matter how convinced of the rightness of its cause, shouldn't be allowed to usurp the prerogatives of the majority. I worry about such humorous political anecdotes, which all too often touch on subjects we are loathe to think about too seriously. They are but ripples on the surface, portending, perhaps, the political *tsunami* that at least this Independent detects forming.

The difference we have enjoyed here in America for making capitalism work, for both itself and everybody else, has been government, like it or not. Many—especially capitalists—would deny this. They don't like rules and regulations. Government has worked because of the sovereignty of the voter, and capitalism, per se, doesn't get to vote—yet (but it sure appears to be trying). This has tended to promote Balance. To the degree that capitalism is able to unduly and unfairly influence government, then both government and those it is primarily intended to represent will suffer negative impact. The truth is so will capitalism, in the end. Then what?

Independents would work to avoid that "then what" scenario.

The difference we have enjoyed in pursuit of the American Dream and the success of capitalism has been government. Marx and history show this pretty clearly. It has worked by providing Balance; by making opportunity available, not necessarily directly, not always by doing (too many) things directly for any one of us. From there, it is up to you; you need to rely primarily upon yourself. The threat to this difference, government that provides Balance, and the opportunity we have enjoyed, is, at least for this Independent, too clearly reflected in my friend's humorous pokes aimed—inaccurately, or narrowly, in my view— at government. To wit:

- The eventual loss of freedom and independence from accepting "free corn"—the feeding of wild pigs
- An unbalanced approach to governing—Paul's support for government at Peter's expense
- Unintended outcomes through the use of the democratic process—two wolves and a sheep

An Independent political option, aware of and concerned about these potential dangers to the difference we have enjoyed, proposes to correct the direction away from Balance our country appears to be heading, by governing to produce a different outcome. Exactly how? Just as we have stated: through a philosophy of governing in a manner that produces the greatest good (happiness) for the greatest number as demonstrated by representing at least most of the people all of the time and all of the people at least most of the time. By their very nature and inclination, partisan options are incapable and really unwilling to do so.

An Independent political option attempts to reinvigorate the link between the trust of the electorate and loyalty on the part of its representatives by committing to the voters as a movement as opposed to on a personal basis, described by Independents as "purpose trumps personality." If you vote for an Independent—any Independent—you know what you are voting for, and why: to achieve a different outcome in the pursuit of better Balance. For whom? For at least most of the people all of the time.

One loose end that continues to bother me, here and in Tocqueville's scenario, is motive, or purpose. Perhaps I can't see the forest for the trees, but it's that question of why someone or some institution or segment of society would want to bring about such "serfdom," as Hayek calls it? To what end? It has to be for some purpose to be a credible theory. I'm reminded of the "Eloi" in H. G. Wells's novel *The Time Machine* when I imagine some purpose for such benevolent, yet malevolent, domination. That's scary, but an unlikely—even unthinkable—scenario, from what we can know today. But was Wells simply projecting and fictionalizing the kind of thinking in these arguments? Probably not ... but I digress yet again.

I cannot at this point conceptualize a rational theory for why one segment of society, or capitalism generally or governments specifically, would consciously want to benevolently transform its fellow citizens into the equivalent of cows in a pasture. Still, a pathological pursuit of power and privilege is of course a possibility—misguided as it might appear, and as contrary to our ideas and ideals of representative self-government, it could be a possible theory; certainly not what I would call a rational one.

The alternative possibility is that *no one* is consciously controlling this; there is no "movement," no conscious intention of causing this erosion, this imbalance. It is simply happening while no one is looking or at least considering the end result. The free "corn" is too tempting (even considered politically necessary, by apparently everybody today). While capitalism pressures government, seeking its favors and preferences, individually or as "interest groups," it is unconsciously driving us in this direction, unwittingly building the fence. This has to be my conclusion. But either way, it doesn't make a real difference. To correct the course of our country, the need for a different outcome seems irrefutable. An outcome that will move us toward Balance, not away from it; an outcome that will short circuit Tocqueville's scenario and validate Hayek's prescription to mend (at least some of) the principles of our policies.

I reiterate: It is unlikely that the growing numbers of political Independents is just happening for no reason. The presence of all us Independents suggests both the evidence for this need to correct the course of our country—as well as the probable desire for it—and the potential means to bring it about. At the same time, given the importance attached to this issue, I'm open to alternative avenues of approach!

Some are going to agree with much if not all that we cover here. But, they may protest, too much change in the real world of politics would be required to achieve these goals, and what we're proposing is but a dream. I admit it does call for change; in fact, change has been the subject here. I wouldn't agree it calls for too much change. If you want change, you have to start someplace—that longest journey begins with the first step. Change requires initiation. Initiation can be inspired by imagination. And imagination is but an extension of what may have begun as a dream. I share with the late Reverend W. B. Clulow the notion that "Nothing so much convinces me of the boundlessness of the human mind as its operations in dreaming." So, if you want to call this a dream, I won't object. But I prefer to call it that first step; the initiation, the option required for change.

Where can you find this option, aside from right here, should you want to support it, further it? Today, you can't but ... maybe tomorrow you can. Currently it doesn't exist in the real world, although as I have said, many would probably say that they are looking for it, waiting for it, so that they can support it. Those in favor of such an Independent political option are not unlike that odd couple Gogo and Didi in Samuel Beckett's cryptic play *Waiting for Godot.* They have, so far, been doomed to wait unendingly in a circular political wasteland; waiting, waiting for an Independent option to appear. And always, the message is, *"Mr. Godot says he can't come today, but maybe he will come tomorrow."*

And so, Independents continue to wait, until next time; an expression, perhaps, of man's absurd political hope. And like in the play, the waiting seems endless. And yet it mysteriously begins again with each election cycle. Maybe it will come next time.

Maybe.

Epilogue

As I wrap this up, the race for the 2008 presidential election is underway. The Democratic entrant of Obama/Biden is already out of the starting gate; the Republican challenger of McCain/Palin is now publicly identified, ready to be anointed by their convention delegates next week, and then they'll be off to officially join the two-horse race. So, what does this mean for what I have written, or, more aptly, what does what I have written mean for this election?

It means that once again Independents, the largest self-identified voting group, will be faced with a least-worse choice. It means, once again, that Independents will be politically used and electorally abused in an effort by just those they are shunning to win office. It means, in all probability, no matter which of the two options eventually prevails, there will be no substantive change in the status quo. No matter the election season orations, promises, finger-pointing, baby-kissing or sleeves-rolled-up common-man-appearance, nothing changes: It is still one party against the other, with neither for a common good larger than their own particular ideology. It is philosophically and hence politically impossible to expect a different outcome—change leading to improved Balance—under our present conservative versus liberal political option. Once the electoral music stops and the chairs are refilled, the same game goes on.

I recognize that this sense of pessimism I exude—nearly fatalism, some might say—is both oppressive and depressive. Is this what we, the greater American public, should expect? Is this all we can expect? Under today's political conditions, I fear so. Usually during the by-now post-election period (as you read this), there will be optimism, enthusiasm, and hope that the new will sweep away the old. But I fear that in our current situation—if history is any guide—what we refer to as the new is simply the old, warmed over; dressed up, and recycled to appear new. There can be no "new," politically and hence governmentally, as things stand. And as sincerely as I believe what has been presented here to be both necessary and, more importantly, doable for that greater American public's future well-being, it's questionable whether we can find leadership that can meet the utilitarian qualifications laid out here. They are demanding. I fear that public choice has come to dominate too much of our professional political thinking. I fear that the "free corn" has already taken its toll.

So, back to the question: "What does what I have written mean for this election?" Nothing. By now that's history; but what about for future elections?

You tell me.

TRH
8/29/08

Notes

Introduction:

iii is currently between 38% to 40%: ANES, Guide to Public Opinion and
Election Behavior, American National Election Studies, Table 2A-1

vi from their own standpoint: Rawls, John, *Political Liberalism*, New
York, New York: Columbia University Press, 1993, p. 16.

vi is made worse off off: Buchanan, James M. and Tullock,
Gordon, *The Calculus of Consent*, Ann Arbor, Michigan:
University of Michigan Press, 1962, p. 172.

vii benefits along with others: Rawls, *Political Liberalism*, p. 50.

vii in benefit to themselves: Ibid.., pp. 50, 51.

vii points of view and of scope: Buchanan, James M. and
Tullock, Gordon, *The Calculus of Consent*, pp. 311–312.

ix has made to itself: Greider, William, *Who Will Tell the People*, New
York, New York: Simon and Schuster, Inc., 1992, pp.14–15.

x *wears the trappings of a democracy*: This quote from Mr. Kaplan is in the author's
notes as from the magazine, *Multinational Monitor*. However, the author has
not been able to confirm this (or any other) source and thus has indicated
the lack of definite identification by stating it is "attributed to Mr. Kaplan." If
one reads Kaplan's article, "Was Democracy just a Moment?" (© 1997 The
Atlantic Monthly Company) his comments and opinions therein appear
to support such a quotation and thus warrant its unconfirmed use herein.

Part One:

2 to use John Rawls' term: Rawls, *Political Liberalism*, note 27, p. 24.

Chapter 1: Why—and Whence—Independents?

5 independents, 6,508: Wypijewsky, JoAnn, Post cards
from Ohio, *The Nation*, 3/17/08, pp. 11–16..

5 of the state at large: "Paint them Blue," *The Economist*, 3/22/08. p. 34. .

6 and 35% in 2002: "Poll finds that 81percent think U.S. is on
wrong track ..." CBS News–New York Times   Poll, 4/04/08.

6 allegiance to neither party: Burns, James MacGregor, *Running
Alone*, New York, New York: Basic Books,   2006, p. 15.

6 double that number today: ANES Guide to Public Opinion and Electoral
Behavior, American   National Election Studies, Table 2A-1.

10 the number really hasn't: "Duverger's law of 2-party domination,"
Executive summary, available at   http://rangevoting.org/Duverger.html

10 much more than against it: Schleicher, David, "Politics as Markets,
Reconsidered: Natural Monopolies,   Competitive Democratic Philosophy
and Primary Ballot Access in American Elections." Supreme Court
Economic review, Vol. 15. Available at SSRN: http//ssrn.com/abstract=740304

Chapter 2: What It Is and What It Isn't

14 would be a good place to start: Brownstein, Ronald, *The Second Civil
War*, New York, New York: Penguin   Group (USA) Inc.,.2007, p. 12.

Chapter 3: The Political Status Quo

18 headed in the right direction: CBS News-New York Times Poll, 4/04/08, op cit.

18 lowest approval rating in 35 years: "Confidence in Congress
Lowest Ever for Any U.S.   Institution," Gallup Poll, 6/20/08.

18 distrust Government strongly: "Turning Left," *The Economist*, 8/11/07.

20 bridge up in Minnesota: "I-35W Mississippi River
Bridge," from Wikipedia at www.wikipedia.org

20 apparently done about this: "Report links money woes to cause
of bridge collapse," *The Wall Street   Journal*, 5/22/08.

20 injuries and losses: "Bridge-collapse victims to receive
$38 million," *The Wall Street Journal*, 5/09/08.

20 now until 2009: "Senate Stalemate Grounds FAA
Overhaul Bill," *The Wall Street Journal*, 5/02/08.

Chapter 4: Politically, Why We Believe What We Do

24 operating in American politics: Sargent, Lyman Tower, *Contemporary Political
Ideologies*, 6th edition,   Homewood, Illinois: The Dorsey Press, 1984, p3–4.

26 overall ideological and social systems: Ibid., pp. 12–13.

26 in a democracy are: Ibid., pp. 33–53.

29 more egalitarian, by design: Thurow, Lester, *The Future of Capitalism*, New
York, New York: William   Morrow and Company, Inc, 1996, p.242.

29 the difference between these poles: *Contemporary Political Ideologies,* pp. 67, 70.

Chapter 5: Democracy and Capitalism

32 view their system: *The Future of Capitalism,* p. 242.

32 without these programs: Ibid., p.245.

33 the provider of last resort: *The Future of Capitalism,* pp. 22, 244–246.

34 to persist and flourish: Ibid., pp. 244–247, 274–276.

35 to exert political influence: *Who will tell the People,* p. 51.

Chapter 6: Why Government Behaves Like It Does

37 should put up with: Zakaria, Fareed, *The Future of Freedom,* New York, New York: WW Norton and Company,   2004, p. 21–22.

39 accorded to five additional posts: "President Bush's Cabinet," available at http://whitehouse.gov/government/cabinate.html

39 position of power or control: *The Random House College Dictionary,* New York, New York: 1988, p.1027.

40 American political activity: "Development of major political parties in America," available at www.123helpme.com/view.asp?=62070

40 party electoral influence: *Running Alone,* p. 92.

41 results are definitely worse: *The Future of Freedom,* p.166.

41 core claims, including these: Hay, Colin, *Why We Hate Politics,* Malden, MA: Polity Press, 2007, p. 90.

44 power and influence of business: *The Second Civil War,* p. 28.

44 defining issue ever since: Ibid., p. 28.

44 dominant politics of this era: Ibid., p. 30.

45 competing societal interests: "Legal Realism," available at www.wikipedia.org/wiki/legal-realism

45 maximizer of self-interest: "Institutional Economics," available at www.wikipedia.org/institutional-economics

46 and Supreme Court decisions: "Intellectual Origins of Modern Law and Economics," available at www.cyber.law.harvard.edu/bridge/laweconomics/origins.txt.htm

46 as the late 1920s: Lloyd, Gordon and Scrivner, MM, editors, "The Two Faces of Liberalism: How the Hoover– Roosevelt debates shaped the twenty-first century," reviewed by Schambra, William, *Claremont Review of Books,* Vol. III. No. 1, Winter 2007–08.

47 unity of government was the rule: "Political Divisions, the U.S. Senate and House of Representatives, 1901–2000," Congressional Directory 1995–96, *World Almanac and Book of Facts:* Mahwah, NJ, 2001 p. 117.

47 evident in our own time: *The Second Civil War,* p. 58.

48 limit economics to markets: "Intellectual Origins of Modern Law and Economics," p. 2.

49 are not blatant Conservatives: Greider, William, "Rolling
    Back the 20th Century" 5/12/03, *The Nation,* Available
    at www.thenation.com/doc/20030512/greider

49 affecting government policy: Ibid., pp. 3–4.

49 by the rest of society: "Income Inequality in the USA," available at
    www.wikipedia.org/wiki/Income-Inequality-in-the-United-States

49 or hyper partisanship: *The Second Civil War,* p. 13.

50 in either party: Ibid., pp. 315, 368.

50 publically acknowledged this: Ibid., pp. 288–289.

50 the two warring parties: Ibid., p. 215.

50 rolled in with the 1930s: "New Nationalism," available
    at www.wikipedia.org/wiki/new-nationalism

53 an underprovided public good: "Public Choice theory" available
    at www.wikipedia.org/wiki/public_Choice_theory

53 own congressional representative: Shaw, Jane S., "Public Choice
    Theory," The Library of Economics and Liberty, available at
    www.econlib.org/Library/Enc?PublicChoiceTheory.html

54 federal public tax dollars are spent: Ibid., p.3.

55 theoretical welfare economics.": Buchanan, James M.,
    "Public Choice: Politics without Romance," *Policy Magazine,*
    Spring 2003, available at www.cis.org.au/policy/spro3

57 million in bribes: "Crooked congressman going to prison," 3/03/08, available
    at www.cnn.com/2006/Law/03/03/Cunningham.sentenced/index.html

57 to refund the money): "A Culture of Bribery in Congress,"
    The Christian Science Monitor, 12/02/05.

57 convicted in criminal court: "Sentences of other congressmen
    convicted of crimes" *The Associated Press,* Available at
    apltbo.com/ap/reaking/MGAYYQVLA4D.html

58 of bribery in congress: "A Culture of Bribery in Congress."

58 Bureau's "top criminal priority": "Legislators Using Law As
    Shield in Probes," The Washington Post, 11/01/08.

58 members of that chamber: "House creates ethics
    panel," *Santa Rosa Press Democrat,* 3/12/08.

59 than a member of Congress: U.S. Representative Murphy, Chris,
    "Dialing for Dollars," *Santa Rosa Press Democrat,* 2/06/08.

Chapter 7: The Rise of the Independent Voter

70 race for the U.S. House: Figures calculated by the author from
    "United States General Elections, 2006" available at www.wikipedia.
    org/wiki/united_states_general_elections_2006 dated 12/04/06.
    These numbers for the popular vote for the House were subsequently
    revised upwards to 80,975,537. However, this does not change the
    relative results as presented. It just makes the numbers a bit larger.

71 to Democrats or Republicans: The ANES Guide to Public
    Opinion and Electoral Behavior," table 2A-1.

71 state a party affiliation: Ibid.

71 remains widely debated: Dalton, Russell J. "Partisan Mobilization,
    Cognitive Mobilization and the Changing American Electorate,"
    2004. Posted at the escholership Repository, University of
    California. Available at www.repositories.edlib.org/csd/04-11

72 largely closed Democrats and Republicans" Magelby, David,
    Keith, Bruce E., et al., *The Myth of the Independent Voter,* Los
    Angeles, CA University of California Press, 1992, p. 4

72 this figure was 10%: "The ANES Guide to Public
    Opinion and Electoral Behavior" Table 2A-1.

75 only come election times: Abramowitz, Alan, "The
    New Independent Voter," 4/26/05. Available at www.
    emergingdemocraticmajorityweblog.com/donkeyrising/...

76 his recent book, *Running Alone: Running Alone,* p. 3.

Chapter 8: Independent Parties and Support Groups Today

82 political necessity of the day:"Information Sheet," Independent Voice.
    Available at www.independentvoice.Org/free-details.asp?id=22

83 independent political movement: "Information sheet," independentvoting.
    org. Available at www.independentvoting.org/about

84 that further these objectives: "IPPN Mission Statement,"
    available at www..ippn.org/article.php?id=Mission

84 local issues and candidates: "The Integrity Party of New York State
    Information Sheet." Available at www.twinforks.com/nyspolitics

84 how this is best done: "Mission Statement." Available at www.3rdparty.org
    major parties tend to do: Vandehei, Jim, "From the Internet
    to the White House, *Washington Post,* 5/31/06.

85 defeat in its efforts: Sifry, Micah L., "They like
    Mike," *The Nation,* 2/11/08, p.24.

86 combined getting just 1%: "Presidential Election of 2004, Electoral and
    Popular vote Summary." Available at www..infoplease.com/ipa/Ao922901.html

87 the two major parties: "Duverger's law, how and why it occurs."
    Available at www.wikipedia.org/wiki/duverger's_law

87 their privileged standing: Schleicher, David, "Politics as Markets'
    Reconsidered: Natural Monopolies, Competitive Democratic
    Philosophy and Primary Ballet Access in American Elections."
    Supreme Court Economic Review, Vol. 15, pp. 4, 5.

88 is difficult to dispute: Ibid., p. 34.

Chapter 9: The Independent Voter: A Profile and a Purpose

95 a major protection for freedom: *Contemporary Political Ideologies,* p. 35.

95 of the competing elites: Ibid.

96 for the benefit of all: "Is Government run for the benefit of all, 1964–2004," The ANES Guide to Public Opinion and Electoral Behavior, Table 5A-2, The American National Election Studies.

98 according to its core criteria: "Intellectual Origins of Modern Law and Economics, p. 2.

101 two sides of the same coin: *Who Will Tell the People,* p. 59.

102 this question of confidence: "Confidence in Congress: Lowest Ever for Any U.S. Institution," Gallup Poll.

104 55% in presidential years: Calculations by the author from statistics provided in "National Voter turnout in Federal Elections: 1960–2004." Available at www.infoplease.com/ipa/AO781453.html

Chapter 10: An Independent Political Option

112 won by write-in candidates: "Electoral Fusion." Available at www.answers.com/topic/electoral_fusion

114 by a 6-3 margin: New Party (USA), "U.S. Supreme Court case, Timmons v. Twin Cities Area New Party. Available at www.en.wikipedia.org/wiki/new_party_(USA)

Chapter 11: The Superstructure: How It Fits Together

118 for the greatest number: *Oxford Dictionary of Philosophy,* New York: Oxford University Press, 1996, p. 41.

121 in terms of maximizing utility: Ibid., p. 388.

121 if they had a choice: *Oxford Dictionary of Politics,* New York, New York: Oxford University Press, 2003, pp. 552–554.

123 being questioned by some: *The Economist,* 1/13/07, p. 73.

125 in the past thirty years: Meyer, Dick, "A Third Way." Available at www.cbsnews.com/stories/2006/00/07/Opinion/meyer/main1692378_page2_html

128 a politics of national purpose: Emanuel, Rahn and Reed, Bruce, *The Plan: Big Ideas for America,* Jackson, TN: The Perseus Book Group, 2006

128 only a very limited sense: *Contemporary Political Ideologies,* p. 35.

134 as to minimize domination: Shapiro, Ian, *The State of Democratic Theory,* Princeton, NJ, Princeton University Press, 2006, p. 3.

134 preferences and desires: Ibid., p. 4

135 of a weakening force: "Duverger's law." Available at www.wikipedia.org/wiki/duverger's_law

136 latest poll was conducted: Leonhardt, David and Connelly, Marjorie, "81% in poll say nation is headed on wrong track," *The New York Times,* 4/04/08.

136 is seriously broken: NBC News/*Wall Street Journal* poll, conducted by polling org of Peter Hart(D) and Bill McIntruff (R), December 14–17, 2007.

Chapter 12: An Independent's View of the Propriety (or Impropriety) of Special-Interest Influences on Government

141 passion, or of interest: Madison, James, "The Federalist #10," *The Federalist Papers*, New York, New York: Bantam Books, 1982, p. 51.

142 convened for the purpose: Ibid., p. 55.

142 interests of the people: Ibid., p. 56.

143 more money than ever: Mulling, Brody, "Groups unveil plans to bankroll Democrats," *The Wall Street Journal*, 3/19/08.

143 and the national parties: Ibid.

145 But it is, so it's not: "A tap on the wrist," *The Economist*, 5/20/06, p. 36.

146 are seeking to represent: "The Rise of the Donor Class," *The Wilson Quarterly*, Summer 2008, p.68–69.

148 in taxes and fees: Meckler, Laura, "Why Big Airlines Are Starting a Fight with Business Jets," *The Wall Street Journal*, *The author has the article in his working papers, but unfortunately neglected to note the exact 2008(?) date*

151 writing in *Capitalism Magazine*: Oliva, S. M., "Nike, Free Speech and the Constitution," *Capitalism Magazine,* 3/26/03.

152 freedom of speech: "Campaign Finance Reform," The Government Sector, Devolving Authority and Democratizing Decision making. Available at www.newrules.org/gov/buckley.html

155 electoral system effective: "Corporate Personhood Debate." Available at www.wikipedia.org/wiki/corporate_Personhood

Chapter 13: An Independent Tax Solution

157 and manifestly unfair: Kemp, Jack, "Flat Tax Revolution," 11/11/03. Available at www.freedomworks. org/Informed/issues_template.php?issue_id=2024

158 additional reforms are desirable: "Individual Income Tax Policy," Statement of David M. Walker, Comptroller General of the United States before the Committee on Finance, U.S. Senate, 8/03/06.

158 the next few decades: Ibid., p.1.

161 estimate for 2007): Calculations by the author from figures on tax receipts Table 2.1, Federal Receipts by Sources, 1934–2012, Available at www.qpoaccess.gov/usbudget/fy08/hist.html

161 to be filled out: Edwards, Chris, "Outrageous Facts about the Income Tax," 4/15/03, The Cato Institute.

161 to pay in taxes: "How Fair Are Our Taxes?," Roper Center for Public Opinion research, 1995, as reported in *Readers Digest*, February 1996, pp. 57–58.

161 too far from those figures: Shapiro, Isaac, "Overall Federal Tax Burden on most Families—including Middle Income Families—at Lowest Levels in More Than Two Decades.," 4/10/02, Center on Budget and Policy Priorities paper. Available at www.cbpp.org/4–10–02/tax.html

164 presidential tax commission: Carroll, Robert, et al, "A Summary of the Dynamic Analysis of the Tax Reform Option Prepared for the President's Advisory Panel on Federal Tax Reform," 5/25/06, Office of Tax Analysis, U.S. Department of the Treasury.

164 conducive to economic growth: "Executive Summary, Understanding Tax Reform: A guide to 21st century alternatives," September 2005, The American Institute of Certified Public Accountants–AICP.

165 book, *The Delicate Illusion*: Harry, Thomas Richard, *The Delicate Illusion: (Dialogs with Myself) Solutions from an average American on How to Reverse our Incredible Shrinking Democracy*, St Louis, MO: Mamco International, 1999, Chapter VII.

173 to the individual income-tax: "Individual Income Tax Policy, Streamlining, Simplification, and Additional Reforms are Desirable," 8/03/06, Testimony before the Committee on Finance, U.S. Senate by David Walker, Comptroller General of the United States, p.18.

173 have yielded to the government: Ibid., Table 1, p. 18 and Table 464, *Statistical Abstract of the United States, 2006*. Calculations by the author.

174 alone will increase savings: Esenwein, Gregg A., "Federal Tax Reform and its Potential Effects on Savings," 1/26/2006, Congressional Research Service and The Library of Congress, Report for Congress.

Chapter 14: Social Security

178 and to 14.6% by 1940: "Employment and Unemployment in the U.S., 1900–2004," *The World Almanac and Book of Facts*, 2006, New York, New York: World Almanac Books, p. 129.

178 expenditures are 2017 or 2018: "Social Security, Analysis of Issues and Selected Reform Proposals," 1/15/03, Testimony before the Special Committee on Aging, U.S. Senate, by David M. Walker, Comptroller of the Untied States, p. 3.

179 into this twenty-first century: *Who Will Tell the People*, pp. 92–93.

179 almost until the year 2042: John, David C., "The top 10 myths about Social Security reforms," 9/30/04, The Heritage Foundation Policy Research and Analysis.

179 and depreciation benefits expanded: Greider, William, *Who Will Tell the People*, p. 93.

179 from Reagan's income-tax reductions: Ibid., p. 92. on a grand scale: Ibid.

180 on those 1982 changes: "Social Security Trust Funds, Old Age and Survivors Insurance Trust funds 1940–2004," *The World Almanac and Book of Facts*, 2006, p. 399.

181 million in 2004: Ibid.

182 benefits paid a year: Source: CSR Report for Congress (94–27 EPW), 5/01/98, Social Security Brief. Available at www.digitallibrary.unt.edu/govdocs

184 supports this assertion: "Individual Income Tax Policy, Streamlining, Simplification, and Additional Reforms are Desirable," p. 4.

184 surplus (unaccounted for) of $159,153: "U.S. Budget, Receipts and Outlays 2000–2005, CBO, *The World Almanac and Book of Facts,* 2006, p. 90.

185 in excess of one trillion dollars: Source: U.S. Social Security Administration, "Annual Report of Board of Trustees."

187 about $81 billion a year: "Individual Income Tax Policy: Streamlining, Simplification, and Additional

Reforms are Desirable," p. 11.

188 restructure of Social Security: "Social Security: Analysis of Issues and Selected Reform Proposals," p. 14.

than if we wait: Ibid., p. 13.

Chapter 15: Working Poverty

191 to the federal wage: "Labor, Immigration and Retirement Policy (U.S.) Portal," The Citizen's Encyclopedia on Congress. Available at www.sourcewatch.org/index.php?title=U.S._minimum_wage, p. 1.

192 has been difficult to verify: Zycher, Benjamin, "Minimal Evidence—Impact of Minimum Wage Increases," 1995, Reason Foundation; also: Mrkusen, Ann, et al., "The Case for a Substantial Minimum Wage Hike for Minnesota," February 2004. Brief written for Growth and Justice and Jobs Now.

193 remained until July 2007: "History of Federal Minimum Wage Rates under the Fair Labor Standards Act 1938–2007," 12/25/07, U.S. Department of Labor.to $7.25 per hour: Ibid.

193 during this same period: "Historical U.S. Inflation Rates, 1914 to Present—Consumer Price Index (CPI-U)," U.S. Department of Labor Statistics, available at www.inflationdata. com/inflation/inflation_rate/ Historical_inflation

197 public financial reports: Nutting, Rex, "Profits Surge to 40 Year High," 3/30/06, *Market Watch.* Available at www. marketwatch.com/news/story/story.aspx?guide

198 the historical average of 9%: Tully, Shawn, "Big Profits=Danger Ahead," 3/19/07, *Fortune Magazine.*

199 solid bipartisan support: Greenstein, Robert, "The Earned Income Tax Credit: Boosting Employment, Aiding the Poor," 8/17/05, Center for Budget and Policy Priorities, p. 1.

200 about $41 billion by 2008: Budget of the United States Government, FY 2004: analytical perspectives, table 6-1.

202 wage distribution scale: Holt, Steve, "The Earned Income Tax Credit at age 30: What we know," February 2006, Metropolitan Policy Program, The Brookings Institution, Washington, DC. (www..brookings.edu/metro)

202 between 1990 and 2004 decreased: "Federal Income Tax Receipts as a share of Gross Domestic Product, 1942–2004." Office of Management and Budget and the U.S. Department of the Treasury. Available from the Center on Budget and Policy Priorities.

204 voluntarily or otherwise: Franc, Michael, "Minimum-wage Hike would Hurt Low-wage Workers," 7/29/06, The Heritage Foundation, Washington, DC.

204 three person households: Calculations by the author.

204 in poverty in 2004: Calculations by the author.

204 hiking through the muck: "The new (improved) Gilded Age," 12/22/07, *The Economist*, p. 122.

207 $6.15, for example: "Minimum Wage in the States," 7/24/07, Labor, Immigration and Retirement Policy (U.S.) Portal, p. 7.

208 by the Department of Labor: Ibid., pp. 6–7.

209 a 1% incremental cost: Author's calculations.

Chapter 16: A Conclusion and a Message

213 or just democracy itself: Fried, Charles, *Modern Liberty, New York, W.W. Norton 2007, p. 165*

214 some of his thinking here: de Tocqueville, Alex, *Democracy in America*, Garden City, NJ: Doubleday and Co. Inc. 1969 re-print, pp. 691–694.

216 to the 1976 edition: Hayek, F. A., *The Road to Serfdom, Text and Documents, The Definitive Edition*. Routledge: London, England. *The Collected Works of F. A. Hayek*, Caldwell, Bruce, editor: The University of Chicago Press, 2007, pp. 54, 55.

218 wishful thinking to him: *Contemporary Political Ideologies*, pp. 88–89.

219 experienced and witnessed it: "Karl Marx." Available at www.wikipedia.org/wiki/Kark_Marx, page 5.

219 unready to deal with: "How the Netherlands fell out of love with Europe," 5/03/08, *The Economist*, p. 62.

222 such benevolent domination: Wells, H.G., *The Time Machine*, London, England: William Heinemann, 1895.

224 as its operations in dreaming: Catrevas, A.B., et al., *The New Dictionary of Thoughts*, The Standard Book Company, 1957.

Bibliography

Blackburn, Simon. *The Oxford Dictionary of Philosophy*. Oxford,
New York: Oxford University Press, 1996.

Brownstein, Ronald. *The Second Civil War*. London: The Penguin Press, 2007.

Buchanan, James M. and Gordon Tullock. *The Calculus of Consent*.
Ann Arbor: University of Michigan Press, 1962.

Burns, James MacGregor. *Running Alone*. Cambridge, MA: Basic Books, 2006.

Cable, Vincent. *Globalization and Global Governance* (Chatham
House Papers). London, New York: Pinter, 1999.

Fried, Charles, *Modern Liberty,* New York, London:
W.W. Norton and Company, Inc., 2007.

Graetz, Michael J. *The U.S. Income Tax*. New York, London:
W.W. Norton and Company, Inc., 1999.

Greider, William. *Who Will Tell the People*. New York:
Simon and Schuster, Inc., 1992.

Hamilton, Alexander, James Madison and John Jay. *The
Federalist Papers*. New York: Bantam Dell, 2003 ed.

Harry, Thomas R. *The Delicate Illusion*. St Louis: Mamco International, 1999.

Hay, Colin. *Why We Hate Politics*. Malden, MA: Polity Press, 2007.

Hayek, Friedrich A. *The collected works of F. A. Hayek, volume 2,
The Road to Serfdom, Text and Documents*. Bruce Caldwell,
Ed. London: University of Chicago Press, 2007.

Henry, William A. III. *In Defense of Elitism*. New York: Doubleday, 1994.

Iacocca, Lee. *Where Have All the Leaders Gone?* New York: Scribner, 2007.

Keith, Bruce E., et al. *The Myth of the Independent Voter*. Berkeley and Los Angeles: University of California Press, 1992.

McGeveran, William A. Jr., Editorial Director. *The World Almanac and Book of Facts 2006.* New York: World Almanac Education Group, Inc., 2006.

McLean, Iain and Alistair McMillan, eds. *The Concise Oxford Dictionary of Politics.* New York, Oxford, UK: Oxford University Press, 2003.

Phillips, Kevin. *Arrogant Capital.* New York, Toronto, London: Little, Brown and Company, 1995.

Rawls, John. *Political Liberalism, Expanded Edition.* New York: Columbia University Press, 1993.

Russell, Bertrand. *A History of Western Philosophy.* New York: Simon and Schuster, 1945.

Sargent, Lyman Tower. *Contemporary Political Ideologies,* 6th edition. Homewood, IL: The Dorsey Press, 1984.

Sen, Amartya and Bernard Williams, eds, *Utilitarianism and Beyond.* Cambridge, New York: Cambridge University Press, 1982. (1999 ed.)

Shapiro, Ian. *The State of Democratic Theory.* Princeton and Oxford: Princeton University Press, 2003.

Stockman, David A. *The Triumph of Politics.* New York, Cambridge: Harper and Row, 1986.

Thurow, Lester C. *The Future of Capitalism.* New York: William Morrow and Company, Inc., 1996.

de Tocqueville, Alexis. *Democracy in America.* Garden City: Anchor edition, 1969.

U.S. Census Bureau. *Statistical Abstract of the United States 2006.* Washington: U.S. Gov. Printing Office, 2006.

Zakaria, Fareed. *The Future of Freedom.* New York, London: W.W. Norton and Company, 2004.

www.ingramcontent.com/pod-product-compliance
Lightning Source LLC
Chambersburg PA
CBHW061345280526
45784CB00001B/139